JACK CRISTIL

VOICE OF THE MSU BULLDOGS

Revised Edition

by

Sid Salter

University Press of Mississippi • Jackson

DEDICATION

This book is dedicated to: Emmaline Leilani Salter, my wonderful wife, my constant friend, and my date on trips to Fenway Park; Katherine Brantley Salter, my sweet and funny daughter who has grown into a young woman of substance, talent, and grace like her extraordinary mother; and to the memory of my persevering mother, Alline Haskins Salter, who taught me to love books.

www.upress.state.ms.us

The University Press of Mississippi is a member of the Association of American University Presses.

Copyright © 2015 by Sid Salter
All rights reserved
Manufactured in the United States of America

First printing 2015
∞
Library of Congress Cataloging-in-Publication Data

Salter, Sidney L. (Sid)
Jack Cristil : voice of the MSU bulldogs / by Sid Salter. — Revised edition.
pages cm
Includes bibliographical references and index.
ISBN 978-1-4968-0500-3 (pbk. : alk. paper) — ISBN 978-1-4968-0501-0 (ebook) 1. Cristil, Jack.
2. Sportscasters—United States—Biography. 3. Mississippi State University—Football. 4. Mississippi
State Bulldogs (Football team)—History. I. Title.
GV742.42.C75S25 2015
070.4'4979609—dc23
[B]
2015015796

British Library Cataloging-in-Publication Data available

Photos that appear in this book are from the personal collection of Jacob S. (Jack) Cristil family, used with permission of *The Northeast Mississippi Daily Journal*, or the combined collections of Mississippi State University. No part of this book may be reproduced, stored in a retrieval system or transmitted in any form or by any means electronic, mechanical, photocopying, recording or otherwise without permission of the copyright owner. Cover photo by the late longtime MSU photographer Fred Faulk.

CONTENTS

Foreword by John Grisham. 5

Introduction. 9

Chapter 1 – Last Call in Knoxville 17

Chapter 2 – The Immigrants' Son 45

Chapter 3 – "A Pretty Good Shoe Salesman" 59

Chapter 4 – Finding His Voice 75

Chapter 5 – "Cut Out The Bull!". 87

Chapter 6 – A Lady Named Mavis 95

Chapter 7 – Shalom, My Friend 143

Chapter 8 – The Coaching Carousel. 153

Chapter 9 – The Final Season 191

Chapter 10 – "Wrap This One in Maroon and White!" 209

Epilogue – Signing Off On His Own Terms 221

Bibliography. 243

Index. 248

FOREWORD

My first recollection of doing anything in this world is that of a small boy sitting on the front porch of a sharecropper's house in the cotton fields of northeastern Arkansas, listening to a Cardinals game on the radio as my mother and grandmother shelled butter beans and my father and grandfather talked about Stan Musial. I knew Musial's background long before I was exposed to important historical figures like Robert E. Lee, Elvis, or even Moses. I also knew I did not want to be a cotton farmer.

The year was around 1960. As with most of those early, clouded memories, I've never been sure of the exact date. The first game blurred into the second, then third, and so on, and I vividly recall sitting there on those hot, endless nights listening to the games.

The date is not important. What I remember is the magic of radio. The announcers were Harry Caray and Jack Buck, calling the games on station KMOX out of St. Louis, a city that seemed a million miles away. The languid pace of baseball allowed them plenty of time to fill in with history, statistics, all manner of colorful stories. Then you could hear the crack of the bat, the roar of the crowd, and Harry Caray, always easily excitable, was yelling into his microphone with a dramatic description of the action. Even as a small boy, I had a hyperactive imagination, and as I listened to the call I could visualize what was happening up there in St. Louis. On that old front porch, there were moments of unbearable tension.

Eventually, mercifully, we left the farm, and for most of my childhood we lived in small towns in Arkansas, Louisiana, and Mississippi. We never left Cardinal country, and the game, every game, was listened to with a loyalty that today is hard to believe. If we were in the car, the radio was on and the entire family listened. If we were at home, my father turned on a radio in the kitchen and we always knew the score. If my buddies and I were playing in a youth league game at the local field, it was not unusual to hear three or four radios at high volume scattered throughout the bleachers.

Then baseball began to change. Free agency arrived, and this year's line-up would not be the same next year. More games were televised, and radio audiences declined. I quit listening to the Cardinals when I went to college.

In the fall of 1974, Mississippi State put together one of its more exciting and successful teams. I was a sophomore at a smaller school and somehow found myself in Memphis on October 19. The Bulldogs – Rockey Felker, Dennis Johnson, Harvey Hull, Terry Vitrano – were playing a good Memphis State team, and the Liberty Bowl Stadium was rocking. A gentleman directly behind me had a large transistor radio, with the volume cranked up, and that was the first time I heard Jack Cristil's voice. Of course, I can't describe it, now or then, but suffice to say it had that unmistakable energy that gave the impression that something dramatic might happen on every play. When State drove 98 yards in the last three minutes to win on a two-point conversion, Bulldog fans were delirious, but their announcer somehow kept his cool. There was no doubt who Jack was rooting for, but, as always, he was too professional to become a fan.

I was hooked. I tuned in to Jack every Saturday afternoon until the end of the season, then transferred to MSU. I'm not suggesting that Jack Cristil was the reason I went to Starkville. The real reasons, though complicated at the time, have now been forgotten.

I'll just say it was not my first transfer.

In those days before cable television, radio was our life line, and Jack Cristil was the voice of authenticity and excitement. We gathered in dorm rooms, frat houses, the student union, and listened and cheered as Jack called the action from Athens, Auburn, Knoxville, and Baton Rouge. We imitated him. We urged him to make good things happen on the field. We marveled at his sentences and one-liners, and we often speculated that he spent hours crafting clever phrases that rolled off his tongue in the thick of the action. He made a difficult task seem so easy.

If we were lucky, we might get two or three State games on TV each season. When they were broadcast, most Bulldog fans watched with the volume turned down and the radio turned up. When the team was at home, radios were abundant in the stands and Jack could always be heard, even in the student section. As we watched the games, we listened to him because he brought even more excitement to the action. He was quick, humorous, entertaining, informative, and he had that gravelly, sing-song voice that left no doubt he was having fun.

He called the game with integrity. There are announcers who tend to exaggerate. Others are so biased you can't always trust them. But not Jack Cristil.

He understood the importance of understatement. There are announcers who yell and get so excited they forget their audience. Others say far too much. But not Jack Cristil.

Occasionally, we did not have the top team in the conference, but we always had the best guy on the radio.

— JOHN GRISHAM
AUGUST 15, 2011

INTRODUCTION

Journalists are storytellers. That's what we do. Mississippi State University is a place that's full of powerful, meaningful stories about faculty, staff, and students who gained knowledge and inspiration on this campus and then moved on to carve out the most magnificent of careers in their chosen fields of study over the course of their lives.

Those stories need to be told. I feel privileged to have the opportunity to tell some of them as the university's first journalist-in-residence.

If there has been a failing over the history of MSU and of the broader state of Mississippi as well, it has been that at times we've done a poor job of telling our best and most uplifting stories. As they told us in Sunday School when I was a child: "Don't hide your light under a bushel." Too many times over the decades, the bright lights of MSU stakeholders didn't receive the attention they deserved not only from the world at large, but from within our own MSU family as well.

One of the benefits of putting a journalist in a university library setting with the time and tools to write is that there exists an opportunity – away from the pressures of daily news cycle deadlines - to develop and tell those stories in context and package them in a way that captures and honors the essence of the subject.

As I began my duties at MSU, one of the more significant developments in the life of the university was taking place – a story that needed to be developed and shared with a broader audience. It was a story that dovetailed nicely with the assets of MSU's Mitchell Memorial Library and with the broader archival assets of the university at large.

That story was Jack Cristil's incredible 58 years of service to MSU and the absolute love that the people of the Bulldog Nation came to feel in return for this unassuming man who has bridged the memories of generations of the MSU faithful.

Jack Cristil is the gold standard of college sports radio play-by-play broadcasting – the last holdout from the old school Golden Age of radio. When sports broadcasting professionals and college sports fans talk about the great radio play-by-play announcers of all time, Cristil's name is a significant part of that discussion and has been for decades. The word "icon" is overused in our hyperbolic society, but it is the accurate word when one is talking about the loyalty and respect that MSU fans and even the fans of rival teams across the Southeastern Conference have invested in Cristil over the last six decades.

When MSU fans think of the essential symbols of their university, they think cowbells, brindle English bulldogs, 3 lb. "cannon balls" of Edam cheese, and the urgent, driving staccato of Jack Cristil's rich baritone voice describing Bulldog football and basketball action in a straightforward manner that was fair, factual, and dignified. Win, lose, or draw – and let's face it, through no fault of his own he's called more losses than wins over the years – Jack Cristil's national acclaim and distinctive identity was a point of significant pride for Mississippi State fans.

Simply put, Jack Cristil was one of the best radio play-by-play announcers in American history and without question one of the best ever to ply the radio broadcasting trade in SEC football stadiums and basketball arenas. Cristil's record of longevity with one university is unlikely ever to be broken in the SEC and is second overall in NCAA history.

Cristil served MSU and the Bulldog Nation with pride, civility, and passion until his health simply would not allow him to continue. Jack's voice never failed him – but the body that supported "The Voice" finally began to break down at age 85.

We live in a microwave popcorn society in which real loyalty is rarely afforded to those who serve or entertain us. This is a country that believes "new and improved" to be an American birthright. Yet after 58 years behind the microphone, Cristil left the stage at MSU with the fans begging for more – just one more game, one more season, one more year.

How much do we really know about this man whose work captivated multi-generational audiences of MSU fans for six decades? What made Cristil's just-the-facts delivery and old school rejection of "homerism" in calling the game as he saw it – rather than as fans and sponsors might want to hear it called – so dear to the hearts of the Bulldog faithful and to sports fans across the South?

What made Cristil's exemplary work on behalf of MSU so valuable that even arch-rival Ole Miss fans grudgingly admitted that Cristil was simply the best at his craft? Why did Cristil reject the lure of bright lights and bigger paychecks calling professional sports to keep the same job in Starkville for 58 years?

Cristil has a story worth telling and a Mississippi life worth celebrating. To tell Cristil's story properly, the most important ingredient was enlisting Jack's genuine interest and active cooperation. Frankly, when MSU President Mark Keenum and MSU Athletic Director Scott Stricklin first approached Cristil about authorizing and participating in a book project, Cristil wasn't too keen on the idea.

"I'm afraid I may forget to recognize someone who deserves credit for whatever success I've had," Cristil told Keenum and

Stricklin aboard a plane from Tupelo to Jackson when Cristil was called for a command farewell appearance before both houses of the Mississippi Legislature after announcing his retirement. "Besides, I can't imagine people being much interested in my life's story." But when Cristil heard that the proceeds of the book would finance a scholarship in his honor at MSU, the octogenarian broadcaster reacted as he always has when the university called on him to serve – Cristil responded with hard work and enthusiasm.

When the time came to begin the interview process, I called Jack in Tupelo and asked for permission to call on him at his home on Marquette Street. "Come on up," he said. "Let's give it a go and see what happens."

The result of that invitation was a remarkable series of interviews at the kitchen table of Jack's home. For this writer, the opportunity to get to know a man who has been a presence in the lives of my family – my late parents, my sisters, my daughter and even my grandson – has been rewarding and inspiring.

I asked questions; Jack answered. He smoked; I took notes. We commiserated on watching our wives battle dread diseases bravely and with hope – and of the despair of watching them lose those battles. We talked of beloved sisters taken from us too soon by brain tumors. We talked of our profound respect for our mothers and the influence they had in each of our lives. For a man born in the "Roaring Twenties" and another born at the end of the Baby Boom, we had more in common than I could ever have imagined.

His voice was the same projecting off the walls of his pine-paneled kitchen as it had been off the windshield of my dad's Chevrolet when we listened – just the two of us and Jack – to so many MSU football and basketball games. The passion about MSU sports, the pride in being given the opportunity to serve the university, and the intensity about getting everything just right was pure Jack Cristil.

What made these visits special was the added element of the visual. Watching Jack's face, seeing his smile, hearing his laughter, and watching those expressive eyes – sometimes sparkling with mirth and occasionally welling with the tears that a long life extracts from those who approach nine decades on this Earth – was moving.

What a privilege this journey has been with this tough old Bulldog. What a class act Cristil has been for the whole of his life and what a tremendous ambassador for Mississippi State University. Politicians talk about "faith and family" during campaign seasons, but Cristil built his life around those concepts. He didn't see broadcasting MSU football and basketball games as a job; he saw it as a dream come true and an opportunity to be affiliated with a great institution of higher learning.

No MSU president, no dean, and certainly no football coach or English professor ever felt a more proprietary interest in Mississippi State than Jack Cristil does to this day. If there was a secret revealed in our interviews for this biography, it is that he saw his role not so much as a play-by-play sports radio broadcaster but as a representative of the university serving the public.

Jack Cristil's loyalty was not to the wealthy alums, to the athletic program's big donors, to the coaches, or to the Legislature. He recognized their importance and appreciated their contributions. Cristil brought a decidedly blue collar work ethic to his broadcasting duties at MSU. His loyalty was to the MSU fan who might not ever have the free time or the money to attend a game in person but who still felt a connection to the university. Cristil's loyalty was to the man alone in the nursing home, the fixed-income widow, the mechanic under the car on Saturday afternoon, the cop on the beat, and anyone who wasn't going to get a first-hand account of the game unless they got it from him on their radios.

Cristil told Marty Mule of *The Times-Picayune* newspaper in New Orleans in an Oct. 20, 2000 interview: "Any radio broadcast, regardless of who you are, is a poor substitute for being at the stadium, watching the event in person. But for those who can't be there, our job is to report those things we see as honestly and impartially as we possibly can, and make it descriptive enough so they can see it through your eyes and your vocabulary. This is the job we're trying to do – paint the pictures for those who can't see the game." He explained to *The* (Memphis) *Commercial Appeal's* Ron Higgins in a 2002 interview on the observance of Cristil's 50th year as the MSU radio broadcaster: "That's my philosophy. I want the listener to see the event as if they were there. I want them to be as near as they can be. That's why I try to be their eyes and ears."

For generations of Mississippians and for countless SEC and NCAA sports fans across the country, Jack Cristil was for 58 years their reliable, recognizable connection to Mississippi State University. The impression those listeners got from Cristil – and, by extension, from MSU – was that the university valued fairness, balance, accuracy, good sportsmanship, and hard-charging competition regardless the outcome.

Cristil's MSU career began with instructions to keep it simple, honest, and direct in the 1950s and ended in a 21st century "sports marketing" environment, where the university athletic program is tethered to the multi-million dollar university and SEC broadcasting contracts and licensing deals that have become the economic lifeblood of major college athletics across the nation. While he adapted to the emerging new technologies right up to the end of his career, Jack Cristil never adapted to modern sports marketing.

He was honest with his listeners, treating them with respect and calling the games in the most straightforward manner possible. He did it in a highly literate fashion and with old world manners. But like a good umpire, Jack Cristil called it like he saw it – and for almost 60 years, those of us who love MSU were fortunate enough to hear what Jack saw. Over time, we came to know that as the picture of the game that he painted developed, we could trust him to tell us the truth even when the truth hurt.

This is Jack's story. His support and cooperation have been generous and selfless. Jack's daughters, Kay Cristil Clouatre and Rebecca Cristil Nelson, were most gracious – as were his sisters, Miriam "Mimi" Cristil Lapides and Zelda Cristil Esgro – in helping this author paint an accurate portrait of Jack's childhood and of his life with his beloved wife, Mavis.

Thanks go to Larry Templeton, Rockey Felker, Straton Karatassos, and a host of others who gave of their time in interviews and provided leads to contact sources. Steve Davenport and Pat LeBlanc at TeleSouth Communications provided audio clips for the book's audio compact disc, as did Random House Audio Books.

This book would not have been possible without the collaboration of so many within the Bulldog family. Let me recognize Scott Stricklin, Mike Nemeth, and John Cade in the MSU Athletic Department; Maridith Geuder and her staff in University Relations; Bennie Ashford, Mike Godwin, and Lewis Halbert at the University Television Center; Steve Ellis and his staff at the MSU campus radio station, WMSV; the late MSU photographer Fred Faulk; David Murray at *Dawgs' Bite*; and Jack Cristil's worthy successor as MSU's broadcaster Jim Ellis.

The steady hand supporting me in this process has been the Mississippi State University Libraries' personnel and resources which have enabled me to successfully orchestrate this collaboration. Dean Frances Coleman has been a driving force, as has Pattye Archer and her staff in the Libraries' fantastic Instructional Media Center – including the yeoman's work of Jim Tomlinson in designing the dust jacket and packaging the collection of photographs for this book. I'm also indebted to Randall McMillen, the Library's digital projects coordinator, for his work on the audio CD, and MSU archivist Mike Ballard. The combined hard work of Kate Salter, Leilani Salter and Lyle Tate in editing and proofing the manuscript was invaluable.

I'm grateful for the support of this project by the MSU Foundation under the direction of John Rush and David Easley. Dr. Jimmy Abraham's support and that of his able staff at the MSU Alumni Association was crucial to making this project successful.

Let me also recognize and honor the many years of faithful reporting by talented newspaper sports reporters and columnists in Mississippi and across the South. In researching this book, I relied heavily on the work of talented sports journalists at *The Clarion-Ledger, The Commercial Appeal, The Northeast Mississippi Daily Journal, Starkville Daily News, Dawgs' Bite,* and countless other publications. Let me especially thank my longtime friend and colleague Rick Cleveland, the dean of Mississippi sports writers at *The Clarion-Ledger,* for his willingness to be a sounding board for me on this project.

To say that fellow MSU alum John Grisham's generous participation in this project was helpful is an understatement, but it turns out John is as rabid a Jack Cristil fan as I am. Most of all, I'm grateful for the encouragement of MSU President Mark Keenum and MSU First Lady Rhonda Keenum, whose shared vision for the university is predicated on honoring the institution's past while building for the university's future.

CHAPTER ONE

LAST CALL IN KNOXVILLE

"We have 3.4 seconds left in the game. Lewis thus far on the day, by the way, has hit three out of four, and his free throw is long, it's not good. Tennessee rebounds it, Hopson grabs it, he's going to fire from midcourt. Missed it. Wrap this one in maroon and white!"

—JACK CRISTIL'S FINAL PLAY-BY-PLAY CALL
MISS. STATE 70, TENNESSEE 69
THOMPSON-BOLING ARENA, KNOXVILLE, TENN.
FEB. 26, 2011

THAT'S HOW 58 YEARS OF JACK CRISTIL'S PROFESSIONAL LIFE AT Mississippi State University ended – in a rush of 55 words.

Two events in Knoxville, Tenn., made national headlines on Feb. 26, 2011 – first, Knoxville Police Department Officer Andrew Olson was shot and seriously wounded during a routine traffic stop by an 18-year-old assailant with a cross tattooed on his face. The other news item of national prominence that day was the last play-by-play radio broadcast or "call" being made by legendary retiring Mississippi State University play-by-play announcer Jack

Cristil at the University of Tennessee's 21,678-seat Thompson-Bowling Arena.

"I had mixed emotions before the game," said Cristil. "I wanted to do well on the air, but I wasn't feeling well. I just had no energy left."

Prior to the tipoff of the last college athletic contest he would broadcast after six decades behind the microphone, Cristil got a standing ovation from an SEC crowd in an opponent's arena. ESPN, the "worldwide leader in sports," interrupted their national broadcast to cut to a live second-half feed of Cristil making his final call of the basketball game between the UT Volunteers and Cristil's beloved MSU Bulldogs. A national television audience heard Cristil's final call.

As hosts, the UT administration and athletic department were deferential and respectful to MSU's retiring broadcaster. "The Tennessee folks and their fans could not have been more gracious in their acknowledgement that I was wrapping it up. And I think having my longtime friend John Ward, the retired UT broadcaster there with me, was helpful. But honestly, I was just so weak and tired," Cristil said.

The TV audience saw a man whose hair was still coarse and thick, but more white than gray. The square jaw that had been so prominent when he wore the uniform of the U.S. Army Air Corps in World War II had softened and rounded. At age 85, Cristil's once broad shoulders had stooped a bit.

Cristil had "known for some time" that the end of his career was approaching. Beyond the undeniable fact of his age, there was the simple physical erosion of a decade of increasingly serious health problems.

On June 26, 2001, Cristil was admitted to North Mississippi

Medical Center in Tupelo for an abdominal aneurysm. The surgery to repair the aneurysm was major and put Jack, then 75, in doubt of continuing his phenomenal streak as MSU's play-by-play broadcaster for the 2001 football season.

In a Sept. 2, 2001 interview with *The Clarion-Ledger's* Todd Kelly, Cristil addressed the illness: "I'd never really had major surgery before, so I didn't know what to expect. I got a little antsy when I stayed weak for some period of time, but I bounced back pretty good once my strength started to come around. It took roughly six to eight weeks."

The 2001 illness got Cristil's attention but not for the reasons he told the media. In that same 2001 interview with Kelly, Cristil said for public consumption: "I guess self-preservation is the first thing that came to mind. You feel a sense of responsibility after all of these years. My friends and neighbors were encouraging me. There were emails from people all over the country. All of that was gratifying, so I'm sure it was a motivating factor."

But the truth was more ominous. Jack Cristil was diagnosed with prostate cancer in 2001. It was that diagnosis that led to the tests that revealed the aneurysm.

Daughter Rebecca said: "Had he not had cancer, his kidney problems would not have been discovered as early, and chances are the aneurysm might not have been discovered in time."

During the battery of tests and x-rays that revealed his dangerous abdominal aneurysm in 2001, it was revealed that his left kidney had at some point either been injured or atrophied and was not functioning. At 75, Cristil was told he had only one functioning kidney.

"That really kind of blew my mind," said Cristil, recounting the event. "At that point, I learned that my left kidney wasn't functioning and that the renal artery to my right kidney was 'kinked up' and had to be straightened out."

Cristil said he'd had no knowledge of any prior kidney injury or disease. "About the only thing I could think of was, back in the 1950s, I was broadcasting a Mississippi State game at the University of Tennessee in Knoxville, and I had a terrible kidney stone attack," he said. "The pain was excruciating. What I remember most about that was that the Tennessee trainer helped us get to the UT Medical Center, and I was treated by a Dr. Acuff, who ended up being a third cousin to the country singer Roy Acuff."

After the initial examination and diagnosis, Cristil said Dr. Acuff asked abruptly: "Mr. Cristil, do you drink beer?"

Jack said he reflected for a time before giving his answer – considering his status as a representative of MSU and considering the odds of that answer getting back to Starkville: "I finally told him that I had a beer every now and again."

"Good," said Dr. Acuff. "Because the best way to pass a kidney stone is to drink all the beer you can get." Cristil said he told Roy Acuff's third cousin: "You're my kind of doctor!"

But the 2001 hospitalization and the sobering news it revealed about Jack's prostate cancer and his kidney disease wasn't his last bout with illness. After enduring a regimen of radiation treatments, Cristil survived the prostate cancer and the public never knew about that health crisis – only his family and his inner circle of close friends and associates. In mid-March in 2005, Cristil – who has smoked cigarettes since his Army Air Corps days – was again hospitalized at 79 for pneumonia.

Each time he was sidelined by illness, Jack would battle back. But the kidney disease continued its steady, relentless assault on his aging body.

Over the two years that preceded what the public perceived as Cristil's abrupt announcement of his retirement, Tupelo nephrologist Dr. Martin Lee had warned the beloved MSU broadcaster of the symptoms that would eventually signal that he would no longer be able to live without engaging in kidney dialysis for the rest of his life.

"At my age, a kidney transplant wasn't an option, and it shouldn't have been an option," said Cristil. "I've lived a good long life. When transplant opportunities become available, they need to go to younger people, not to folks my age."

The classic textbook symptoms of chronic kidney disease are, according to the National Kidney Foundation: fatigue, trouble concentrating, diminished appetite, insomnia, muscle cramps, swelling of feet and ankles, dry and itchy skin, and other symptoms involving the body's ability to throw off toxins.

"Over the six months before I announced my retirement, I had no energy," said Cristil. "I couldn't walk from my house 50 feet to the mailbox without serious fatigue. My breathing was labored, and I just felt washed out. I guess the poisons were just building up in my system."

Doctors in recent months told Cristil that his remaining functional kidney, the right kidney, was functioning at only about 10 percent capacity. The time had come for dialysis. Cristil had decided on his own during MSU's Gator Bowl trip that he would not be able to do more than perhaps complete the 2011 basketball season before dialysis became an inevitable reality in his life.

"I could feel myself losing strength by the day," said Cristil. "Because of the basketball schedule, Jim Ellis and I had flown from Memphis to Charlotte and on to Jacksonville for the Gator Bowl. We had an extra broadcast in Jacksonville the night before the game, and I was simply exhausted. While everyone else was out celebrating, I was holed up in the hotel room reading a John Grisham novel – that's all I had the strength to do other than meet my broadcast obligations."

After the Gator Bowl trip, Dr. Lee and Cristil agreed that finishing the 2011 basketball season would be difficult if not impossible. Still, Cristil wanted to try to complete the season. "You never want to stop what you love doing until circumstances leave you no other choice," Cristil said.

Cristil in 1994 told *The Commercial Appeal's* Ron Higgins that when the time came to step down, MSU wouldn't have to show him the door. "I'm not going to be one of these guys who outlive their usefulness." In the September 2009 edition of *Mississippi Sports* magazine, ESPN's BulldogJunction.com senior writer Paul Jones, in a superb story on Cristil's MSU career, quoted the broadcaster: "I am in the fourth quarter, and the clock is getting in the red, and I am trying to make it to overtime."

But Dr. Lee and Cristil both knew that time had run out and that there would be no overtime – at least not for Cristil's radio broadcasting career. When the time came to step down, Cristil made the difficult decision and orchestrated the announcement after he was convinced that he'd gone as far as he could go and still do a credible job of the broadcast.

"I had been in conversation with my doctors, and it was evident that things were going downhill in a hurry," said Cristil. "Dr. Lee had prepared me over a period of time for this eventual necessity of dialysis, and when I started having these symptoms, he wanted me to begin dialysis immediately. But I put him off two weeks until I could get my ducks in a row."

But Jack Cristil came to Knoxville dressed for work that day –

his last day on the job. He wore khaki slacks, and a tan Mississippi State sweater vest with maroon piping and a university logo over a maroon dress shirt. Despite wearing his university's colors amid a sea of Volunteer Orange-clad Tennessee fans, the fans gathered in Knoxville, and the national television audience on ESPN knew they were seeing greatness and history as Cristil prepared to make his final call as "the Voice of the Mississippi State Bulldogs." The UT fans joined the small contingent of MSU fans in rising to their feet to honor Cristil. Their applause thundered as UT officials invited Cristil to take a pregame bow in front of the 20,777 fans in attendance. The Vols honored Cristil with a video highlight package on their arena's Jumbotron in pregame ceremonies.

Before tipoff, Cristil's on-air MSU colleague Jim Ellis expressed the feelings of Mississippi State fans everywhere when he said on the pregame broadcast: "Jack, it's a funny feeling right now as I say I hope you have a great call and a great game, and I hope that you can wrap it in maroon and white."

On his last day on the job for MSU, Jack Cristil's voice remained the last great voice of the Golden Age of college sports radio in America. At 85, Cristil was the last man standing when the inevitable debates ensued over who really was the best college sports play-by-play broadcaster in the country – not simply the best broadcaster still on the air, but the best college sports radio broadcaster ever.

In the Spring 1992 edition of MSU's *Alumnus* magazine, Cristil told fellow broadcaster and former MSU broadcast coordinator Steve Ellis: "Radio was my first love, and having shared in so many of the things that radio grew to be and to be a part of it is very pleasing to me. In the early days, we would broadcast pep rallies, Christmas parades, things that many people wanted to take part in but might not be able to be there. They may seem unimportant today, but they were very important to people at that time. Everything was a challenge, and a lot of things had never been done before, but we went out and did them . . . it's a real art form."

Before ESPN's *SportsCenter*, before the days of receiving real-time play-by-play texts and RSS feeds via a host of smart phone software applications, and before college football had proliferated several television networks devoted to 24/7 coverage of the game, there was simply a man and a microphone and the imagination of his listeners who had no other means of following the game than the picture that broadcaster painted in their minds.

A lifetime ago on the north side of Memphis, Jack Cristil had grown up listening to the first great voices of the Golden Age of radio. There was Graham McNamee, the medium's first national star. A 1927 *Time* magazine article called McNamee "the chief actor-manager of radio."

The other voices that fired Cristil's imagination as a boy included Bill Stern on the Colgate Sports Newsreel, boxing and horse racing sportscaster Clem McCarthy (the voice of the Pathe News RKO Newsreels), Edward "Ted" Husing of the CBS Radio Network, and "blow-by-blow" boxing announcer Don Dunphy.

Cristil called Stern "an emotional broadcaster, very energetic on the air, and he would let the excitement build, and his broadcast would grow in excitement with it." MSU fans would get brief glimpses of that in Cristil's otherwise steady calls – like MSU's 1980 signature 6-3 football win over Alabama: "Bulldogs recover! Bulldogs recover! Bulldogs recover!"

In his 1999 book *Sports on New York Radio*, David J. Halberstam of Westwood One Sports network dubbed McCarthy's "gravelly voice and dramatic style" as "a whiskey tenor." Halberstam also believed Stern was the forerunner of later radio legend Paul Harvey's no-nonsense, lilting style of delivery – writing that Harvey used many of Stern's broadcasting devices in his performances.

Cristil said that he heard McNamee "primarily calling prize fights." Husing, Cristil recalled, "had an extensive vocabulary and chose the appropriate word for every occasion and circumstance. You never got the idea that he was talking down to you as a listener." Yet Husing had a habit of calling the action as he saw it. Husing was temporarily banned by Harvard University from calling their football games and by the nation's first commissioner of professional baseball, Kenesaw Mountain Landis, from calling the World Series for his frank assessment of the play of individual athletes, teams, and umpires. That broadcast trait of frank and sometimes biting honesty would be a part of Cristil's skill set during his long run at MSU.

There was the inimitable Red Barber, who influenced generations of baseball play-by-play broadcasters. Barber, a native of Columbus, Miss., went on to a legendary career broadcasting the exploits of the Brooklyn Dodgers. Barber coined such phrases to describe a close game as "tighter than a new pair of shoes on a rainy day" and would refer to the ball as "slicker than boiled okra" when a fielder couldn't make the catch.

In analyzing Cristil's broadcasting style as it would evolve, one can hear a number of similarities between Barber's laid-back catchphrases and those that Cristil would offer with growing confidence over the course of his career – despite the fact that Cristil said in 2011 that he rarely heard Barber's broadcasts: "We didn't get a lot of Brooklyn Dodger baseball down in Memphis." But like Barber, Cristil's unique phrasing was memorable. The 1963 Library Bowl in Philadelphia comes to mind, when Cristil observed that the frigid Pennsylvania temperatures had left the playing conditions "colder than a pawnbroker's heart."

Cristil told Ellis in the 1992 *Alumnus* piece that his career influences had been "Ted Husing, Bill Stern, and Clem McCarthy. They were the pioneers in this industry. They were doing things that had never been done before, and they were doing it quite well."

In a special program printed for Cristil's "golden anniversary" celebration at MSU in 2002, former MSU sports information director and then-Big 12 Conference assistant commissioner Bo Carter wrote: "It was while growing up and listening to the radio greats of his youth – Ted Husing, Bill Stern, Clem McCarthy and many of the other classic sports voices of that era – that the MSU legend began molding his style. Many have compared Cristil to the late Stern, whose inflection and genuine interest in every game really did make it feel as if he was talking to the listeners right in their living rooms."

In Carter's heartfelt article celebrating Cristil's 50-year anniversary at MSU, Jack told him: "I have tried to broadcast in a similar style, and I know folks like to listen to someone with some enthusiasm and feel comfortable with the broadcaster. Yelling and screaming just doesn't cut it many times, and people get used to a fluid and professional approach."

Listening to Cristil's broadcasts, it was easy to envision that the influences of Stern, McCarthy, Husing, Dunphy, Barber, and even McNamee were evident in Cristil's courtly on-air manners and in his spot-on command of both a refined vocabulary and memorable phrasings. In all things, Cristil paid deference to painting the most accurate word picture possible.

In that milieu, Jack Cristil wasn't merely an artist, he was Rembrandt. He painted precise, clear, and balanced portraits of the game. Like he was told when he was hired at MSU by athletic director Dudy Noble over a half-century ago on a handshake: "Son, you tell the radio audience who has got the ball, what the score is, and how much time is left, and cut out the bull." For 58 years, he'd done that. Jack Cristil had used an economy of words, a disciplined delivery, and the lessons he'd learned from the old radio masters to meet and exceed Noble's charge to him.

Cristil told Paul Jones in the *Mississippi Sports* magazine article: "I knew what I wanted to do as a youngster, since I was eight or 10 years old. But I never dreamed I would go through and be at Mississippi State for (more than) a half-century."

The tired, ailing man behind the microphone that day in an east Tennessee basketball arena was preparing to end a Mississippi State broadcasting career that he'd begun some 400 miles away in a west Tennessee football stadium 58 years earlier. How does one contain the memories and the emotions of 58-year career in a two-hour radio broadcast of a 40-minute basketball game?

Behind that microphone was a man whose record of both sports broadcasting excellence and longevity in the Southeastern Conference is far and away the best and may literally never be broken. Only one broadcaster in the whole of NCAA Division 1 history – Max Falkenstien of the University of Kansas at 60 years – ever logged a longer record of longevity serving one university as a sports broadcaster than did Jack Cristil at MSU. That's the big picture, the bright line statement of Cristil's remarkable career in Starkville.

Along the way, Cristil earned a multitude of professional honors from his peers and from grateful fans. None tells the tale more succinctly than his 1997 National Football Foundation/College Football Hall of Fame's Chris Schenkel Award, which recognizes broadcasters with direct ties to universities and colleges rather than the national broadcasters. Schenkel was the first winner of the award, receiving the first trophy as it was named in his honor.

Of all the college sports broadcasters in the nation, Cristil was the second winner of the award. Falkenstien earned the third Schenkel Award recognition a year after Cristil.

Yet from a personal standpoint, Cristil was also an octogenarian widower whose health was betraying him, a dignified gentleman who lived alone on a quiet street in Tupelo, Miss., and whose daughters lived far away in Georgia and Louisiana. As Cristil in recent years often told interviewers who asked about his future: "Hell, I don't buy green bananas when I go to the store."

He'd outlived most of his friends and contemporaries and outlasted his professional colleagues. At the age of 85, Jack Cristil's weathered baritone voice and innate talent for painting the unfolding scenes of college football and basketball games for radio listeners had outlasted them all – even Falkenstien's, whose football and basketball broadcasting record at the University of Kansas from 1946 to 2006 exceeded Cristil's tenure at Mississippi State by two years.

"I never met Falkenstien," Cristil would say after his own retirement. "Our paths just never crossed. But 60 years at one school? That's marvelous."

As he prepared for his final broadcast in Knoxville – a Bulldog basketball road game between MSU Coach Rick Stansbury's 14-13 Bulldogs and UT Coach Bruce Pearl's 17-11 Volunteers – Cristil's 58-year career as MSU's play-by-play broadcaster had seen all the legendary college sports radio broadcasters of his generation fall by the wayside to retirement or death.

Some ended their careers graciously on their own terms; others were asked to leave as universities endured the ebb and flow of new university administrations, athletic directors, or coaching regimes. Some retired, and many died.

Falkenstien logged his 60 years at Kansas and retired in 2006. Oklahoma broadcasting legend Bob Barry, Sr. logged 51 years calling college football and basketball in the state of Oklahoma – 12 years for the University of Oklahoma Sooners, 18 years for arch-rival Oklahoma State University Cowboys, and then the final 21 years for OU. Barry retired in 2011 at the age of 80.

University of Minnesota broadcaster Ray Christensen is credited with 50 years as the voice of the Golden Gophers. He retired in 2001. Texas Tech University's "Gentleman" Jack Dale Schmanke posted 50 years of service broadcasting football and basketball games for the Red Raiders before he retired in 2003. At the University of Iowa, Jim Zabel *("Hug and kiss those radios, folks!")* was the play-by-play announcer for the Hawkeyes for 49 years.

University of Idaho broadcaster Bob Curtis logged 46 years calling Vandal football and basketball from 1958 until his retirement in 2004.

Washington State's Bob Robertson has been broadcasting Cougar football since 1964 with the exception of three years for a total of 43 seasons. Robertson quit calling WSU basketball games in 1994. To match Cristil's record, Robertson, 81, would have to continue broadcasting to age 95. Even then, Cristil was a two-sport broadcaster for 54 of his 58 seasons, while Robertson handled two-sport broadcasting duties at WSU only 27 years.

Only three SEC radio broadcasters approached Cristil's record at Mississippi State in terms of longevity at their schools – South Carolina's Bob Fulton, Florida's Otis Boggs, and Georgia's Larry Munson got within 15 and 16 seasons respectively of Cristil's 58-

year mark before they retired. Cristil would stay on the air three seasons past Munson's retirement. In Columbia, South Carolina's Fulton delivered 43 years of service from 1952 to 1995 broadcasting football and basketball as "the Voice of the Gamecocks." Fulton died in 2010 at the age of 89.

"Larry Munson and I go back to 1948," said Cristil. "I was doing Memphis baseball, and he was doing Nashville baseball. I liked him a great deal. He was enthusiastic and full of life. But our philosophies about broadcasting were vastly different. Georgia must have wanted more of a cheerleader, and Larry provided that. Mississippi State didn't." Cristil was friends with Boggs and later Fulton, as well, although South Carolina was a latecomer to SEC play.

Broadcasting for the SEC's "other" Bulldogs, Munson (revered by Georgia fans and loathed by SEC opponents as an admitted "homer" for his UGA Bulldogs) is three years older than Cristil, but didn't begin broadcasting for UGA football until 1966. Munson is best known for his breathless, shrieking calls like his signature classic when Georgia came back from the dead against Florida in 1980 on Lindsay Scott's 92-yard touchdown catch and run off a pass from quarterback Buck Belue to defeat the Gators 26-21: "*Florida in a stand-up five, they may or may not blitz, Belue third down on the 8, in trouble, he got a block behind him going to throw on the run, complete on the 25 to the 30, Lindsay Scott 35, 40, Lindsay Scott 45, 50, 45, 40. ... Run Lindsay, 25, 20, 15, 10, 5, Lindsay Scott! Lindsay Scott! Lindsay Scott!*" Munson served Georgia from 1966 to 2008, putting in 42 years behind the mike. Munson retired in 2008 and lives in Atlanta at age 88.

Boggs, the longtime voice of the University of Florida Gators, served for 42 years as a football and basketball play-by-play broadcaster in Gainesville from 1940 to 1982, when he retired. Boggs died in 2002 at age 82 after a long illness.

Frank Fallon was the "Voice of the Baylor Bears" for 42 years before retiring in 1994. Fallon died in 1997 at his home in Waco, Texas, at the age of 73. Leo W. "Jack" Fleming was a fixture in the West Virginia University football and basketball programs for a total of 41 years with two breaks during the 49 years between 1947 and 1996. Fleming died at age 77 in 2001.

Another Cristil contemporary was Louisiana State University's smooth John Ferguson, who broadcast LSU football for 41 seasons from 1946 to 1987 on WWL-AM's 50,000-watt clear channel station. Ferguson died in 2005 at the age of 86. "John Ferguson represented LSU so well, and I got to hear his broadcasts a great deal," said Cristil. "He was a real pro."

Gentleman John Ward *("It's football time in Tennessee!")*, who was also a lawyer, broadcast University of Tennessee basketball for 33 years and football for 30 years from 1965 to 1999. Ward and Cristil's long friendship and mutual respect was evident in Cristil's final broadcast in Nashville, as Ward showed up from retirement to take part in UT's salute to the MSU broadcaster.

There was Cristil's longtime friend Cawood Ledford *("Hello, everybody, this is Cawood Ledford")*, who delivered the play-by-play radio broadcasts of football and basketball games for 39 years for the University of Kentucky Wildcats from 1953 to 1992. Ledford called 18 Final Fours and 22 Kentucky Derbys during his distinguished career.

So respected was Ledford that following the broadcast of his final game in 1992 when Kentucky fell to the Duke Blue Devils 104-103 in the NCAA East Regional Final at the Metrodome in Minneapolis, Duke head coach Mike Krzyzewski strode to the UK broadcast booth immediately after the game to congratulate

Ledford on his career after Duke won what many Southeastern Conference and Atlantic Coast Conference fans consider the greatest college basketball game ever played. Ledford died of cancer in 2001 in Harlan, Ky., at the age of 75.

"I have a great deal of respect for Cawood Ledford at Kentucky and John Ward at Tennessee," Cristil told Steve Ellis in 1992. "They are from the old school in their approach. They try as best they possibly can to be impartial."

Al Ciraldo called football and basketball games for the "Ramblin' Wreck" at Georgia Tech for 38 years from 1954 to 1992, when he retired. Ciraldo, known for referring to his audience as "brothers and sisters," died in 1997 at the age of 76. "I really liked Al when Georgia Tech was a member of the SEC," said Cristil. "In later years, I'd see him at professional conventions. He was a lot of fun."

The legendary Bob Ufer was the broadcaster for Michigan football for 37 years – from 1944 until 10 days before his death from cancer in 1981. Ufer's son, Tom, told Barry Horn of *The Dallas Morning News* in 2005: "Dad thought football was a religion, and Saturday was the holy day of obligation. He gave a sermon every Saturday. and people actually listened."

Notre Dame's Tony Roberts *("TOUCHDOWN, IRISH!!!")* put up 26 years as the play-by-play broadcaster for the Fighting Irish. Roberts was released by the Westwood One radio network in 2006.

Over the course of Cristil's career at MSU, the University of Mississippi employed a number of radio broadcasters. Bill Goodrich *("Whew-Hoo, Mercy!")* was the "Voice of the Rebels" from 1958 to 1965. The late Stan Torgerson – a consummate broadcaster who was despised by Mississippi State fans *("HE SCORES!!!")* – was the "Voice of the Rebels" for a 17-year period in the 1960s and

1970s. Torgerson logged 61 years in radio and TV broadcasting before his death at age 82 in 2006. Charlie McAlexander, who broadcast play-by-play calls at four different SEC schools over the course of his career, was the Ole Miss sports broadcaster from 1972-78.

The venerable Mississippi journalist and lifetime Jack Cristil fan Orley Hood, writing about Torgerson's death for *The Clarion-Ledger* in 2006, observed that, like Cristil, the Rebel broadcaster was more than simply a distinctive voice. "He knew the best places. He knew the best wines," wrote Hood. "(Stan) built a wine cellar onto his house. He'd serve wine you couldn't get anywhere else in Mississippi and cheese you'd never heard of to clear our palate. And he'd tell tall tales with a twinkle in his eye."

On the eve of Cristil's induction into the Mississippi Sports Hall of Fame in 1992, *Clarion-Ledger* sports writer Mike Knobler wrote that despite their friendship, Cristil had a sense of humor about Torgerson's infatuation with the State-Ole Miss rivalry: "Torgerson remembers walking into McCarthy Gym and being greeted by an extremely loud chorus of boos. The boos continued as he made his way up the stairs to his broadcast table."

Torgerson told Knobler: "When I got to the top, Jack just smiled and looked at me and said 'Welcome to Mississippi State. I hope you like it here.' "

But Cristil's friendships with Rebel broadcasters were sincere and of long standing.

"I knew Bill Goodrich back when he was broadcasting Southern Mississippi games, and we got along very well," said Cristil. "Bill kept an upbeat broadcast. Some of his phrases got redundant, but that's all right. And I really enjoyed my association with Stan Torgerson. Stan and I worked together several years broadcasting the Mississippi High School Activities Association's high school all-star game."

Oxford native David Kellum, the 2011 Mississippi Sportscaster of the Year and a five-time winner of that award from the National Sportswriters and Sportscasters Association, is in his 23rd season as the "Voice of the Rebels." He became the play-by-play announcer for Rebel baseball as a freshman student at Ole Miss in 1978, and he is one of only a few announcers in the SEC handling play-by-play for football, men's basketball, and baseball.

"David Kellum is a true prince of a guy," said Cristil. "He is a really fine broadcaster. David got his start in broadcasting for Ole Miss at a young age, and I'm told he's got a chance to perhaps tie or break my record if he stays at it. If anyone was going to break that record in the SEC, I'd be tickled to death for it to be David Kellum – unless it was broken by my MSU broadcasting partner Jim Ellis."

The University of Alabama's Eli Gold has been broadcasting Crimson Tide games since 1988 and will observe his 23rd year of service to that university during the 2011 season. During the Bear Bryant era, Alabama broadcaster John Forney logged 19 years broadcasting play-by-play for the Crimson Tide audience. Forney died in 1997.

Paul Ells was the "Voice of the Arkansas Razorbacks" from 1978 until his death in a car crash in 2006 at the age of 70. Jim Fyffe served as the "Voice of the Auburn Tigers" for 22 years from 1981 until he died of a brain aneurysm prior to the 2003 football season.

Vanderbilt's Joe Fisher is in his 13th season as the "Voice of the Commodores," and, like Mississippi's Kellum, he is a three-sport broadcaster. Not only is Cristil's two-sport longevity in the college football and basketball ranks impressive, his record of service to MSU is notable even when compared with national and international broadcasters of professional sports. Irish Gaelic Athletic

Association football broadcaster Sean Og O'Ceallachain served Ireland's RTE (Ireland's public broadcasting network) listeners on his *Gaelic Sports Results* program for 63 years from 1948 to 2011 and retired at the age of 88 – a job he "inherited" from his father of the same name.

Vin Scully's 62 seasons with the Dodgers (1950–present) is the longest continuous gig of any broadcaster with a single club in the history of professional sports. ABC's Keith Jackson *("Whoa, Nelly!")* posted 54 years covering college football but not for one school.

As he prepared to retire, Cristil said he thought about his broadcasting colleagues – past and present: "There was never enough time to share with your friends and counterparts in the business. The broadcasts kept getting longer and longer – pre-game, the game, post-game – they just kept growing. At this age, you regret not having more fellowship and time with your friends and colleagues."

But to Cristil, the statistics, awards, and accolades of his craft were just that. Cristil told Barry Horn of *The Dallas Morning News* in his 2005 story on the gray eminences of college football radio broadcasts in which the MSU broadcaster figured prominently: "Let me be modest. The recognition was nice. But it's not like anyone knows me nationally. Unless you are a Mississippi State fan, I don't think I'm famous. If you root for the Bulldogs, you might know who I am."

John Pruett, the respected sports editor of *The Huntsville (Ala.) Times*, begged to differ. In a 1996 column celebrating the role radio played in the enjoyment of college football in the South, Pruett offered this terse assessment: "The SEC is blessed with some of the finest play-by-play football announcers in the country, including two of the best – John Ward of Tennessee and Jack Cristil of Mississippi State. Cristil, in my view, is the best pure football announcer I've ever heard."

In May 2011, a multi-engine Internet search of the terms "Jack Cristil & retires" three months after Cristil retired after the MSU-UT basketball game in Knoxville in February, 2011 generated 99,200 hits – clips and video of stories and packages from all across the nation. News of Cristil's retirement made ESPN's *SportsCenter* and was front-page news across Mississippi.

In the minds of Cristil's radio audience, the drama of Cristil's final call had been established just days before the looming MSU-UT basketball game that night in Knoxville. Again, he had painted the picture as only he could. Following a dismal MSU basketball 84-82 loss to LSU in the Humphrey Coliseum on Wednesday, Feb. 23, 2011, Cristil made the "honest and heartfelt" announcement that stunned most of the Bulldog Nation:

"I'm not going to talk basketball for the next couple of moments. I certainly would like to have a personal message with you. I have been privileged for the past 58 years to have the opportunity to represent Mississippi State University as their broadcaster for football and basketball.

"All good things, as they say in the trade, have to come to an end sooner or later. Please accept my sincere, my genuine, my honest, and heartfelt thank-you for all the kindness you have displayed to me over these past 58 years. It has been one genuine pleasure to be associated with such a magnificent university as this with the administration, the faculty, its students, and the Mississippi State family.

"The reason I am stepping down at this particular point, in conference with my physicians, Dr. Martin Lee in particular of Tupelo, Mississippi, it's been determined because of a deteriorating health situation in which I'm experiencing, that it is necessary for me to immediately start some

kidney dialysis, and in so doing, this treatment will restrict me to the point where I cannot represent this university the way it should be represented. And when I cannot do that, I have told many people over the years that I would step aside, and now it's time to step aside.

"Please, ladies and gentlemen, accept my genuine, my honest, my heartfelt thank-you for all the kindness, the courtesy, and the encouragement that you have given to me and to my family over these years. The Mississippi State University family is second-to-none, and as a family, I know you understand. Thank you very much. May God's blessings be upon you and your family. Thank you. That concludes our broadcast of Mississippi State basketball from Learfield Sports."

Cristil said he hadn't given a great deal of thought to his retirement announcement. "I didn't know what to expect," he said. "I hadn't thought about it. I really had no idea what to expect, but I really didn't think it was particularly newsworthy beyond MSU fans. I knew it would be news to them, but I didn't expect anything beyond that."

Kay Cristil Clouatre of Baton Rouge, La., Jack's eldest daughter, had let her friends on Facebook know of her father's decision to step down from his duties in a 4:35 p.m. post on her wall before the LSU game:

"Today's post is by far the hardest and most emotional post I think I will ever write on FB. I debated for several days as to whether posting on FB would be the 'right' thing to do. But, then I thought: You on FB are my family and true friends. So, with that being said, here it goes: Tonight is Jack Cristil's last night to ever call a game for Miss. State University. Due to health issues (beginning of dialysis), he has made the decision that the game tonight will be his last. I hope with all my heart and soul that we win tonight. I want to hear him say 'wrap it in maroon and white' one last time. To you, he will always be the Voice of the MSU Bulldogs. To

me, he is Daddy."

Kay's Facebook post set off a viral reaction on social media, sports message boards, newspaper sports blogs, and the like. An honest miscommunication between father and daughter – corrected by a conversation with Kay's younger sister, Rebecca Cristil Nelson in Augusta, Ga., less than two hours later – left Kay under the impression that the LSU game would be her father's final broadcast. By the time Jack Cristil actually made his eloquent radio announcement, the state's media was in full frenzy, and the news had made ESPN.

But Kay's poignant announcement lit a social media wildfire, and particularly among MSU fans. The fact that it was indeed the Tennessee game in Knoxville three days later that would mark Cristil's last call only gave State fans time to process the news and to prepare to experience a separation anxiety that most truly could not imagine.

"The national attention surprised me when I learned about it, but to tell the truth I really wasn't aware of all that while it was happening," Cristil said. "I had only told the girls (his daughters) and Jim (Ellis). So I had no idea of the extent of the news coverage."

Beyond the conversations with daughters Kay and Rebecca, Cristil said the hardest part of revealing his decision to retire was telling his longtime broadcast partner Jim Ellis.

"I wanted to tell Jim eyeball-to-eyeball, because I think he deserved that," said Cristil. "I had told him in the past about the kidney disease and the eventual dialysis, so I don't think he was totally surprised. He'd been my roommate on the road, and he knew. But I wanted to tell Jim first and foremost how much I appreciated working with him for 30 years. Jim's as dear a friend as I've ever had. It's been such a privilege to work with Jim. He's so outstanding."

Jack had been broadcasting MSU games longer than most MSU fans had been alive. Cristil's tenure at MSU had spanned the services of 11 MSU head football coaches, nine head basketball coaches, 11 university presidents, 11 U.S. presidents and 13 Mississippi governors. Cristil had called MSU games from the end of the Korean War through wars in Vietnam, the Persian Gulf, Iraq, Afghanistan, and the 1983 invasion of Grenada – the Caribbean island, not the Mississippi town on I-55 North.

Cristil's tenure at MSU began in 1953 – a year before the invention and mass production of pocket transistor radios by the Regency Company in 1954 and six months before FM radio began to enjoy any substantial commercial success in the U.S.

The MSU broadcaster carried his audience through wars and the protests of wars, from the most dangerous and violent days of the nation's civil rights era of a segregated South with segregated teams to an era in which African-American athletes dominated the rosters of MSU's football and basketball programs by the time he retired. Cristil's career lasted through the Cold War, the Space Race, Jack Kennedy's "New Frontier," and LBJ's "Great Society" to lunar landings, the fall of Saigon, and the shame of Watergate. Cristil's voice was constant through Jimmy Carter's "malaise," the Reagan administration, the "Me" Generation, the invention of cell phones and texting, the Monica Lewinsky scandal, the 9-11 attacks, and the election of Barack Obama as the nation's first African-American president.

Cristil's 1953 hiring was typed and distributed by teletype over the news wires. Cristil's retirement was "tweeted" on Twitter and posted on Facebook.

To put Cristil's tenure in proper perspective, consider this: When Cristil broadcast his first MSU game on Sept. 19, 1953, Dwight Eisenhower was in his first term as president, Nikita Khrushchev had taken control of the Soviet Central Committee 12 days earlier, Queen Elizabeth II had been on the throne of England less than three months, and Sir Edmund Hillary had scaled Mount Everest with Sherpa guide Tenzing Norgay just four months earlier.

Tennessee, the state of Cristil's birth, had always been a place of significance for his storied broadcasting career. MSU – at that point still called the "Maroons" because the official adoption of "Bull-dogs" as the school mascot was still eight years in the future – won Cristil's debut MSU football broadcast in that Sept. 19, 1953 game against Memphis State University by a score of 34-6. When Cristil added basketball play-by-play to his MSU repertoire four years later during the 1957-58 season, his first MSU basketball broadcast was an 80-56 Maroon victory over Union University in Jackson, Tenn. – the same town where Cristil's professional radio broadcasting career had begun a decade earlier in 1948 when he made his professional debut calling KITTY League (Class D Minor League) professional baseball games.

Yet that day in Knoxville it must have seemed both poetic and ironic that after 58 years spent calling 636 MSU football games and 1,538 MSU basketball games, Cristil's final broadcast came down to calling this last game in Tennessee – where both his professional dreams and their ultimate fulfillment had begun.

As a matter of fact, Cristil's final call – his final opportunity to say "you can wrap this one up in maroon and white" – would come in Knoxville, the place where Cristil told one interviewer that he began using his career-defining catch phrase. In 1992 in the *Alumnus* magazine interview, Cristil told Steve Ellis: "I probably used it (first) in 1986 when we played Tennessee in Knoxville be-cause everything in Knoxville is 'Big Orange.' That's all you hear, that's all you see, that's all that is talked about is 'Big Orange' this or 'Big Orange' that.

"I guess when Don Smith made that run and MSU won 27-23, it was just the fact that 'Big Orange' was second that day. You can wrap this one up in maroon and white! There's something in this world besides 'Big Orange!' And on that particular day, it was maroon and white!"

Or perhaps that phrase began in another Bulldog contest. A decade later, Cristil told *Dawgs' Bite* in the Nov. 9, 2002, edition: "The phrase 'wrap it in maroon and white' came about by accident. I can't even remember when it started or why. It just came out, it seemed appropriate at the time. And it's been sort of a signature ever since."

Whatever the genesis of the Cristil catchphrase, Bulldog fans were greedy to hear it just one more time in Jack's last game. A thunderous dunk from Wendell Lewis with three seconds left and the failure of Hopson's half-court prayer of a shot on the final play sealed the deal for the Bulldogs to take a 70-69 win. *The Clarion-Ledger's* Brandon Marcello captured the moment in his game story: "And off to the side, soaking it all in, was a smiling Cristil, who was able to cap his final game as the voice of the Bulldogs with his favorite phrase – 'Wrap this one in maroon and white.'" MSU's point guard Dee Bost said MSU was "fighting" for Cristil in trying to find a way to give the esteemed broadcaster a win in his final MSU call.

Beyond Cristil's final call, State's Feb. 26 win in Knoxville snapped a five-game Bulldog losing streak and moved the team back into a two-way tie for second in the SEC West and kept MSU's SEC tournament hopes alive. The Bulldogs finished the season 17-14 overall and 9-7 in the SEC West to take second place in the division and an SEC tournament bye. The Vanderbilt Commodores sent the Dogs home for the season with an 87-81 loss on March 11.

But MSU head basketball coach Rick Stansbury said in Knoxville,

Cristil's retirement was a motivating factor, and he told Cristil's audience that during his postgame interview with the broadcaster: "These guys had a little something extra in them tonight, and that was because of you (Cristil). We were disappointed Wednesday night that we couldn't send you out a winner in the Hump (MSU's Humphrey Coliseum). But really, we couldn't have picked a better place to go on the road in this league to fight and find a way to win a game on the road. And Jack, this one was all for you."

Across the South, on computers through Web streaming, on satellite radio, and on the old standby AM and FM radios in homes and cars, the Mississippi State faithful gathered as families to listen to Cristil's last broadcast. Many wept.

But Cristil said his only particularly deep thoughts on the night of his final MSU broadcast were two distinct but disjunct memories – one was of his travels from Tupelo to Knoxville for the second MSU football game he ever broadcast – a 26-0 Maroon victory over the Volunteers in Knoxville the year after Gen. Bob Neyland stepped down as UT's head coach.

"I thought about my trip, the drive from Tupelo to Corinth to catch the train and the train ride to Knoxville," said Cristil. "I got to the hotel, found (MSU sports information director) Bob Hartley, got in the room, and cleaned up and broadcast the game. Then there was the long train ride back to Corinth and the drive back to Tupelo. That train trip long ago was on my mind that night."

The second memory Cristil lingered on the night of his final broadcast was yet another MSU-UT football game – this time a 14-9 Volunteer win over the Maroons – on Oct. 5, 1957. "I don't remember a thing about that game, but I remember that the Russians put up Sputnik, the first artificial satellite to orbit the Earth the night before the game," said Cristil. "The whole country was absolutely mesmerized by that fact. Some were scared, but it was hard to keep a football game interesting when the whole country was talking about that kind of technological marvel. I don't know why I remembered that on my last night, but I did."

In the minutes before the broadcast, Cristil said he realized: "You don't readily accept that you're riding off into the sunset, but it's another phase in a lengthy process. I tried to read up on what was ahead of me with dialysis. You try to learn something about the unknown."

Just as Cristil was preparing to enter another phase of his life, Bulldog fans were uneasily wondering about what the new phase in their lives would be like – life and MSU sports without Jack Cristil.

Rick Cleveland, the dean of Mississippi sportswriters at *The Clarion-Ledger*, summed up the feelings of many sports fans when he wrote on the morning prior to Cristil's last broadcast: "For many of us, it will be like hearing Sinatra sing his last song. For three generations of Mississippians, our introduction to the Deep South's regional pastime of college football often has been Cristil's gravelly, baritone voice telling us about a 6-tall, 180-pound halfback from Amory or Ackerman or Moss Point. Doesn't matter which university you pulled for, you listened to Cristil. You listened because he put you there, in the stadium. He described the weather and the setting. Told you which team was going which way. He gave you the uniform colors and context of the game he was describing. His voice was so distinct, you could almost taste the cigarettes he was smoking."

For many State fans, Cristil's retirement felt almost like a death in the family. The news left 60-year-old men and women with no appropriate frame of reference for their connection with Mississippi State football and basketball – for they'd never heard anyone but Cristil calling the action. Most MSU fans had such confidence in Cristil that even 'if Mississippi State was playing in a nationally televised game – with supposedly the best team of college sports announcers that money could buy assembled to serve them – that they would turn the sound off on their televisions and watch TV while listening to Jack.

In a 2008 oral history interview with former MSU interim president and longtime university administrator Roy H. Ruby for the MSU Congressional and Political Research Center, Ruby asked Cristil about whether that put additional pressure on the announcer to be "up to snuff" on the action he was calling: "They're listening to you because they can't be at the game. And you owe it to them to give them that ball game as accurately and as picturesquely as you possibly can."

So what were Jack's thoughts at the end of the last broadcast? What was on his mind after 58 years of calling 636 college football games and 1,538 college basketball games?

"I was tired, completely worn out. All I could think about was getting to the bathroom and the bus," Cristil said. "No deep thoughts, no regrets, I was just so pleased that we won the ballgame. I was ready to get on the bus and head for home and get on with whatever awaited me."

For the fans, Cristil's retirement was a bittersweet moment involving a beloved figure in their lives. For Jack, retirement marked the beginning of a new and uncertain time in his life. It marked the beginning of a new regimen of kidney dialysis that would tether him to a machine for hours on a regular basis. It marked, more than anything else, an erosion of the independence and self-reliance that has marked Cristil's life – lessons Jack learned at his mother's knee on the north side of Memphis in the late 1920s and early 1930s.

CHAPTER TWO

THE IMMIGRANTS' SON

"Even a secret agent can't lie to a Jewish mother."

—PETER MALKIN
ISRAELI SECRET AGENT AND MEMBER OF THE MOSSAD
1927 – 2005

WHILE IT WAS "THE VOICE" THAT BROUGHT JACK A MODICUM OF FAME
and a good living, it was his great heart – strengthened by
hardship, obstacles, love, and loss – that led this humble son
of Eastern European Jewish immigrants to the very top of his
profession. At the essence, Cristil's career was about a man and a
microphone. But Jack Cristil's extraordinary life – defined not by
his career but by his friends, family, and fans – is about so much
more.

Jacob Sanford "Jack" Cristil, the son of Mollie Kabakoff Cristil
and Benjamin Herman Cristil, was born Dec. 10, 1925, in Memphis, Tenn.

Family records supported by U.S. immigration and census records indicate that Mollie Kabakoff – Jack's mother and a woman

he would call "the central figure in my life" until his marriage –
was born May 26, 1890, in Dokshitsy, a village that had historically
been a center of mostly Hassidic Jews that was located less than a
mile from the source of the Berezina River in the Vitebsk region of
present-day Belarus in the former Soviet Union. After the Second
Partition of Poland in 1795, the village was included in the Russian empire and bordered the Vilna District. The village was near
Borisov, the site of one of Napoleon's greatest military disasters
during his retreat from his 1812 invasion of Russia.

According to historian Alexander Mikaberidze in *Napoleon's
Great Escape: The Battle of Berezina*, the Russian Cossacks sought
to pin the French forces against the river, but despite losing some
25,000 soldiers – half his army – Napoleon was able to cross the
Berezina to the west and escape into Poland. More than a century
later, Dokshitsy would be the scene of a Nazi atrocity when on
May 23, 1942, most of the Jewish residents of Dokshitsy were
herded into a ravine near a Jewish cemetery and shot dead by the
Germans and their sympathizers in a massacre.

BelaPAN, the Web presence of the Belarusian Information
Company, reported that a May 23, 2008, unveiling of a Holocaust
memorial to the Dokshitsy Jews slain in 1942 by the Nazis was
organized by the local government and an American pharmacist
from Massachusetts named Aaron Ginsburg. An account of the
1942 Nazi atrocity made the day of the 2008 memorial in Dokshitsy offered this chilling narrative:

"A horrible fate awaited most of those who remained in Dokshitsy and Parafianov (a nearby city). After the Germans invaded in
June, 1941, the Jews were terrorized. They were herded into dense-
ly populated ghettos in September, 1941, with inadequate food.
In Dokshitsy during Passover, 1942, 65 Jews were killed. A month

later, 300. Finally on Log B'Omer (May), 1942, approximately half of the 2,800 remaining residents were marched to a pit across the street from the cemetery and shot. The remaining half were killed a few weeks later. . . about 97 percent of the Jewish residents (of Dokshitsy) on the day of the German invasion were killed."

More than 800,000 Jews were slain in Belarus during the Holocaust. Ginsburg, an amateur genealogist whose research already had developed extensive information about American Jews whose roots were in Dokshitsy, formed the Friends of Jewish Dokshitsy (https://sites.google.com/site/friendsofjd/home) and offers the following insight into why the Jews emigrated from Dokshitsy:

"Many Jewish residents of Dokshitsy left in the late 19th and early 20th century, mainly for the United States. Part of the impetus for this was the Russian draft. The Russian army was not friendly towards Jews. Russia was clearly a country in turmoil. Many of the residents of small towns would have moved to larger cities as part of Russia's modernization. For Jews from Dokshitsy, as from many other areas, and for other nationalities, it made just as much sense to leave the country entirely and to move an ocean's breadth away from the turbulent and inhospitable early twentieth-century Russia. In the U.S., many immigrants settled where their (countrymen) went. In the case of the Dokshitsy area, in addition to New York City (Brooklyn), we find groups in Sheboygan, Wisconsin; Newport, Rhode Island; Waterbury, Connecticut; eastern Connecticut; Cleveland, Ohio; and Memphis, Tennessee. Jews also went to England, South Africa and Australia. They also went to parts of the Soviet Union including Russia and the Ukraine. And Dokshitzers moved to towns near and far."

Mollie Kabakoff's 1909 exodus from Dokshitsy, the small village near Minsk (the largest city in Belarus and the nearest town of any substantial size to Dokshitsy), was an incredible odyssey for a 19-year-old woman. Jack recounted his memories of his mother's stories of her emigration from Russia to the U.S. to Steve Ellis in his 1992 *Alumnus* magazine interview – telling Ellis that his Grandfather Kabakoff learned that the Russian authorities were looking for his mother because of her involvement in revolutionary activities against the Romanov dynasty and Czar Nicholas II in the first Russian Revolution. "Her father took her by wagon to the Polish border, where she was escorted on to Hamburg, Germany. From there, she traveled by cattle boat to New York, then on to Memphis to join a sister who lived there," Cristil said.

In 2002, Cristil told David Murray at *Dawgs' Bite*: "Momma was a revolutionary, evidently. This was when the czar was in power, in her teens she got involved with a group of revolutionaries. She was told one day the troops were looking for her, she had to get out, and they ran her through what we would call the underground. She was taken to Minsk, across Poland and Germany, and left from Hamburg and eventually docked in New York where she had family. I'm not really sure how she made her way to Clarksdale." The 1920 U.S. Census records reveal that Mollie Kabakoff Cristil's immigration was registered in 1909.

Jack's sister, Zelda Cristil Esgro of St. Louis, Mo., said their mother lived for a time in New York City with her brother Mendel Kabakoff who had preceded her in passing through Ellis Island. Mendel helped Mollie find work in New York's Garment District where she learned to be a seamstress – the trade that would sustain her and her family in the years to follow after she joined her sister Esther Kabakoff Ziskind in Memphis and her brother Jacob Kabakoff in Clarksdale, Miss. Mollie's sister Sarah Kabakoff Tzuchman settled in Israel, and her brother Schmuel would eventually settle in South Africa, according to Mrs. Esgro.

Miriam "Mimi" Cristil Lapides, Jack's younger sister, said she had heard her mother say she lived in Brooklyn while in New York and that she "had pictures of Momma made with her cousins in Brooklyn." While the pictures remain, Lapides said she heard her mother say little about her emigration to the U.S. from Dokshitsy, Belarus.

"Most immigrant families didn't talk about their backgrounds or their problems," said Mrs. Lapides. "They wanted to be assimilated, wanted to be totally Americanized. My parents spoke Yiddish but never spoke it to us. I think that's true of immigrants from many ethnic backgrounds from that era in America."

The certitude with which Mollie Kabakoff Cristil's heritage can be traced is near 100 percent. The Kabakov/Kabakoff genealogical website www.kabakoff.com traces the descendants of Lebya Kabakov of Dokshitsy, Belarus, principally Zvi Hersh "Herschel" Kabakoff and Shabsai "Shepsel" Kabakoff. From her grandparents, Shepsel Kabakoff and Sara Liba Tabachnik, was born Mollie's father, Yehoshua Zalman "Zelik" Kabakoff. Her mother was named Stirka "Tillie" Motlin. Kabakoff family genealogical records hold that Zelik Kabakoff, the father who spirited Mollie out of Belarus across the Polish border and on to freedom through the port of Hamburg, Germany, was later killed in a Russian *pogrom* (a government sanctioned mob attack against a particular group) by crucifixion as the authorities nailed him to a tree.

Benjamin Herman Cristil, Jack's elusive father, was born April 2, 1888. His World War I U.S. Civilian Draft Registration records show what he was born in "Zager Kovno, Russia," but Cristil family records indicate he emigrated from Riga, Latvia. The 1920 U.S Census records show that Ben Cristil's immigration was registered in 1901 at Ellis Island. While the discrepancy between Benjamin Cristil's U.S. draft registration, the U.S. Census records and his family records might seem contradictory, there is a plausible explanation. First and foremost, Riga, Latvia, was the closest port city for a young man who was emigrating from a town on the Latvian-Lithuanian border.

"Cristil, of course, is an Anglicized spelling of the name," Jack told *The Northeast Mississippi Daily Journal's* John Armistead in an Aug. 26, 1995, interview. "I've seen it spelled different ways. It just depended on how the Ellis Island official did it."

"Zagory" was the Polish spelling for the city of Zager (Yiddish spelling) in the state or district of Kovno in northern Lithuania. The city was on the border between Lithuania and Latvia and was a major settlement of Orthodox Jews and Jewish scholars. Yehuda Slutsky of the Jewish Virtual Library, an online project of the American-Israeli Cooperative Enterprise, wrote of Zager: "It had two separate Jewish communities: Old Zager and New Zager . . . After World War I, during the existence of independent Lithuania, the communities declined. The Jewish population of the two communities numbered 5,443 in 1897 (or some 68 percent of the total population) and 1,923 in 1923 (41 percent of the total population). After the German occupation of Lithuania in 1941, a ghetto was set up in the town, in which Jews from the neighboring localities were also interned. At the beginning of October 1941, the inhabitants of the Zager ghetto were murdered." The Association of Lithuanian Jews estimates that "in this place (Zager) on 2 October 1941 the Nazi executioners and their local helpers massacred about 3,000 Jewish men, women and children" from the area around Zagere, the present-day spelling of old Zager.

Jack's sister Miriam "Mimi" Cristil Lapides said that later in life she received a photo of her father from cousins in Indiana who said that the photo showed a young Benjamin Cristil with his family in Lithuania. "We had all been told he emigrated from Latvia, but so much of the information at Ellis Island got changed for so many immigrants. I believe he was indeed from Lithuania," said Mrs. Lapides.

Roy Hiller of Nashville, Tenn., Jack Cristil's nephew and the son of his late sister, Charlotte Cristil Hiller, said his grandfather made contact with his brothers Sol and David after arriving in the U.S. at Ellis Island, rendezvousing with them in Evansville, Indiana, where the brothers had a scrap business. "My understanding is that he (Benjamin Cristil) was a good businessman but not such a good gambler," said Hiller. The Ben Cristil family moved several times before settling in Memphis.

In a 2002 column written to honor Jack Cristil on his 50th year of broadcasting at MSU, gifted *Clarion-Ledger* columnist Orley Hood wrote: "How lucky we are that Jack's dad, who was from Latvia, met Jack's mom, who was from Russia, back in Memphis · before World War I, when the 20th century was young and frisky."

The irony is that the Russian empire was so vast at the time that Jack Cristil's parents emigrated to the U.S. that his memories and their census and immigration documents tell the tale of two Eastern European Jews who were born – as the crow flies – about 175 miles apart in Zager, Lithuania, and Dokshitsy, Belarus – both as citizens of the broader Russian empire. They emigrated eight years apart, yet they found each other in the close-knit Jewish community of Clarksdale, Miss., and later married in 1915 in Friars Point in Coahoma County, Miss.

"My mother's brother Jacob Kabakoff lived in Clarksdale, and Momma came to his wedding and met my father at that wedding," said Mrs. Lapides. "That's what she told me."

Ben, 27, was working in the fur and hide business and as a pecan trader, and Mollie, 25, was a seamstress from the skills she'd learned in New York while living with Mendel. Ben's business – buying hides and furs from trappers and selling them to furriers – kept him traveling. After a few moves back and forth between Indiana, Kentucky and Tennessee, the couple settled in Memphis and set about raising their family.

Ben Cristil was a dark-haired man of average size and build who was a devout Orthodox Jew. Mollie Kabakoff Cristil was a lovely woman with dark hair and an indefatigable work ethic who followed her husband's lead in the Orthodox practices but was far less dogmatic and severe in the practice of her faith, according to Jack.

The Cristil family grew quickly. First came a son, Harold, in 1916, followed by daughter Charlotte in 1918, son Stanley in 1919, daughter Zelda in 1922, son Jack in 1925, and daughter Miriam in 1927. The six Cristil children were close and congenial, and Jack recalled "a happy home life" in their small frame house on Galloway Street. Jack remembered "a sort of shotgun house that had running water and a bathroom, a little front porch, a sort of living room-dining room combo. I remember I slept on a fold-out sofa bed."

Jack characterized his family as "poor as church mice" and said flatly but with a smile: "We didn't have anything and didn't know we were supposed to have anything." He said he never knew if he was born at home or in a hospital. "One of my early memories is that my sister Mimi and I somehow came into possession of a penny, and there was some spirited debate over just what treasure we'd acquire with that penny," Jack said. "Finally, we decided to go in together and buy this big cookie, and we split it. Man, you talk about feeling rich!'"

When speaking of his mother, Jack Cristil's tone is consistently reverential and reliably light-hearted. It is obvious that he adored and respected his mother and marveled at her ability to raise six children with little help from his father.

"She was an extraordinary woman of strong will," Cristil said in 2011. "Momma supported the family. Momma raised the six children. She was without question the central figure in my life until Mavis and I got married." Despite Cristil's love for his mother, she maintained discipline in their relationship.

"Momma insisted that we accept responsibility," Jack said. "We each had various chores around the house, and she expected us to complete them. She was concerned that we did well in school. Whatever marks we brought home, she'd always ask: 'Is this the best you can do?' She taught us to respect one another and, most of all, to think for yourself and take care of yourself."

So, Cristil said, as soon as he was able he "got busy taking care of myself."

"I worked because every little bit I could earn eased the burden on Momma," Jack said. "It was the Depression; nobody had any money. Roosevelt's 'New Deal' was on the table with the WPA [Works Progress Administration] and the CCC [Civilian Conservation Corps], and everyone was trying to go back to work. I can't really say the Depression impacted me one bit. I'm sure it hurt my family, but our circumstances weren't such that the stock market was of much concern to us."

Mrs. Cristil worked as a seamstress in the alterations department of the high-end Memphis women's clothing emporium Levy's Ladies Toggery. "It was where all the belles of the Delta shopped," Jack said.

But Jack's devotion to his mother was constant as a child. "I remember that Momma used to get off work late and ride the street car that was two long city blocks from our house," he said. "My job was to meet her at the street car and walk her back to the house. Somehow, she always managed to make us dinner after she'd worked all day. On the few occasions when Daddy would be home, there would be chocolate pie and lemon pie, and that was a real highlight. But I always got lemon pie as the youngest boy because the chocolate pie was spoken for by the older boys and my father."

Jack Cristil's relationship with his father was far more complex than the one he enjoyed with his mother, and that complexity was based in far more than missing out on a slice of chocolate pie. Benjamin Cristil contracted tuberculosis soon after his marriage and was sent to a sanatorium in Denver, Colo., for treatment. The elder Cristil would make a few trips home to visit his wife and children, but he spent the majority of Jack's life battling tuberculosis before his death in 1939. The Mayo Clinic defines tuberculosis as "a potentially serious infectious disease that primarily affects your lungs. The bacteria that cause tuberculosis are spread from person to person through tiny droplets released into the air through coughs and sneezes."

In the late 1800s and into the first half of the next century, tuberculosis was a widely misunderstood and feared disease that was commonly called "consumption" because of the nature in which the disease "consumed" its victims through weight loss, fever, night sweats and "frequent blood-tinged sputum." Victims of tuberculosis were feared as carriers and referred to through the term of derision "lungers." Tuberculosis was the leading cause of death in the 19th century.

While family records are unclear as to the exact date that Benjamin Cristil began his treatment in the Denver sanatorium, there is little doubt where Cristil received his treatment. By virtue of his Jewish faith, his humble economic circumstances and his growing family, it's almost certain that Benjamin Cristil first received his sanatorium treatment at National Jewish Hospital in Denver – a project that was funded by the national Jewish organization B'nai B'rith. A September 2004 study by the Colorado Department of Public Health and the Environment documents the opening of the National Jewish Hospital in Denver in 1899 as the "first sanatorium in the state (of Colorado) and perhaps in the country that was dedicated to treatment of indigent TB patients. Its motto was "None May Enter Who Can Pay – None Can Pay Who Enter." National Jewish primarily accepted "incipient" TB cases or those who were likely to recover, according to the 2004 Colorado DPHE study.

Yet both of Jack's sisters, Zelda and Miriam, remembered that letters from their father in Colorado and the return mail to him from their home in Memphis bore the address "Spivak, Colorado" – a locale now identified as a former western suburb of Denver on West Colfax Avenue in Denver proper – that was the location of the Sanatorium of the Jewish Consumptive Relief Society that was founded in 1904 by Dr. Charles David Spivak, a Russian Jew, to accommodate the many Jewish consumptives who did not seem likely to recover but had nowhere else to go.

Spivak's TB sanatorium likely appealed to Benjamin Cristil's dogged devotion to his Jewish faith. Records from Jefferson County, Colo.'s official website offers the following glimpse of the Spivak's Jewish Consumptive Relief Society facility: "There were 34 tents used for 15 years. Doctors and volunteers responded with their skills and money. The farm raised grains and food, they ran a dairy and poultry farm, a book bindery, a print shop, and a general store. One two-story building was destroyed by fire in 1920. Dr. Spivak toured the country and came back with money to build a bigger hospital to serve 204 patients."

Like Benjamin Cristil, Dr. Spivak was an Eastern European Orthodox Jew and spoke Yiddish. Born Chaim Dovid Spivakofsky in Russia in 1888, he later shortened his name to Spivak after leaving Philadelphia and heading west to Denver, according to historian Jeanne Adams in the 2009 book *Dr. Charles David Spivak: A Jewish Immigrant and the American Tuberculosis Movement*. Abrams noted that while National Jewish Hospital had "no kosher kitchen" in the early years, Spivak's facility did.

Jack Cristil was a small boy during these years, and his memories are scant of the specifics of his father's illness. "All I know is that he spent five or six years in a sanatorium in Denver, Colorado, and that he died there," said Jack. "They shipped his body home on the train." The elder Cristil died July 18, 1939, at the age of 51 and was interred in the historic Baron Hirsch Jewish Cemetery in Memphis.

Jack Cristil was 13 years old when his father died.

"I didn't know Daddy," Jack recounted in 2011. "He would come back periodically for only a few weeks or months. My father was a sick man, and I've found that sickness brings out the worst in some people. He was arrogant and domineering. When he did come home, everything revolved around him. As well as I can remember, I just tried to stay far away from him."

Asked about the impact of his father's death at such a young age, Jack said: "I don't know that his death really affected me. The truth is I remember that I kind of felt a sense of relief that his visits were not going to upset the household and Momma anymore."

Zelda Cristil Esgro said that none of the Cristil children really knew their father.

"Jack was about four when Daddy went into the sanatorium the first time in 1929," said Zelda. "The six children were between ages 15 and two. I don't think Daddy meant to be unpleasant, but he was really not physically able to be otherwise. Daddy was gone, Momma was gone a lot because she had to work, and it was really a tough time for all of us. We all thought Momma was a fantastic person to have raised six children on her own. In those years, there was no government program, nothing. She had to do it on her own, and she did it."

But Jack's older sister had some pleasant memories of her father as well. "I can remember that he had a car, an electric car, and on Sundays we would go for drives," said Zelda. "That electric car, sometimes on the hills – well, it wouldn't quite make it to the top, and we'd all have to push. I also remember that Daddy bought and sold nuts, and on Sunday afternoons, we'd crack pecans in the kitchen and have a party."

Benjamin Cristil's devotion to Orthodox Judaism was also an obstacle in his relationship with his youngest son. Jack said he chafed under the dogma of the Orthodox practices and particularly under his father's refusal to explain the tenets of the religion or answer his son's questions about it. "I went to synagogue with my father in the practice of Orthodox Judaism, and he was intolerant of other religions," said Jack. "Orthodox Judaism is very stern. There are no adjustments. The attitude was 'what's been done for 4,000 years is what's done today,' and when I asked questions, he only said, 'That's the way it is.' That didn't sit very well with me. I remember Daddy's funeral as an Orthodox service right down to throwing dirt on the coffin. I left the Orthodox church when Daddy died, and I never went back." Yet in 2011, Cristil is a lay leader of the reform congregation of Temple B'nai Israel in Tupelo.

Despite their difficult relationship, Jack Cristil did believe in his father's intelligence and that he had his family's best interests at heart in the long run.

"Daddy could speak Russian, Hebrew, Yiddish, and German, but he would not permit anything but English to be spoken in the house because we were in America, and English would be spoken in our lives," said Jack. "Once in a while, Daddy and Momma would speak Russian or Hebrew if they didn't want the children involved in the conversation." Jack would tell Steve Ellis in the 1992 *Alumnus* interview that he "regretted to this day" not learning to speak Russian from his parents.

Cristil said in 2011 that his boyhood neighborhood was "a Duke's mixture" of varying religions, ethnicities, and nationalities. Cristil told David Murray of *Dawgs' Bite* in 2002: "The street we lived on was paved, two city blocks long, but the intersecting street had never been cut through, so it was a lengthy street. The lamp posts were 50 yards apart, so two lamp posts were your football field out in the street. Everybody went into everybody's house, nobody locked up anything. We had families from all extractions there. Most of the parents were first-generation from the old country. There was Greek, Hebrew, and Italian talked on the street, even some English. But everybody got along famously."

Life holds a lot of lessons for a boy who loses his father at the age of 13, but with the strong guidance of his mother and sharing her work ethic, Jack Cristil would learn two distinct life lessons in the next years of his life: first, that he was absolutely mesmerized by one final gift to the family from his parents' union – a radio purchased by his parents during Ben Cristil's final visit home two years before his death – and second, that the youngest son of Mollie Kabakoff Cristil was "a pretty good shoe salesman."

CHAPTER THREE

"A Pretty Good Shoe Salesman"

"There is man in his entirety, blaming his shoe when his foot is guilty."

—Samuel Beckett
Waiting for Godot, Act I

Zelda Cristil Esgro, Jack's older sister, described her kid brother as someone who always knew exactly what he wanted. "Jack always, always wanted to be a sportscaster," Zelda said. "It was the neatest thing; Jack always had a tennis ball, and he'd throw it against the wall or the sidewalk or the steps and pretend he was calling a ball game on the radio. He never tired of it, and you really could actually hear him getting better at it, although the whole thing was happening within his imagination. Now, I don't mean that Jack wasted his time; he didn't. But there was no secret to us what he wanted to do with his life."

In his 1992 interview with Steve Ellis, Cristil told basically the same story: "I would take a golf ball or tennis ball and simulate a game, you know, broadcast it. In fact, the junior high football coach lived across the street from us when I first went out for football. He later told me he couldn't wait for me to join the team so he could work my tail off. He said he got sick and tired of me broadcasting those imaginary games up and down the street. That was the only way he could get back at me."

A decade later, Cristil would tell Rick Cleveland of *The Clarion-Ledger*: "Here I was in Memphis and I was absolutely enthralled with the idea that a man could be sitting in some stadium in New York or Chicago or Boston, telling me about a game. It was like magic. I was enchanted by it. It captured my imagination to the extent that I knew right then and there that's what I was going to do. I was six years old, but I knew what I was going to do for a living and I never changed my mind."

Jack Cristil began his formal education in first grade at Leroy Polk Elementary School on Chelsea Street in Memphis in 1931 but would spend most of his elementary school years at Maury Elementary on North Bellevue Blvd. in Memphis. As most boys learn at an early age, some lessons are more expensive than others.

He would tell David Murray of *Dawgs' Bite* in 2002: "At Pope School, we played marbles at recess and I couldn't shoot marbles but I could 'lag to the line' and the one closest to the line won the marbles. Well, I had a bag full of them in my pocket and my first recess at Maury School, somebody told somebody and they told the principal, Mrs. Riley. When I got ready to leave there after the sixth grade she called me to the office, reached in her desk drawer and got those marbles and said 'they're yours, take them.' I said 'No, ma'am, you kept them five years, you can keep them' and turned around and walked out. I remember that like it was yesterday."

At age 11, Jack remembered being enlisted by the men of the neighborhood to help fill sandbags on Chelsea Street, as the floodwaters of the Great Flood of 1937 saw the Mississippi swell to the point that the big river's tributaries – the Wolf River, Loosahatchie River, Nonconnah Creek and Big Creek – all overflowed their banks. The 1937 flood saw the Mississippi River rise to 48.7 feet in Memphis and create a "lake almost as large as Ireland" that sent 60,000 refugees into temporary Red Cross barracks at the Memphis Fairgrounds.

But the dominant theme in Jack's memory over the decades in all of the interviews granted by Cristil has been of his family – his mother and his five siblings.

Jack's oldest brother, Harold, represented not a "father figure" to Jack after his father's death, but an "authority figure." Harold was the only one of the Cristil children born in Clarksdale, Miss.

"Harold had more of Dad's traits than he did Mom's traits," Jack said. "It was the Depression, he was 15 years old when we lost our father, and he had a lot of responsibility placed on him. Harold was a deep thinker, adamant, argumentative, and ambitious. I think the combination of the Depression and no father put a lot of stress on him. You got the feeling that at times he felt over-burdened, and he should have. Harold was always productive."

The eldest Cristil son worked his way through high school and four years in the Reserve Officer Training Corps (ROTC) at L.C. Humes High School. Jack said he remembered Harold's playing the tuba in the Rotary Club Band. He had a job with a company making doors that supplied doors across the Mid-South. "I remember Harold helped make a lot of the doors that went to Tupelo to help rebuild after the 1936 tornado there," Jack said.

Drafted into the U.S. Army, Jack said Harold was a "90-day wonder" and exited his training as a second lieutenant in the Signal Corps. Harold Cristil spent the bulk of his three years of overseas service leading a crew stringing wire and cables from French West Africa to the Mediterranean.

"When he got out of service, Harold got a job back in Memphis but also enrolled in law school at night," Cristil said with obvious pride in his oldest brother. "He became a very accomplished lawyer and did a lot of his work in real estate."

But as he had with his late father, Jack chafed under Harold's role as the "authority figure' in his life. "I remember coming home one night, and Momma had put on a pot of new potatoes, you know, unpeeled potatoes, on the stove for our supper after having worked hard all day," said Jack. "Harold said to Momma 'that's the lazy way to do it.' I guess I was about 22 then, and I'd heard about enough of that kind of talk to Momma. It reminded me of something Daddy would have said to her years before. I told Harold that we'd take that discussion outside, and we did!"

After a distinguished career as a lawyer, Harold Cristil died in 1994 of heart failure at the age of 78.

Charlotte Cristil Hiller was born in 1918 in Bowling Green, Ky., and was the first of Jack's siblings to die, in 1979, at the age of 60 of a brain tumor. "Charlotte was just so sweet," Jack would say in 2011. "More than anything, I think Charlotte was affected by the conditions in which we lived. Early in the war years, she moved to Washington, D.C., and lived there and worked as an administrator for the War Department during the war. After the war, she married Nathan Hiller, who also died young. He was a merchant. They had three boys."

"Mimi" Cristil Lapides said her sister Charlotte "was beautiful and popular, she looked like the movie star Olivia de Havilland."

Jack's brother Stanley Cristil was born in 1919 and is clearly someone his brother loved and admired deeply. "Stanley was one of the most loveable people you'd ever want to meet," said Jack. "He was soft-hearted, interested in doing things for others, was a real independent thinker, and was intensely loyal."

As a boy, Jack was most proud of Stanley's athletic notoriety. "Stanley was a really good athlete," said Jack with a laugh. "Humes High played at one time in the old "Boss" Crump Stadium in Memphis. Stanley held the record for the longest punt ever kicked in that stadium – 86 yards – I guess you could say ole Stanley got all the roll out of that punt." After high school, Stanley served in the U.S. Army during World War II. Jack said that returning servicemen in that era had an opportunity to join the "52/20 Club" – a provision of the 1944 Servicemen's Readjustment Act commonly known as the "G.I. Bill." The law afforded returning honorably discharged servicemen looking for work $20 per week for 52 weeks. Yet less than 20 percent of the government funds set aside for the "52/20" provision was ever collected by servicemen, as most either found jobs or enrolled in college.

Jack recalled: "After we had both been discharged from service and were back in Memphis, Stanley went down to collect his $20 and found a long line. He said, 'I've been standing in line the whole time I was in the Army, and I'm tired of standing in line. I'm going to get me a job!'"

On the way home from that experience, Stanley passed Farber Brothers, a company that made seat covers and other products for cars. "Stanley went in, got a job in their shipping department in 1945, and stayed with them for 40 years, retiring as their vice president for sales and product presentations," said Jack. Stanley Cristil died in 2006 at the age of 86 of kidney failure.

Middle sister Zelda Cristil Esgro was born in 1922 in Memphis. "Zelda had a great sense of responsibility for our family, and I can't remember as a child when she wasn't working," said Jack. "She worked at Sears and went to school full-time from the time she was 14." After marrying her husband, Sam Esgro, they moved to California and later to St. Louis, Mo., where they spent most of their lives in the appliance and RCA electronics business. "Sam was significantly involved in signing Elvis Presley with RCA," Jack would say in 2011.

Sam Esgro, now 90 and still living with Zelda, 89, in St. Louis, Mo., was one of two RCA field representatives who went to Memphis to close the deal with Col. Tom Parker, Sun Records owner Sam Phillips, Gladys and Vernon Presley, and, of course, Elvis, on Nov. 21, 1955, that sold the young Presley's Sun Records contract to RCA for $35,000, according to music critic and historian Andrew Vaughan of Nashville, Tenn., writing for guitar company Gibson USA's website on Nov. 21, 2010. Documents reproduced on the elvispresleymuseum.com website also confirm the transaction. History would prove the transaction to be momentous, as Elvis went on to sell over a billion records, including the second song he recorded for RCA called "Heartbreak Hotel" – the Tupelo, Miss., native's first gold record.

Rounding out the Cristil household was Jack's youngest sister Miriam "Mimi" Cristil Lapides, the baby of the family. Jack and the rest of the family called her "Mimi," and 85 years later, it is clear that Mimi remains a close confidante and the repository of many of Jack's memories about his family. "My sister Mimi and I were always very congenial," said Jack. "She's always been so easy to get along with and so gracious. Mimi's very artistic and just had a wonderful mind."

Mimi was the only one of the Cristil children to attend and graduate from Memphis Technical High School, so that her interests in the arts could be nurtured at a school that offered art instruction. "I wanted to take classes from this Tech art teacher name Mike Abt," said Lapides. "Funny thing, when I got there and took art classes, I found out that one of Abt's main jobs was building all the floats for the Cotton Carnival Parade, so he didn't do a whole lot of art teaching." But Mimi Cristil's childhood interests in the arts would never wane, studying art at the University of Memphis after high school. She later graduated with a bachelor's degree in fine arts from Memphis College of Art. In 1952, she married Max Michel Jr., and they made their life in Memphis until Max's death in 1989. She had been "a serious painter." Mimi later became managing director of Opera Memphis and after Max's death, assistant managing director of the Opera Company of Philadelphia.

Mimi would later marry Bernard Lapides of Isola, Miss., and they lived happily together before his death in 2005. In 2006, Lapides would move to Denver to be close to her married daughter there and her two grandsons. She is 84 years old.

During his childhood in Memphis, Jack Cristil likely couldn't have conceived that his little sister Mimi would ever be 84 and retired in Denver. On April 19, 1935, when Jack was nine, *The Commercial Appeal* would report this news item: "Wee Willie Duke hit a home run over the right field fence with Kirby Ferrell on third yesterday to defeat Little Rock 3-2 in the home debut of the Memphis Chicks this season and to send the team's new manager, Freddie Hofmann, and 8,433 fans, including 2,100 Chickasaw Buddies, jumping with joy."

The minor league Memphis Chickasaws or Chicks, playing at Russwood Park near Baptist Hospital in Memphis, had a promotional membership club for children called "Chickasaw Buddies" that allowed kids into the games free if they wore their beanie caps and sat in the left field seats. The color of the caps changed every year, according to Mrs. Lapides.

"One of my earliest recollections of Jack was watching him wear his Chickasaw Buddies cap and bouncing a tennis ball against the steps as he pretended to broadcast a game he was creating solely from his imagination," said Mrs. Lapides. "Jack called every player in the lineup – both teams, every small detail of the game he saw in his mind. I marveled at his concentration. He could tell the way the ball hit the step what kind of 'hit' the team had gotten. He could tell. That's what he did." But his kid sister said Jack Cristil occasionally had other headgear as well.

"Jack and I were very close as children; we were playmates," said Mrs. Lapides. "But when Jack got to be about six years old, he sort of lost interest in playing with me and got interested in boy things. That's about the time he started wearing this leather aviator's cap with goggles. Wore them everywhere he went. I really hated those things because he had no interest in me if I saw him in that aviator's cap. But he was a really good brother."

A look of true nostalgia swept over Cristil's face when asked about his days as a Chickasaw Buddy: "You could join for $1, and for that dollar you got a beanie and an identification card. With that card and the beanie, you could get into the game free on 'Chickasaw Buddy Days,' which were Wednesdays and Saturdays. So before the season, boys would collect bottles, scrap iron, or whatever they could find to sell to make a $1 to join."

Not every boy was able to raise that dollar. "There were more than a few kids who went in with a rock in their pocket that they would use to pass their beanie and card through the fence back near a ditch behind right field to help their friends get in the game," Cristil said.

Jack described his life as a school boy in this way: "You had an opportunity to go to school, and you were expected by everyone to do the best you could do. I enjoyed the activities. There was always a ball game going on, and that was always a challenge, as I saw it. You're trying to be successful. In baseball, I was a good catcher and a fairly decent hitter. At times I could control where I hit it, but I never had a lot of speed or quickness."

Cristil said his entry into L.C. Humes Junior High and later Humes High School was something he'd long anticipated. "I'd looked forward to it. At home, I'd heard stories about some teachers and some classes, and I wanted to compete in the classroom. The athletic teams had coaches and wore uniforms. I couldn't wait to get out there. My brothers and sisters had sort of paved the way, and I wanted my shot at it," Jack said. "I wanted to do well and carry on the family tradition."

At 5'7" and 150 lbs., Jack played a year of basketball and four years of high school football. "In my day, it was the old single-wing," said Jack, who was a blocking back and a punter – as brother Stanley had also been – for the orange and white Humes Tigers. "I played for Coach Hiltpold and then for Coach Jack Nix, who played at Mississippi State and graduated in 1943. I didn't know how successful he had been at State. But we pretty much played 'three yards and a cloud of dust' football at Humes." Cristil told Steve Ellis in their 1992 interview that he wasn't a very good athlete: "I knew what you were supposed to do. I just didn't do it very well."

Nix, the Moselle native, played one season in the NFL for the old Cleveland Rams in 1940. At State, Nix was a rangy halfback that MSU head coach Allyn McKeen – who led MSU to its only SEC football championship in 1941 – said had "tremendous physical ability" and captained the 1939 Maroon squad. Cristil said his introduction to Nix gave him his "first real knowledge of Mississippi State football."

"By the time I was playing high school football, Mississippi State was having some real success, and I admired how Coach Nix handled himself," said Cristil.

While enrolled at Humes, Jack also spent a year in the school's glee club. "I'm not sure why I did the glee club," Cristil said. "Let's just say I'm not musically inclined." But Jack liked music – particularly Big Band era tunes played on record players at Saturday night neighborhood dances and the pretty girls that frequented those dances. "It was mostly the Jitterbug and ballroom dancing," he said. In those days, Jack's attentions were focused on two girls – sister Mimi's best friend, Bonnie Smith, a petite blonde from down the street that he dated "off and on through high school" and who he said "was just a knockout and a very sweet girl." Another regular girlfriend was Florence Siegal, who Jack said was his high school ROTC sponsor. "Most of the functions at the high school, Florence would be my date," Jack said. "We shared a locker and had some classes together."

Scholastically, Jack enjoyed math and science but wasn't fond of literature or writing. "I did well in school, and I enjoyed it, but I already knew what I wanted to do, and nothing was going to change that," he said. "English was always difficult for me, but my teachers helped."

Jack was also introduced to his first substantial work beyond the household chores assigned him by his mother. "I got my first job when I was in the 10th grade at Broadnax Jewelers on Main Street in Memphis in the fall of the year," said Jack. "I was a runner in an upscale jewelry, gift and fine china shop. People would make their selections from the clerk. Then we'd run up the stairs to the 5th floor and get a new item from the warehouse. I also worked at Krieger's, a general merchandise store on North Main as a stock boy, but I'd clerk the overflow. Then I worked at Slater's Shoe Store, an independent shoe store."

Jack said Mr. Krieger taught him to stay busy, to have a sense of responsibility and the value of learning people's names and greeting them accordingly. "People like to hear their names," Jack said. "That carried over into my own professional life."

While selling Flagg Brothers shoes, Jack's natural talents in retail became obvious even to a school boy, who told Ellis in 1992 that he became "a pretty good shoe salesman."

One teacher in particular taught Jack a lesson that was off the subject matter of his class, but the teacher stirred in Jack a gift that would serve him all of his life – the gift of confidence in his ability to sell.

"The chemistry teacher at Humes was Sim Winfield," said Jack. "I was selling shoes at the independent store, and he came in complaining that his shoes hurt his feet. I remember even now, the shoes he had were too small. I measured his feet and found he needed a brown size 8B wingtip, and I got it for him and made sure it was a good fit. Well, he later became my teacher, and he kept me after class one day the first week of school. He said: 'These are the best shoes I ever had. My feet feel good.' And I knew I had a good grade coming in chemistry. I found most people didn't like to clerk in stores. But I saw that the good ones made money by helping people. When you think about it, it's not a bad way to make a living, helping people. Of course, that was back when a dollar was a wagon wheel."

After graduation in 1943 from Humes High School in Memphis

armed Jack Cristil with a high school diploma to compliment the lessons he'd learned as a "pretty good shoe salesman" from his mentors in the downtown Memphis business community, Jack faced his next crucial decision. What next?

"From the age of 14 on, every decision I made in my life I made on my own," said Jack. "Did I consult others? Sure. But I made the decision." The decision, as Jack saw it, was to enlist in the U.S. military at the height of World War II or wait to be drafted.

As had been the case since childhood – first with his late father and later with older brother Harold – Jack didn't particularly like being told what to do. He joined his brothers and brothers-in-law in service of their country. Cristil enlisted in the U.S. Army Air Corps, the forerunner of the U.S. Air Force, hoping to be a pilot. How could a young man who'd worn a leather aviator's helmet with goggles "constantly" as a little boy hope for anything else?

Cristil enlisted in downtown Memphis on Dec. 7. 1943 – two years to the day after the Japanese bombed Pearl Harbor. Three weeks later, he was at Camp Shelby, south of Hattiesburg, Miss., preparing for transport to Miami Beach, Fla., for basic training. His next transfer was to Moody Field at Valdosta, Ga., where training continued in preparation for Air Corps ground school. Next came Winthrop College in Rock Hill, S.C., where an appendectomy sidelined Jack for six-to-seven weeks and separated him from his unit.

Winthrop College had been South Carolina's women's university, but the Army Air Corps eventually chose Winthrop as the base of the Corps' Aviation Cadet Program.

"I don't remember if my appendix ruptured or what, but I was pretty sick, and it took me six or seven weeks to get back on my feet, and by then, my original unit was gone," said Cristil. But Cristil was sent to Shaw Field at Sumter, S.C., where he began crewing aircraft. "That's where I finally completed ground school and actually started working on single-engine aircraft engines. It was mostly AT6 aircraft, and pilots used them for final training, and we used them for on-the-job training in repairing and rebuilding engines."

The Army Air Corps first received the AT6 planes (originally designed as a light attack aircraft) from North American Aviation in 1939, and the AT6 is generally believed by military experts to have been the best-known training aircraft of all time. The plane was powered by the 600-horsepower Wright R-1340-7 engine, could attain speeds of 200 m.p.h. and could be mounted with .30 caliber machine guns forward and aft, according to the Aviation History Museum. Most, however, served as basic training planes for fighter pilots and for aviation mechanics.

Cristil would then be sent to Randolph Field in San Antonio, Texas, where he would learn to work on multi-engine aircraft. His final duty station was Kelly Field at San Antonio, where he received his final training and prepared to ship out for service in the Pacific.

"That's when they dropped the atomic bomb on Hiroshima and Nagasaki," said Cristil. "I guess that decision saved a million lives, and mine might have been one of them, but it meant that I would not be sent overseas to do the job I'd trained to do."

Jack would tell former MSU sports information director Bo Carter that his days in the U.S. Army Air Corps gave him "a great respect" for flying. Cristil told Steve Ellis in 1992 that he wanted to become a pilot but that the Air Corps wouldn't "grant him flight status because he was color blind." Cristil told David Murray of *Dawgs' Bite* in 2002: "I joined the service right out of high school. My time in the service was a marvelous experience. I was an aircraft and engineer mechanic and a damn good one, too. It was all piston engines. I never saw a jet until after the service. It was basically what I'd call production line maintenance. For the first time in my life, I had tools, which I haven't had since and don't intend to because I found out there were other ways to make a living without manual labor!"

Beyond tools, Jack picked up something else in 1943 after enlisting in the Army Air Corps – cigarettes. "They told us 'smoke 'em if you got 'em' back in service, and in both instances, the answer was 'yes' for me," said Jack. "I've been smoking ever since."

Cristil called his time in service "uneventful" but also said it allowed him to travel and to feel he had "met my obligations to my country" by answering the call with the rest of his generation.

One memory from his service days remains vibrant with Jack in 2011: "I remember learning that Franklin Roosevelt had died at Warm Springs. None of us had ever known anyone but FDR as president. None of us, not a one, had ever heard of Harry Truman, and now he was the commander-in-chief."

Cristil was honorably discharged from the U.S. Army Air Corps on Oct. 31, 1945.

He told David Murray at *Dawgs' Bite* in 2002: "I mustered out in Amarillo (Amarillo Army Air Field) and we 'stood retreat' that afternoon. I had a little weekend bag with some shirts and some skivvies and headed for the main gate with $200 pay. I'd never heard of that much money in my life. Old Route 66 was at the main gate. I didn't know whether to go east or west, and if someone had walked up to me and said 'Son, don't you want to re-enlist?' I'd probably have signed back up right then and there."

"I was completely lost," Cristil said in 2011. "I had no idea where I was going to go and what I was going to do. So I decided to head back to Memphis, go to Momma's house, and get my ducks in a row."

Jack recalls one post-war incident that seared into his memory. Mollie Cristil had never become a naturalized citizen until after World War II. Son Harold, the lawyer, eventually handled his mother's naturalization application and helped her complete the necessary steps to become a U.S. citizen in a ceremony in Memphis. Afterwards, Harold suggested a celebratory lunch. Mollie Cristil said: "First, where do you register to vote? Then, we have lunch."

But one thing was certain in Jack's mind – radio, broadcasting and sports announcing would be his future. From being a Chickasaw Buddy at Russwood Park in his Memphis days to standing on Route 66 at Amarillo with his muster pay in his pocket after World War II, a career in radio had been his singular dream.

"I never gave the future much thought," said Jack. "That last trip home, Mom and Dad bought that radio. I just fell in love with it and knew that's what I wanted to do if the opportunity presented itself. It was what I wanted to do – broadcast sporting events – and I set out to find that opportunity or to make that opportunity."

But in an April 6, 1992, interview with Mike Talbert of *The Northeast Mississippi Daily Journal*, Cristil gave a sign of his zeal to get into radio: "When I was in service and my best friend and I were hitchhiking home, I would be giving him a play-by-play. He would tell me, 'You're driving me crazy!'"

In the 2002 book *Shalom Y'all: Images of Jewish Life in the American South*, Cristil told photographer Bill Aron and writer Vicki Reikes Fox: "I was going to broadcast ball games. I mean, it was just that simple. I never thought of anything else. I wasn't going to be a brain surgeon or ditch digger – I was going to be a broadcaster. And radio was big in those days. It was before the advent of television."

Little did Jack Cristil know that his dream of broadcasting ball games would come true in a way that took him across the South and back again to the scenes of his halcyon days as a Chickasaw Buddy and to the city where his mother met his father back in 1915 – Clarksdale, Miss.

CHAPTER FOUR

FINDING HIS VOICE

"Why, no, I think I'll just win this one for ole Bobo."

—LOUIS NORMAN NEWSOM

AFTER JACK CRISTIL GOT OUT OF SERVICE, HE RETURNED HOME BRIEFLY and resumed his former career selling Flagg Brothers shoes in downtown Memphis. He also went to a Veterans Administration counselor to research where he could take his G.I. Bill education benefits and get the training necessary to get into the broadcasting business.

"Things weren't radically different than they had been before the war," said Cristil. "I made good money selling shoes. I lived at home with Momma." Asked if his mother was glad to have him home and have his feet under her table again, Jack flashed a grin and said: "She never did say." But in the post-war days, Mollie Cristil's home was "central headquarters" for her sons returning from service. Harold was in a VA hospital nursing shrapnel wounds to his shoulder. Jack had his job selling shoes, but he still ached to find his calling in radio.

Cristil made the rounds to the Memphis radio stations seeking advice. He visited WMC-AM and WREC-AM and met and talked with people already making a living in the broadcasting field. "I didn't think I needed to have any illusions about what I was getting into, so I just asked them about the 'real world' of radio, and they told me," he said.

In the late summer of 1946, Jack said he was ready to chase his dream by enrolling at Northwestern University. He took a train to Chicago and spent the night at the YMCA. His luggage was light, and among his possessions were his high school transcript from Humes and his military records and honorable discharge.

As Jack told Steve Ellis in 1992: "I wanted to go to college to study radio, and I'd heard that Northwestern University in Chicago had some broadcast journalism courses. So, I caught the train in Memphis and went to Northwestern and found out they were not accepting out-of-state students. But they told me (the University of) Minnesota was, and I asked them 'where's that?' I didn't have enough money to catch another train, so I hitchhiked the 400 miles to Minneapolis. I enrolled and stayed two years, taking all the broadcast journalism courses they had to offer."

Cristil would say in 2011 that Northwestern, like many universities, was full of ex-soldiers back from the war taking advantage of their G.I. benefits and getting an education. "There was a large influx of G.I.s after the war, and Northwestern wasn't the only school turning out-of-state students away," Cristil said. The news left him disappointed and in no small amount of financial discomfort.

Cristil told David Murray at *Dawgs' Bite* in 2002: "Radio school was fascinating. They had some equipment there, people who'd been in the broadcast industry. We did get to go out to the Triple

A park in Minneapolis and they had some spindle-wire recorders in those days. Students would do an inning or two. And we went to basketball games where the Minnesota Lakers played. Radio stations were beginning to come into being; there weren't any "stringing" personnel so they'd call the schools and you'd send them an audition on acetate discs. I remember simulating a game between the New York Giants and the Brooklyn Dodgers."

Asked why he didn't stay and complete his undergraduate degree at Minnesota, Jack said: "An academic degree was never my goal. I'd already been out in the world of work and spent three years in the military. I felt like an old man at that point. What I had on my mind was getting qualified and trained to broadcast baseball; that was for me."

Cristil said he lived in a boarding house owned by the Hewittson family on the corner of 39th and Upton streets in Minneapolis – living on his $65-per-month G.I. pay and the $100 he earned monthly selling Nunn-Bush brand shoes for a local men's store called Carr, Dolan & Hahn.

The brutal Minnesota winters were something totally foreign to Cristil, whose life and military service had been spent in the South. "It was my first real experience with winter weather, and I really wasn't prepared," said Jack. "I remember on Thursday nights, the store where I worked was open until 9 p.m. I met some friends at Snyder's Bar and Grill for a beer after work. Usually, I rode the street car to within five or six blocks of where I lived. But one night, the street car wasn't running. I walked home and woke up in terrible pain. Mrs. Hewittson knocked on the door and checked on me. She knew I'd gotten close to suffering frostbite. They rubbed my legs down with snow. Suffice to say I had enough winter while I lived in Minneapolis to suit me for a lifetime."

After taking all the broadcast journalism courses offered at Minnesota, Cristil headed back south to accept his first job as a professional announcer out of college broadcasting KITTY League or Class D – the lowest of the low in professional baseball – in Jackson, Tenn.

Jack told *The Commercial Appeal's* John Branston in an Aug. 19, 1984 interview: "We used to recreate baseball games from the bare essentials the Western Union guys would give us. And the quality of the broadcast depended a lot on whether the guy tapping out the wire was a fan and how descriptive he was. Some of them would write 'so-and-so hit a screaming liner to left' and others would just say he flied out. At the time, you had to have a lot more knowledge of the game than you do now. You had to anticipate what the manager was doing, and you had to know your players. You couldn't have the steal sign on with some jug-legged catcher at first base."

Cristil next moved to Anniston, Ala., to call the games of the Class B Anniston Rams in the Southeastern League. At its apex in the late 1940s and early 1950s, Anniston competed with teams in Pensacola, Fla.; Meridian, Miss.; Montgomery, Ala.; Jackson, Miss.; Vicksburg, Miss.; Selma, Ala.; and Gadsden, Ala. Cristil recalls the Rams as "not very good, and by the end of the season, they had the attendance to match their skills. Most people called the Rams the 'Ramblers' behind their back, because the players didn't stay in one place very long and certainly not on one team." Cristil said the team was on the road more than they were at home because of scant interest from the fans.

Jack's next minor league stop took him back to his Chickasaw Buddy roots, as he got two years behind the microphone broadcasting the Class AA Memphis Chicks, the team that once lured

Jack as a child to wear their colorful beanies. The Chicks played in the old Southern League. In his 1992 interview with the *Clarion-Ledger's* Mike Knobler, Cristil offered this glimpse of his minor league days: "It's probably the most fun I ever had."

Knobler recounted how Cristil recreated action from the Western Union ticker tape: "He'd tap his wallet for the sound of ball hitting glove and tap an aspirin can for the sound of ball hitting bat. Crowd noise was on a turntable." Cristil told Knobler that the ticker tape broke down frequently, but that it really wasn't a problem. "The beauty part about it, the games were always played in the Mid-South area, where there's always a 20 percent chance of showers." No ticker tape? Then tell the listeners the old "rain delay" story.

One favorite Cristil tale from his minor league days with the Memphis Chicks is the Bobo Newsom story. Louis Norman (Bobo) Newsom, also known by some fans as Buck Newsom, was a Major League pitcher who at 6 feet and 200 lbs. was a large player for that era – and had an even bigger mouth. Newsom's nickname came from his annoying habit of refusing to learn the names of his teammates or his adversaries, calling everyone "Bobo" and eventually seeing that nickname stick to him instead.

So famous for running his mouth and for occasionally backing it up with truly heroic pitching was Bobo Newsom that he was immortalized in the famous 1949 Ogden Nash poem "Line-Up for Yesterday": "N is for Newsom, Bobo's favorite kin, you ask how he's here, he talked himself in."

Despite his braggadocio and eccentricity, Newsom was a solid Major Leaguer. In the 1940 World Series, Newsom pitched a shutout in the opener for the Detroit Tigers. Newsom's father died while watching the game. He told the press before pitching a win in Game Five that he would win the game for his daddy. Called upon to pitch Game Seven, reporters asked him if he'd win that game for his father as well. "Why, no, I think I'll win this one for ole Bobo." The Tigers lost the game and the series. But in a 20-season career, Newsom posted a 211–222 record with 2,082 strikeouts and a 3.98 earned run average in 3,759.1 innings pitched. Newsom made the American League All-Star team from 1938–1940 and in 1944. With 211 wins, he is one of the 100 winningest pitchers of all time. His 222 losses also make him one of only two major league pitchers to win 200 games and still have a sub .500 career winning percentage – and he's the only player mentioned in Nash's famous baseball poem still not elected to the Baseball Hall of Fame.

Cristil told *The Commercial Appeal's* Branston in 1984 about the time visiting Chattanooga Lookouts players set him up with a live interview with a player who could not speak a word of English, only Spanish. In 1992, he told the *Clarion-Ledger's* Mike Knobler more of the same story. At the end of a storied big league baseball career, Bobo Newsom had been sent down to the minors and was playing for the Chattanooga Lookouts against the Memphis Chicks. Cristil recognized Bobo, so when Bobo introduced Jack to who he claimed was a phenomenal new player for a live interview and then walked away, Jack thought nothing of it: "(Turns out) this guy doesn't *spraken zee English*; and I don't *spraken zee Spanish*. He's going '*Si, si, senor.*' The guys (with Bobo) were rolling in the dugout."

Newsom's renown wasn't wasted on Cristil. He knew, like most, that Newsom was in the shank of a long but productive career in baseball. Newsom signed with the Washington Senators five different times in his career, leading him to boast that he'd had more terms in Washington "than President Roosevelt." But when pranked by Bobo Newsom, Cristil never let anyone see him sweat the exchange. He simply improvised five minutes worth of questions that required only one-word responses: "Si."

But it was Ellis in 1992 that got the "rest of the story" on Cristil's brush with Bobo Newsom. Jack told Ellis: "Out of the corner of my eye, I can see Bobo and the other guys hollering and laughing and I knew I'd been had. I stumble through this thing, and of course, the guys are laughing over in the dugout. I finally get through with the interview, get off the air, and I go over and cuss Bobo real good." Despite the fun, the Memphis Chicks were not immune to the wonders of televised baseball and affordable home window air conditioning units – the deadly combination that Cristil says eventually crippled minor league baseball in America.

Cristil left Jackson, Tenn., seeking to advance from D League to B League baseball. He left Anniston for better pay and more league stability with the Chicks in his hometown. But a Chicks team ownership change saw the former Chickasaw Buddy's relationship severed with the team, as the new owners cleaned house and brought in their own people. Leaving the Memphis Chicks gig was tough, Cristil admitted in 2011: "It was a defining time in my life. It was the first time I'd ever had enough money to sort of live comfortably. I worked, lived at home with Momma, saved some money, and basically did as I pleased. I remember that I bought four suits of clothes at one time during that period. Four! I'd never owned four suits of clothes before, much less bought them at one time."

The final stop on Cristil's minor league baseball announcing career carried him to Clarksdale, Miss., and the Class C Cotton States League featuring teams like the one whose action Cristil was broadcasting – the Clarksdale Planters – along with the El

Dorado Oilers, the Greenwood Dodgers, the Helena Seaporters, the Hot Springs Bathers, the Natchez Indians, and the Pine Bluff Cardinals made up the league in 1948, according to league records. In Clarksdale, Jack was employed by the WROX-AM radio station. "I sold radio advertising during the day, did my prep work in the afternoon for the baseball broadcast, then broadcast the game," said Jack. "I was friends with some of the players, particularly Joe Kopach. Kopach was originally from Pennsylvania and was a pitcher and an outfielder. He was playing ball to get out of the coal mines and steel mills back home – but he ended up right back there. We stayed in touch for several years."

Cristil remembers his minor league days as a succession of bus and train rides in which he slept, read, talked, and played cards with the players, coaches, and other minor league team associates. "I remember we 'recreated' most of the road games in the studio," said Cristil. "In Memphis, the team was playing on the road in Little Rock in the final game of the season. There was also an exhibition professional football game being played that same night in Little Rock. We had no listeners, no fans, for either team. They moved up the start of the baseball game to avoid competing with the football game. I recreated that nine-inning game in its entirety in 54 minutes."

During those days, Jack was driving his first car – a black 1948 Plymouth with a radio and heater. "It was fully equipped," Jack deadpans in 2011. In addition to selling ads for WROX and calling minor league baseball, Jack was broadcasting high school football and basketball games. As his former teacher Sim Winfield had told him about his ability to sell shoes, Cristil found that he was a pretty good ad salesman as well. "The fundamentals were the same," said Jack. "The product has a purpose. You talk to the customer about how that product will benefit them and hopefully you close the sale." He called on all types of accounts – retail, financial, institutional accounts, service businesses, heating and air-conditioning, auto sales, and repair.

"I enjoyed it," Jack said. "Soon, I'd met about half the town and perhaps more that that in the business community. I knew their families, their friends, and that helped me to have friends." He lived with the Baker family on Catalpa Street for a time and then moved in with the McMillin family in a rooming house situation.

The year was 1953. Jack Cristil was 27 years old, single, good in his chosen profession, and making a name for himself in the Mississippi Delta in his job at WROX. His life was all out in front of him. With no obligations or responsibilities, Cristil could choose his own path.

WROX was owned by Birney Imes, Jr., of Columbus, Miss., who purchased the station from founder Robin Weaver in 1944. Imes, an innovative newspaper publisher, had begun to acquire broadcast stations and envisioned building a radio network in the state. The Imes media company would eventually include daily and weekly newspapers and multiple radio and TV stations.

In 1953, Imes had hired Bob McRaney to manage his radio stations and to set about building a statewide radio network. Cristil told David Murray of *Dawgs' Bite* in 2002: "Imes owned a five-station network at the time, headquartered in Columbus, and he sent McRaney to make the rounds once a month. In April, maybe May of 1953, I was called into the office. I had no idea what McRaney wanted. He told me the Mississippi State football job was available. I'd never dreamed of doing college football. He asked if I'd like to audition and I said 'Sure.'"

Mike Talbert of *The Northeast Mississippi Daily Journal* reported

in a 1992 story that Cristil's opportunity at MSU developed because former play-by-play announcer Dick Crago had decided to
move back to Florida. Crago would go on to a 40-year career as the
public address announcer for Holman Stadium in Vero Beach, Fla.
– "Dodgertown" – in Major League Baseball's "Grapefruit League"
spring training venue for the Los Angeles Dodgers. Crago was the
announcer for the final out at "Dodgertown" in 2008 when the
Dodgers closed Holman Stadium and moved their spring training
program to Glendale, Ariz. Crago remained active in the leadership of the Florida Sports Hall of Fame until his death from cancer
on July 1, 2011.

Described as "imposing" and "thoughtful," Crago began his
broadcasting career while a student at the University of Florida,
where he earned Phi Beta Kappa status. During World War II,
Crago served in the U.S. Army in the 88th Infantry Division, the
first to enter Rome. After several post-war radio play-by-play announcing gigs, including time at both his alma mater and at MSU,
Crago worked for a number of Florida radio stations and eventually acquired his own station in Vero Beach, Fla. So influential was
Crago's work in the MLB's Grapefruit League that at his death at
age 85, former Major League Baseball Commissioner Fay Vincent
wrote in *The Vero Beach Press Journal* on July 4, 2011: "In every
sense, Dick led a good and noble life. He was a loyal churchgoer
and committed Presbyterian who carefully ran the good race, and
one knows his reward awaits him. In my last phone call to him a
few days before he died, he told me calmly he was 'at the end.' I
urged him to find good seats at the ball park where he was headed
and save a place for me. 'If I have any say, I will do just that,' was
his assurance. I am in good hands."

Crago broadcast MSU games for five years and Ole Miss games

for two years before returning to Florida, he confirmed in an interview with the Ft. Pierce, Fla.-based Indian River State College radio station WQCS.org in an oral history interview five years before his death.

Bulldog Club and MSU Athletics Department staff member Bart Gregory – who will join MSU's men's basketball broadcasts in the 2011-12 season – encountered Crago at "The Swamp" at the University of Florida in Gainesville, Fla., on the night of State's 2010 10-7 football victory over the Florida Gators. Gregory brought Crago to meet MSU Athletic Director Scott Stricklin – who later issued a tweet on Twitter regarding meeting Cristil's broadcasting predecessor at MSU: "Who knew such a person existed?"

Without Crago's departure from Starkville to return to his native Florida, who knows what would have become of either Jack Cristil or of MSU's sports broadcasting fortunes over the next six decades? But Crago did return home to Florida, and the powers that ruled the Imes family radio empire in Mississippi nudged Cristil toward the opportunity at MSU that Crago's absence created. The rest, as they say, is history.

Cristil told multiple interviewers over the years that with the active support of Birney Imes, McRaney was a prime mover in helping him get a shot at the MSU gig. By early August 1953, Cristil got a call from McRaney asking him if he'd go to Starkville and meet Coach Dudy Noble to discuss accepting the college's broadcasting duties.

Jack said his first response was: "Where's Starkville, and how do I get there?"

CHAPTER FIVE

"CUT OUT THE BULL!"

"Serendipity. Look for something, find something else, and realize that what you've found is more suited to your needs than what you thought you were looking for."

—LAWRENCE BLOCK
NOVELIST

ON THE 145-MILE DRIVE FROM CLARKSDALE TO STARKVILLE, JACK Cristil thought about this "Coach Dudy Noble" character in a Mississippi town that Cristil had never before visited. His image of what a successful leader of an organization looked and acted like was modeled in great measure upon the image of Bob McRaney, the general manager of the small Mississippi radio network where Cristil worked. McRaney was tall, nattily dressed, and immaculately groomed. McRaney, Cristil recalled, was a man who was smooth, polished, and knew how to close the deal. From McRaney, Cristil learned the value of finesse and a light touch in business.

However, in Mississippi State University athletic director Clark

Randolph "Dudy" Noble, Jack Cristil found exactly none of those qualities. Noble – who had earned 14 varsity letters in football, basketball, baseball, and track – graduated in 1915 from Mississippi A&M when the school's athletic teams were known as the "Aggies." As a player, Noble's Aggie squad had led a 65-0 rout of Ole Miss. He entered the coaching ranks soon after graduation, serving as head coach at Mississippi College in 1916, the University of Mississippi in 1917-18 and at his alma mater in 1922 – compiling a decidedly underwhelming 9-14-3 overall record as a head football coach and a 3-4-2 record at A&M. He was 0-3 at Ole Miss as a basketball coach in 1918-19 while also serving as the Rebel baseball coach. But Noble's baseball fortunes were significantly better than those enjoyed in football and basketball, and he served his alma mater as head baseball coach from 1920-43 and from 1946-47, building a lifetime head baseball coaching record of 277-205-9. He served as MSU's athletic director from 1938 until 1959 – and it was in that role the Noble left his distinguished mark on the university's athletic program.

Never let it be said that Noble was confused regarding his loyalties, despite the diversity of his early Mississippi coaching stints. "I know what hell is like," Noble once intoned. "I once coached at Ole Miss."

But the Dudy Noble who greeted Jack Cristil in 1953 in Starkville at what was then called the New Gym on the Mississippi State campus was a far cry from the gifted athlete who served A&M so gracefully in 1915. Noble was heavy set with a shock of grayish black hair and rather rumpled. The university was now known as "Mississippi State College," and the athletic teams were now known as the "Maroons." In the waiting area at the gymnasium, Cristil remembered seeing the 1941 Orange Bowl trophy inscribed: "Mississippi State 14, Georgetown 7."

Cristil would share this frank assessment of Noble with *Dawgs'*
Bite's David Murray in 2002: "I'd envisioned a young, energetic
businessman-type person, maybe in his late 30s or early 40s in
a trim suit, neat hair-do, all the things you saw in the world of
business at that time. This was not the case. Mr. Dudy Noble was
over six feet, quite hefty, attired in an old cotton shirt and britches
baggier than what I had on. He said 'boy" . . . (I later learned that
he called a lot of people boy if he didn't know their name or didn't
care) . . . he said 'boy, I understand you want to do these football
games.' I said 'Yes, sir, I certainly do.' I was eager to please him. He
said 'We've decided to give you the opportunity.' I was beaming
inside, trying to keep a straight face, and he said 'I'll tell you what
we want you to do.' I thought here comes some words of wisdom
I can use. And they certainly were."

"He said: 'You tell that radio audience what the score is, who's
got the ball and how much time is left, and you cut out the bull.'
We shook hands. Later, I was told what I'd get paid. I never signed
a contract," Cristil said. Cristil told *The Clarion-Ledger's* Mike Knobler in 1992 that Noble finally told him: "Well, we're going to give
you a try."

At 27, Cristil said he felt apprehensive meeting Noble for the
first time. He told the MSU *Alumnus* magazine in 1969: "When
I had my interview session in his office, with him behind that
big mahogany desk in the athletic building, I was nervous as any
young man would be in such an endeavor. He gave me some very
sage advice which I still try to heed. He told me he wanted me to
report what was happening truthfully. That was the first thing."

Yet, as he told Paul Jones of the *Mississippi Sports Magazine* in
2009, Cristil didn't approach the meeting as if it had life or death

consequences: "I didn't know what to expect or anticipate in that interview. I had never stepped foot on the campus at Mississippi State. Heck, I didn't even know what an athletic director did. So I put my best clothes on and walked in with a smile on my face. And what do ya know, he actually hired me."

As Cristil has told and retold the story of his encounter with Noble over the years, he has confirmed to multiple interviewers what Noble actually told him that day. "Bull" made a better read for family newspapers, but even after years of telling the story, Cristil still delights in giving reporters whom he trusts the un-expurgated quote from old Dudy – in which the curmudgeonly athletic director instructed his new charge to dispense with what he considered the bovine residue of extraneous radio broadcasting chatter. Cristil told Knobler in 1992: "The thought never entered my mind 'How long is this going to go on?' When you're youthful, you don't worry about those things. Here's an opportunity. You grab it. You run with it. You do the very best you can."

The late Bob Hartley, the legendary longtime MSU sports information director, told Knobler for that story: "It was one of the best decisions that Clark Randolph 'Dudy' Noble ever made." Bo Carter, the Hartley acolyte who would go on to a magnificent career in his own right in major college sports media, wrote in 1992 of how Cristil took Noble's charge to heart on the occasion of Jack Cristil's 50th year of service to MSU: "Jack even used the radio maxim of placing an egg timer in front of his broadcast position to remind avid listeners about the score, time remaining, site of the contest and specific situations every two minutes during the broadcast."

Carter also wrote reverently of the mutual respect and abiding friendship Cristil shared with Hartley after Jack told him: "I considered Bob Hartley as the man who made my transition from minor league baseball and local sports to announcing at MSU as smooth as possible. We spent many an hour in a car or on a plane or even in the old days on trains and he was a true friend . . . and he was always a gracious gentleman to my family."

In his 2008 oral history interview with Dr. Roy Ruby, Cristil spoke again of his relationship with Hartley: "Bob was a very unique individual. And he made you feel very, very comfortable although you may not have known him for five minutes. [Hartley] probably made more friends for Mississippi State when they needed friends than anybody else had ever done for the university. And I can't say enough about him. He led and guided and directed me in the infancy in this business as to how to conduct myself and those things you needed to do. He never, as such, and no one for that matter at Mississippi State, ever told me how to broadcast a game. The only thing I was ever instructed to do, Coach Noble told me [in his office]."

Cristil's compensation in 1953 was $25 per game plus mileage and other travel expenses. In the 1957-58 season, he would also be put in charge of Maroon men's basketball broadcasts for $10 a game plus travel. In 2011, Jack reflected on what he considered the greatest misconception that MSU fans had about his career as their announcer: "My association at Mississippi State University was never my primary source of income. It wasn't in 1953, and that was true up until my retirement from broadcast sales. I dare say that for the whole of my career, I was probably the lowest paid announcer in the SEC. I don't know; I never checked it out, but I'd say that's a fair conclusion. In 1953, anyone trying to make a living doing sports announcing alone in Mississippi would have starved to death. But the MSU affiliation did open so many doors for me as someone selling radio and later television advertising.

Not only did it help me with the Mississippi State fans in the business community, it didn't hurt me with the Ole Miss folks, either. As the announcer for Mississippi State, I was a known commodity; someone who merchants believed might have a little more on the ball than some of my competitors by virtue of that affiliation. From that sense, it contributed significantly to my overall income. No, I never got rich broadcasting for MSU – but I was able to make a good living and support my family, which was my goal for my career."

As Orley Hood noted in his 1992 tribute to Cristil: "The first Mississippi State game he saw, he broadcast." In his 1992 interview with Steve Ellis, Cristil talked about that 1953 first season calling MSU football. His first MSU game was a road game in his native Memphis against the Memphis State University Tigers. MSU Head Coach Murray Warmath's Maroons cruised to a 34-6 win, but Jack has virtually no recollection of the game. He told Ellis: "I do not remember the first game. For years and years, I thought it was against Tennessee at Knoxville. We went up there and beat UT 26-0, and at the time it was the worst opening day defeat Tennessee had ever suffered. It was our second game. I didn't realize it for years and years, but we had already played Memphis State at the old Crump Stadium. Evidently, my mind was on Tennessee more than Memphis State, for whatever reason."

Warmath's 1953 Maroon team would post a 5-2-3 mark in Cristil's first season. The team was led by one of MSU's all-time greats, All-American quarterback Jackie Parker. In the 1952 season, Parker scored 120 points on 16 touchdowns and 24 PATs – a league record that stood for 40 years before Georgia's Garrison Hearst broke it by scoring 21 touchdowns in 1992. In Bill Sorrels' 1975 book *The Maroon Bulldogs*, Warmath said of Parker: "He was the greatest clutch player I ever saw in football. When it had to be done, he would do it."

But Warmath departed Starkville for Cristil's alma mater, the University of Minnesota, in the spring of 1954. Noble brought back a former MSU assistant, Darrell Royal, from the Canadian Football League's Edmonton Eskimos to succeed Warmath, who first brought Royal to MSU in 1952 as his assistant. With a stable of athletes that included Bobby Collins, Art Davis, Hal Easterwood, Scott Suber, Bill Dooley, and Dinky Evans, Royal posted back-to-back 6-4 seasons in Starkville in 1954-55 before departing for the University of Washington. Royal would go on to win three national championships in football at the University of Texas in 1963, 1969, and 1970. A new coach would follow Royal, but in his early years at Mississippi State, Cristil's attention was increasingly diverted from the coaching carousel at MSU and even from his duties at WROX by a young lady he'd met in Clarksdale. As surely as Jack had known as a child that he wanted to be a radio announcer, he would say decades later that he came to know this lovely young woman he'd met – Mavis Kelly – "was the one" to be his bride.

CHAPTER SIX

A LADY NAMED MAVIS

*"Men forget everything. Women remember everything.
That's why men need instant replay in sports."*

—RITA RUDNER
COMEDIENNE

JACK CRISTIL MET MAVIS KELLY IN 1952 IN CLARKSDALE. "MAVIS HAD A
brother, James, who was playing football at Ole Miss. That's how
I met James. I was calling Clarksdale High School football and
basketball on WROX. James introduced me to Mavis, and I liked
her right off the bat."

In 2011, Cristil said their courtship took the normal path in the
1950s. "I really took a liking to Mavis, and we started dating, going
to dances, the movies, and out for a beer. It really wasn't that long
before I knew she was the one. Mavis was even then an intelligent
person who made her own decisions. She was compassionate
and understanding, open-minded, and not at all dogmatic in her
thinking. She was stern when she knew she was right, and in those
instances, no one could move her. She was just so pleasant to be

with, so comforting, and she was strong enough not to be anyone's 'yes man.' Mavis had such a positive attitude."

Mavis Kelly was born Nov. 21, 1926, in Mathiston in Choctaw County, Miss., to a working class family. Her parents moved to the Delta and also spent time in Pascagoula before settling in Clarksdale. Her father had an auto body shop, and her mother worked in a department store. Mrs. Kelly also made custom drapes and curtains. Mr. Kelly worked for a time in a bakery. The Kellys were Baptist, and the family was active in their church.

"I loved Mavis, and I really enjoyed her family – and she seemed to enjoy mine," said Jack. "There was nothing really dramatic about our courtship. I just think we both knew that marriage was the next step for both of us."

The couple married on Jan. 30, 1955, at Temple Israel in Memphis. "Mavis was late," fumed Jack in 2011. "If she'd been 10 minutes later, there wouldn't have been a wedding." A stickler for punctuality, Cristil has a broadcaster's sense of time and the necessity of not only being punctual, but early if possible. Yet when he speaks of his wife, one gets the sense that he would have waited far longer for his bride than his protestations indicate.

"I don't know that we had a honeymoon as such," said Jack. "I got transferred to Tupelo. I moved and went to work. Mavis didn't join me for five or six months. She had a good job at Planters Manufacturing Company in Clarksdale, where they made cotton seed oil and other products. During the season, the girls in the office were working 13, 14, sometimes 15 hours a day. They'd go early and stay late. Mavis was really good at her job, and she enjoyed it."

Shortly after their marriage, Jack was asked to go to Tupelo to broadcast high school basketball tournaments for radio station WELO, a "sister" station to WROX in the Imes-owned MidSouth

Radio Network. It was to have been a temporary assignment.

Jack told David Murray in 2002: "When I found out I was going to be transferred to Tupelo to WELO, I didn't want to go without Mavis and why she elected to come I don't know. I never did understand why she married me, she was an intelligent woman. And I mean that sincerely. She had a nice job with the company processing cotton seed oil, a better job than I had. When I moved to Tupelo, I thought it was going to be temporary." Cristil told Ellis in 1992: "In those days, you did everything yourself. You worked on a shoestring; you didn't have a lot of money to spend. You would try to get everything by writing a letter to each team's sports information director. Bob Hartley was a tremendous help. He introduced me around the league and made everything a lot easier."

In those days, Jack and Mavis bent their social life to his professional life. "She'd go with me to ball games on Friday and Saturdays. We'd have cookouts in the summer, and Mavis worked a lot in her flower beds," said Jack. "She always raised the most beautiful flowers. After she joined me in Tupelo, we went to Clarksdale often to visit her family there. I really enjoyed being part of the Kelly family."

But Cristil's career was demanding. Jack was calling Itawamba Community College games on Thursday nights, high school games on Friday nights, and college games on Saturday nights. With those games came long distance travel. Jack was on the road constantly, plus maintaining a job at WELO that included advertising sales, shifts in the station's main studio, and the various "live remote" broadcasts from county fairs, concerts, and the like. It was in this role that Cristil would interview Elvis Presley in 1956 after he performed at the Mississippi-Alabama Fair in a triumphant return to the singer's hometown. Cristil told *Dawgs' Bite* in 2002:

"It was as difficult an interview as I've ever had, trying to make an interesting interview with him . . . I did do the interview, but I was never really proud of it, not necessarily because of the person I was interviewing, but because I thought I'd failed in what I attempted to do. And I'm not one who likes failure."

Another star turn for Cristil came when he interviewed Hollywood icon Joan Crawford in the late 1950s while she was on a publicity tour for Pepsi Cola. Crawford married Pepsi chairman Alfred Steele in 1955 and claimed to have traveled over 100,000 miles promoting the soft drink – and one of those trips carried her into Cristil's orbit in Tupelo. Photographs of Cristil interviewing the *Mommie Dearest* inspiration/*Mildred Pierce* star hang near the kitchen table of his home today.

In an Oct. 23, 1996, story in *The Northeast Mississippi Daily Journal*, Bobby Pepper wrote this description of WELO's working environment in the 1950s and early 1960s: "WELO, which was then on 1490 on the (AM) dial, broadcasted from a building on South Spring Street. Where the building once stood is now the parking lot for the Peoples Bank and Trust Company's downtown headquarters. From sunrise to sunset, WELO presented a variety of programs: news, weather, sports, live music, women's programs, community information programs, market reports, farm news, teenage news, church services, regional and national news from MidSouth and Mutual radio networks, and live remotes from events such as store openings, the courthouse on election night, and the annual Mississippi-Alabama Fair."

Cristil told Pepper the facts about his job in that era: "I was involved in sales and sports, but I also did a board shift. When you ran a board shift, you did what was on the schedule. You gave the news, played music, read market reports, whatever it called for on your shift."

The realities of Jack's career did not threaten his marriage to Mavis. Divorce rates among media personalities ran high in those days as they do today.

"Mavis was the dominant person in our household," said Jack. "She never complained about me being gone. We never even talked about things like that. We really never talked in terms of my 'career' except when opportunities were before us. Mavis was all about grace and class. When you came in off the road, things would be normal, no fussing and fighting. Even at home, the job was always a factor. The travel took time. The preparation took time. But Mavis took it all in stride. When you got home, things would be pleasant and normal."

Cristil told David Murray in 2002: "I've often said the only reason a person in my situation would enjoy any degree of success is first and foremost a loving and understanding family willing to give you 100 percent support. If you don't, it is an impossible job. Because if there's a crisis at home, you're never there. When the washing machine breaks down, when the plumbing goes bad, when the roof leaks, when the youngsters get sick you're never there. Fortunately, I married a very intelligent lady who could handle it and who never once to my knowledge complained about me being on the road."

Jack and Mavis had their first child on Feb. 3, 1959, when they welcomed daughter Kay. A second daughter, Rebecca, would complete the Cristil family on Feb. 17, 1963.

The one exception to Mavis Cristil's mastery of the home front while Jack pursued his career was the morning routine. While Mavis was pregnant with Kay, Jack got in the habit of making her breakfast every morning. Daughter Rebecca said: "The habit never stopped, and that's why he was in charge of getting the house running every morning. There's a story about Kay getting in the car one day after school and exclaiming to Mama, 'Can you believe there's a girl in my class who says her mother cooks breakfast?!?' Mama responded, 'I've never heard of such a thing.'"

Jack's assumption of the lead in the family's morning routine must have suited Mavis.

"Mavis did well during the pregnancy, but Kay's delivery was difficult," said Jack. "I saw Mavis after, and she was just so washed out that it really frightened me." But Mavis recovered, and the Cristils adapted to a growing family. They lived in an apartment on Jackson Street in Tupelo and bought their first window air conditioner. "We told each other it was for the baby, and it was, but I guess we enjoyed it as well," Jack grinned. "Before Kay was born, we got a boxer puppy; and Mavis named it Susie. Susie was Mavis' baby until she had a real baby.

Mavis, born working class Baptist in rural Mississippi, converted to Judaism in 1963. "There was no argument, no big discussion," Jack said. "She became active in the local synagogue, with the schools, and with the Girl Scouts."

"She started a Girl Scout troop and carried that same group through their senior year in high school," Jack said. "For three years prior to that 1976 bicentennial year, she worked to raise funds for a trip to Washington, Philadelphia, and Williamsburg. She chartered a bus from John L. Long of Starkville, and he and I were the only two men to make that trip with 40 ladies and girls. Mavis did that all by herself."

When not taking care of the girls, Jack said Mavis enjoyed pop music from the Big Band era and played the organ. "Mavis was a wonderful dancer. She read a lot, books and newspapers. She did a lot of knitting, needlework, and really enjoyed genealogy. She also took care of the family finances. I didn't know if we had a nickel or a dollar."

Over the course of her life, Mavis Cristil was an active member of Temple B'Nai Israel in Tupelo and president of the Temple Sisterhood. She was a troop leader and advisor for the Prairie Girl Scout Council in northeast Mississippi. Her interests in genealogy led her to membership in the Northeast Mississippi Historical and Genealogical Society, the Daughters of the American Revolution, and the United Daughters of the Confederacy. She was a past president of the Tupelo chapter of Beta Sigma Phi, the international "friendship organization" that holds the motto: "Life, Learning and Friendship."

Rebecca Cristil Nelson speaks of her mother's curiosity and intellect: "My mama was one tough cookie. She could handle anything. Even though she never went to college, Mama was more educated than most adults I know. She was smart, and if she was curious about a subject, she'd teach herself what she needed to know. She also enrolled in some courses at Itawamba Junior College (now Itawamba Community College), including speech and Spanish. I remember that one of her speech assignments was a demonstration speech. She wanted to do something different than the usual "how to make a cake." She decided to demonstrate masonry. So she taught herself how to build a brick wall, practiced in the back yard, and delivered her speech to the class. She got an A."

The Cristils traveled across the U.S. visiting relatives and taking the girls to see the sights. There were regular trips to the Mississippi Gulf Coast, to Shiloh Military Park in Tennessee, and there were trips to Arizona, Colorado, Nashville, Chicago and other destinations. There would be a memorable trip to Europe as the

Cristils visited England, Scotland, Ireland, and Wales.

Opportunities would come to Jack Cristil in the 1960s. Cristil was invited to interview with brothers Bill and Charlie Bidwill, owners of the old St. Louis Cardinals, for a spot at KMOX in St. Louis doing football play-by-play for the Cardinals and working as a fill-in baseball announcer for Harry Caray and Jack Buck on Cardinals baseball broadcasts. After several days of talks, Cristil turned the opportunity down. "Mavis and I had brought a couple of children into the world by that time. That's an awesome responsibility. Mavis and I focused our decision on what was in the best interests of our family. I'm convinced that it was the wisest thing I never did, not getting into that rat race."

Cristil told Ellis in 1992: "Once I make a decision, I never look back at what might have been. We enjoyed Northeast Mississippi and the relationships with our friends and the people I worked with. I never had the delusions of grandeur of being a network broadcaster, so Mavis and I just made the decision to stay where we were."

Not all of Jack's decisions won praise. Daughter Rebecca offered this evidence: "Mama was also the typical housewife . . . cooking supper, doing laundry, cleaning the house, washing dishes, shopping for groceries, etc. She did have the help of us girls, but she did NOT have the help of a dryer or dishwasher. She claimed all those years that she didn't want either one, but I think it has something to do with Daddy's frugal ways. When Mama was in the hospital in 1988, Aunt Mimi came to Tupelo for a few days to help Daddy. After doing the laundry one day and hanging the clothes on the line, she said, 'Jack, whatever it is that you've been trying to prove all these years by not having a dryer, you proved it. Now get a dryer.' He still doesn't have one."

Mavis Cristil's independence was not wasted on her children. Daughter Kay Cristil Clouatre recalls this life lesson: "As a Girl Scout leader to my troop, she was always finding things 'outside the box' of the usual Girl Scout activities. About the time everyone was turning 15 and getting a driver's license, Mama decided that as young women learning to drive and being behind the wheel, we all needed to learn more about driving than just turning the key and pushing a pedal. She was determined that each of us would learn to change a flat tire in case we ever got stranded and didn't have a 'man' to help us. So, she got permission from the manager at Gibson's to use their parking lot for this experience. I am not sure how many cars we had there, but we all watched and took turns going through the motions of changing a tire. A few weeks later, a group of us went traveling to Pontotoc for a party at Julie Tutor's house, and on the way, I had a flat tire in Mama's car. Amazingly, each of us in the caravan of cars remembered bits and pieces of our 'tire changing lesson,' and we did a remarkable job of changing that tire. When we got back to Tupelo and told Mama that her car had the flat tire, and we all changed the tire ourselves, she was so proud."

Of all Jack Cristil's memories of his wife of 33 years, the one he has shared most often – in most of the comprehensive biographical articles written about him by David Murray, Steve Ellis, and others – is the story of Mavis Cristil's encounter with the legendary University of Kentucky head basketball coach Adolph Rupp. Cristil last told the story publicly during a June 20, 2011, ceremony honoring him in Starkville. Rupp, in 41 seasons, won 879 games and four national titles and was a four-time National Coach of the Year selection. At Kentucky, Rupp captured 27 Southeastern Conference regular season titles and won 13 SEC tournament titles.

Cristil recounted the tale to a rapt audience in Starkville: "In our early days of broadcasting, we were working with what we now call the McCarthy Gym. We had a location midway between the rollaway bleachers and the permanent bleachers on top, and there were two seats reserved behind us at a little desk for visiting scouts. At that time we were playing Saturday-Monday basketball. We were paired with Ole Miss, Tennessee, and Kentucky. And Ole Miss and Kentucky played on Friday night in Jackson for some reason rather than on Saturday in Oxford. On Saturday, we played Tennessee. Well, with Kentucky having played, Coach [Adolph] Rupp and Coach [Harry] Lancaster, the athletic director at Kentucky, came to Mississippi State to scout in person on Saturday night prior to the Monday ball game. They took seats immediately behind us. Well, Mavis had brought her knitting. She's sitting there knitting while the team is warming up. And this got to Coach Rupp, who said, 'Lady, do you intend to knit during this basketball game?' She didn't know who he was. She said, 'Mister, if you had seen as much basketball as I have, you could knit and watch it at the same time.'

"Well, they carried on a conversation throughout the course of the ball game. As it ultimately turned out, our game went to double overtime. Tennessee gets a two-point lead and the ball, and our gym is as quiet as this room is right now. This ball game is over. There was no shot clock in those days. Tennessee had the possession of the ball with a two-point lead. Mavis turns to Coach Rupp and she pops him: 'Well, State just won the game.'

"'Lady, how are they going to win the game? Tennessee has got the two-point lead and the ball.'

"She said: 'You see that man down there in the brown suit.' She pointed to Coach (Babe) McCarthy.

"'Yeah, I know Coach McCarthy.'

"'He's telling that group of kids what to do. They're going to get that basketball, and they're going to win this game.'

"As it ultimately turned out, that's exactly what happened. State did get the basketball, and we did win the basketball game, and it was absolute bedlam in that arena.

"We had to do a little postgame show when it was over. Of course, Coach Lancaster and Coach Rupp had left, and I asked Mavis, 'Who was that man you were talking to?' She says, 'I don't know.' I said, 'That was Adolph Rupp. He probably knows more basketball than any man in the world.' Mavis said, 'Well, he learned a lesson here tonight.'"

Cristil tells that story with a mixture of mirth, pride, and sadness when trying to communicate to people the type of woman he married. And he speaks often of her friendship in that era with MSU sports information director Bob Hartley's wife, Jean.

Jack and Mavis Cristil's daughters share in their father's memories of their mother. Kay Cristil Clouatre, 52, is a special education language arts teacher in Denham Springs, La., and makes her home in Baton Rouge. She is the mother of Jake Clouatre, 18, Jack's grandson and a freshman at Northwestern State University in Natchitoches, La. Rebecca Cristil Nelson, 48, is an English teacher in Augusta, Ga. She is the mother of Lindsey Newhall, 12, a sixth-grader in Augusta, Ga. Asked about their father, each daughter had a different story to illustrate the same devoted dad. Each daughter also bore the scars of loss and regret from their mother's death in 1988 in different ways but with equal result.

Kay Cristil Clouatre recounted this story: "Growing up, I always had crushes on movie stars, entertainers as young kids did – Donny Osmond, The Jackson Five, The Partridge Family, etc. – but none of my crushes were as great as the crushes I had on MSU football players. I didn't date much in high school, and I never had a boyfriend, so in my pitiful little teenage mind, admiring football players from afar seemed innocent enough. I had the biggest crush on Terry Vitrano (MSU running back, 1974-77, the Most Valuable Player of the 1974 Sun Bowl). I thought he was the 'hottest thing since sliced bread.' I never really talked about my crushes with Daddy or even the boys that I liked, but I talked enough openly that these crushes were not a secret. So, on a football trip on a flight to somewhere for a game, Daddy sat next to Terry Vitrano on the plane. He apparently mentioned to Terry how much I adored him, and at that moment Terry wrote me a personal note. Daddy and Mama woke me up when he returned from that trip to show me the note. I still have that personal handwritten note in my scrapbook, and I have always thought that was one of the coolest things Daddy ever did. He didn't embarrass me, he didn't quiz me about my crush, and he didn't tease me about it. He just took the time to put a special smile on my face that I have never forgotten."

Rebecca Cristil Nelson told this story: "In the summer of 1976, Mama and some other Girl Scout leaders were taking some scouts from throughout Prairie Council to Our Cabana, which is an international Girl Scout house in Mexico. They would be gone 10 days. I was to spend those 10 days with Daddy. Part of that time we would be in St. Louis, where we would visit Aunt Zelda and Uncle Sam. Everyone met at the Memphis airport on the given day, and we all waited at the gate until the scouts departed. Since I had been away at camp the previous four summers for two weeks each time, I was completely fine knowing I would not see Mama for 10 days – or so I thought. When it came time to board, I burst into tears and begged Mama not to go. She said I would be fine and that I must have been crying because I was left alone with Daddy. Everyone chuckled at that.

"So Daddy and I went to St. Louis, and among our activities was a trip to Six Flags over Mid-America. Daddy was game to ride whatever I wanted to ride (probably knowing that I'm a chicken where roller coasters and such are concerned): the Tilt-A-Whirl, the Scrambler, the Himalaya. He even let me drive when we rode in the tin-lizzie. But the best part to me was the log ride, where the log follows a winding course then ends with a slow climb to the top and a plunge to the bottom, causing everyone aboard to get completely soaked. After we rode that, I said, 'That was FUN!' Daddy said, 'Do you want to ride it again?' I was somewhat surprised. We are not a 'repeat' sort of family. We never even got beverage refills in restaurants. But we spent the rest of the afternoon riding the log ride over and over and over. Pure joy for me . . . and I think for Daddy, too. It's just one of those memories that have remained in my heart all these years," Nelson said.

In the 1980s, the Cristils saw their lives rocked by an intruder that none of them had anticipated when Mavis Cristil was diagnosed with lupus. According to the Lupus Foundation of America, lupus "is a chronic, autoimmune disease that can damage any part of the body (skin, joints, and/or organs inside the body). Chronic means that the signs and symptoms tend to last longer than six weeks and often for many years. In lupus, something goes wrong with your immune system, which is the part of the body that fights off viruses, bacteria, and germs ('foreign invaders,' like the flu). Normally our immune system produces proteins called antibodies that protect the body from these invaders. Autoimmune means your immune system cannot tell the difference between these foreign invaders and your body's healthy tissues ('auto' means 'self') and creates autoantibodies that attack and destroy healthy tissue. These autoantibodies cause inflammation, pain, and damage in various parts of the body."

While not universally fatal, lupus can result in death for some afflicted with the disease as a result of damage to vital organs. That was the case in Mavis Cristil's battle with the disease. Jack Cristil said the onset of the disease in 1982 caught him by surprise.

"Mavis at first just seemed to have gotten bogged down and tired," Cristil said. "But soon after that, she had gotten sick, very sick," Jack said. "I had been on the road, and Mavis had a problem with her heart. My neighbors down the street, Charlie and Kay Robison, came to the house and took her to the hospital. The sac around the heart, the pericardium, was enlarged. She lost the function of two chambers of her heart in that episode and really never recovered her strength. A pacemaker was installed to help her deal with the damage to her heart, but the doctors told us that she would only last four or five years, and they knew exactly what they were talking about – that's how long she lasted. She slowed down; fatigue was constant, and Mavis just didn't have the pep she'd always had."

There were frequent hospitalizations. Medication was increased but to no real avail. In January of 1988, Mavis Cristil entered North Mississippi Medical Center in Tupelo for her final hospitalization. "I missed a number of games during that time," said Jack. "Jim Ellis handled everything in his inimitable fashion, and that was such a help to me. Sometimes I would go and broadcast the games and come straight back, but it depended on the situation. But broadcasting the games at that time in our lives was the only time I left town."

Mavis Cristil battled lupus there for 77 days, and many of those days she was on a ventilator. Jack maintained a vigil at her bedside. He'd work at his job as WTVA-TV's sales manager and spend time at the hospital. At night, he slept on a cot at her bedside. In the pre-dawn hours of April 3, 1988, Jack was awakened from an exhaustive sleep to face his worst nightmare.

"She died at 3:33 a.m.," said Jack. "Earlier that night, I knew that time was short, that she would not last long, and I feared the worst at any minute. But I guess I was just so beat down and weary that I fell asleep on the cot. The doctor woke me up and told me that Mavis had died. My first reaction was that it was a blessing. It had hurt me to see her deteriorate to that state."

The impact of Mavis Cristil's death fell hard not only on Jack but on his daughters.

Jack told David Murray in 2002: "It was a difficult time for the kids. Rebecca was a student, and Kay was teaching in Louisiana. But the neighbors were wonderful. It was a severe loss to the family, but thanks to so many friends and associates, it worked out as well as it could. I couldn't tell you how many people I heard from personally or through letters, phone calls, genuinely and sincerely asking to help. It was deeply appreciated."

Daughter Kay Cristil Clouatre said: "My mother's illness and death is not an experience I would wish on my worst enemy. To watch my mama die at such a young age is a visual I have never forgotten. I wasn't as strong as I wanted people to believe. I tried to ignore the fact that Mama wasn't getting any better. In my mind, I lived in Baton Rouge, and because I wasn't there at the hospital every day, maybe it would just go away. I remember Mississippi State offering to send their plane for me to fly home one weekend, and I graciously said 'no.' I didn't want to go home. I really didn't

want to face Mama's situation. I am not sure in my mind at that
time what Daddy was going through. Neither Rebecca nor I was
married at that time, and I felt so alone those few months and
after Mama's death. When Mama passed away, I remember feeling a relief and a release – a relief that her suffering as well as ours
was over and a release from all the misery this illness brought to
everyone. For anyone who hasn't experienced a lengthy illness of a
family member, it is absolutely draining for the patient and everyone in the family. After the funeral, I was standing at the end of
the driveway, and Daddy walked up to me and said: 'Nothing has
changed except you can't pick up the phone and call your mother.'
I didn't want to hurt his feelings with what I was thinking, but my
thought process was 'everything has changed.'"

The funeral was held at Pegues Funeral Home in Tupelo with
interment in Lee Memorial Park at Verona, Miss. Former MSU
President William Giles and then-MSU President Donald W. Zacharias led a large contingent of MSU mourners. The university sent
three buses to Tupelo for the services. Hundreds passed through
the funeral home visitation line to express their condolences.
With the leadership of Tupelo businessman Buzzy Mize, the Lee
County Chapter of the MSU Alumni Association established the
Jack and Mavis Cristil Endowed Scholarship Fund "in memory of
Mrs. Mavis Cristil and in honor of Mr. Jack Cristil's many years of
service to Mississippi State University as the 'Voice of the Bulldogs.' The scholarship is available to freshman students who have
academic eligibility but do not have the financial resources to
attend college and who have a 3.0 GPA or equivalent at the high
school level."

Jack's sisters remained with him for a couple of weeks after
Mavis died to help with the adjustment, and the broadcaster was

grateful. He was also grateful for his daughters.

"But when things settled down, I was absolutely lost," said Jack. "All I could think was where do I go from here without her. I had relied on her for so long. There was a time that I just couldn't think rationally. I was never so lonesome in my life."

Daughter Rebecca Nelson said: "After Mama died, Daddy was lost. He had spent every day and almost every night since January at the hospital, and now he was home with essentially no purpose. His world had absolutely crashed. The first time I saw Daddy after Mama's funeral was in May 1988. I was in Starkville for a wedding, and afterwards I headed to Dudy Noble Field for the baseball regionals. Daddy and I had decided to meet there and watch the game together. I cried as we hugged, and he may have shed a tear or two as well. With no spoken words, each knew what the other was thinking – I'm grateful that this first meeting was in the midst of our Bulldog family."

Kay Cristil Clouatre remembers her father's stoic nature after her mother's death: "Daddy didn't cry around Rebecca and me until the day of Mama's funeral, and even then he kept his tears to a minimum until he saw his brothers and sisters walk into the funeral home, and even then he was trying to be strong. I did ask Daddy later why he didn't cry, and he replied: 'I've cried every night.' My mama was everything to my daddy. He placed her on a pedestal and revered her as every man should revere his wife. She was his best friend. For the first time in a very long time, he didn't have his best friend. He was lost. Mama kept the house, cooked, paid the bills. Daddy didn't have a clue how to keep a checkbook or pay the bills. I worked with Daddy on this, and eventually he got the hang of it. He stayed busy with MSU and his men friends, and I know that they were a huge part of his moving forward and getting on with his life.

"He still mentions their wedding anniversary as if they are still celebrating. And for a very long time, when he would call, he would hang up by saying 'we love you.' Daddy has survived as we all have, but there has always been that void in our lives. Even after all these years, not a day goes by that I don't think of her or talk to her and ask her opinion or what she would do in a certain situation. Of course, she has never directly answered me, but in my heart, I get the answers I need. I still find myself picking up the phone to ask about a recipe or talk about a TV show that she liked. I personally always felt like life cheated me for taking my mama. I was 29; she was 61. I was supposed to have had my mama with me forever. She wasn't here to see me get married, but the fact she wasn't here for the birth of Jake and never getting to know him absolutely kills me. She would have loved him so much."

Both Kay Cristil Clouatre and Rebecca Cristil Nelson have gone through divorces. Their father, both report, stood by them as adults facing problems as he did when they were children.

Rebecca said: "Because Daddy was on the road so much, we did not get to spend as much time with him as our friends spent with their fathers. Likewise, Daddy missed out on some time with his children. Even when we traveled with him, it was still a business trip, and the name of the game was getting the job done. Even so, his impact on me was tremendous. As adults, Daddy gives us full support in whatever we choose to do. In many instances he simply does not know what to do, whereas Mama would have, but he reminds us that he is available and will help any way he can. He knows he has reared two intelligent, well-adjusted children who must ultimately make their own decisions, and he is confident we

Jack Cristil photographed in 1992 by the late MSU staff photographer Fred Faulk.

Jacob Sanford "Jack" Cristil, age 1, is pictured in a chair in the yard of his family home on Galloway Street in Memphis, Tenn.

Cristil, age 5, with his mother, Mollie Kabakoff Cristil, and sister Miriam "Mimi" Cristil in 1930 in Memphis.

Cristil's parents, Mollie Kabakoff Cristil and Benjamin Herman Cristil, circa 1932, in Memphis.

Cristil, age 13, a student at L.C. Humes Junior High School in Memphis. Cristil lost his father to ulosis in 1939 just months before this photo was taken.

Cristil enlisted in the U.S. Army Air Corps in 1943 during World War II, where he served as an aircraft engine mechanic.

Jack Cristil married Mavis Kelly of Clarksdale on January 30, 1955, at Temple Israel in Memphis. Their marriage lasted 33 years until her death from lupus in 1988.

Jack and Mavis Cristil at the Kelly home in Clarksdale, Miss., in the late 1950s.

Cristil in 1957 at radio station WSSO in Starkville.

MISSISSIPPI STATE COLLEGE   FOR IMMEDIATE RELEASE
Athletic Publicity Department

        STATE COLLEGE, Miss., Sept. ____. — Jack Cristil, sports director

of station WROX in Clarksdale, Miss., will air all of Mississippi State's 1953

football games over a state-wide Mississippi network.

        Cristil, a native of Memphis, played football at Humes High and later

played service football at Lubbock Army Air Field in Texas in 1945.

        A graduate of radio school in Minneapolis, Minnesota, Cristil has done

                                          (WROX-Clarksdale   — WREC-Memphis — Anniston
extensive sports announcing and radio work in Mississippi, Tennessee and Alabama   baseball
                                          WELO-Tupelo   — Jackson, TN   team
for the past five years.

        During this time he has been at the mike covering football, baseball,

basketball and boxing for Mid-South sports fans.

        Cristil's first assignment following the Maroon grid fortunes will be

broadcasting the Mississippi State-Memphis State game from Memphis Saturday.

        He will then follow the Maroons broadcasting the road games with

Tennessee, Kentucky, Alabama, Texas Tech, Tulane and LSU along with the three

campus games with North Texas State, Auburn and Ole Miss.

                                    ####

Copy of the official university news release when Cristil was hired by MSU in September 1953.

Cristil in 1953 shortly after accepting the job as MSU's play-by-play radio broadcaster.

Cristil, standing at right, with his siblings and his mother in the late 1960s. Standing: Harold Cristil, Stanley Cristil, Miriam "Mimi" Cristil Lapides, and Jack Cristil. Seated: Charlotte Cristil Hiller, Mrs. Mollie Cristil, and Zelda Cristil Esgro. Jack's mom died in 1982 at age 91.

Cristil during his days as a radio broadcaster in Clarksdale at WROX, wearing the "horse collar" microphone in the early 1950s.

Cristil broadcasting a high school basketball game for WELO radio in Tupelo in the early 1960s.

Cristil, third from left, broadcasts MSU's 16-12 win over North Carolina State in the 1963 Liberty Bowl from Philadelphia Stadium in Philadelphia, Penn. - a game which Cristil told listeners was played in conditions "colder than a pawnbroker's heart." Distinguished MSU alumnus U.S. Sen. John C. Stennis, second from right, was in the unheated broadcast booth for the game.

Cristil, right, with longtime former MSU sports information director Bob Hartley during a MSU team photo session at Scott Field in the early 1960s.

Cristil, left, with comedian Bob Hope, center, and longtime former MSU radio network producer and director Joe Phillips of Starkville. Cristil interviewed Hope during halftime of the MSU 35-6 loss to Alabama in the former Denny Stadium in Tuscaloosa on Oct. 31, 1970.

Cristil, right, with Larry Templeton. Templeton, who was a spotter for Cristil as a kid, later became MSU's athletic director for 21 years before becoming a consultant to the Southeastern Conference.

Mavis and Jack Cristil in the stands at the 1974 Sun Bowl in El Paso, Texas, the only football game Cristil didn't call during his 58-year career. Cristil was sidelined because of pre-existing broadcast rights.

The Jack Cristil family in 1973: From left, Kay, Jack, Mavis and front center, Rebecca, during a family outing to the Shiloh Military Park at Pittsburg Landing, Tenn.

Cristil, right, with legendary University of Kentucky broadcaster Cawood Ledford in the early 1980s.

Cristil sporting a "Go to Hell, Ole Miss" button at Mississippi Veterans Memorial Stadium in Jackson in the 1970s.

Cristil at work at WELO Radio in Tupelo in the mid-1970s. He broadcast Tupelo High School and Itawamba Community College football and basketball games from 1955-1985.

In later years, Cristil, center, shared MSU football broadcast with color analyst Jim Ellis, left, and sideline reporter John Correro, right.

MSU Network officials inked a pact with Richard Redd, center, who was a major sponsor of Bulldog radio broadcast in the early 1970s. Shown are Joe Phillips, Jack Cristil, Redd, former MSU athletic director and head football coach Charlie Shira, and former MSU head football coach Bob Tyler.

Cristil with former MSU head football coach Emory Bellard in 1980.

Cristil was inducted into the Mississippi Sports Hall of Fame in 1992, the first non-athlete or non-coach to be so honored.

Cristil with former MSU head football coach Rockey Felker in 1986.

Cristil with former MSU head basketball coach Richard Williams in 1996.

Cristil with daughters Rebecca Cristil Nelson, left, and Kay Cristil Clouatre, right, on Rebecca's wedding day in 1991.

Cristil with his longtime friend Waurene Heflin, her daughter Rhiannon, and former MSU head football coach Jackie Sherrill.

Jack Cristil in the booth with the man who will succeed him as the "Voice of the Bulldogs" during the 2011 football and 2012 basketball seasons, longtime color analyst Jim Ellis.

Jack Cristil on Scott Field as MSU honors him on 50 years as the "Voice of the Bulldogs" in 2002. Shown with Cristil are former MSU president Charles Lee, center, and former MSU athletic director Larry Templeton.

Cristil with former MSU head football coach Sylvester Croom.

Jack Cristil receives his honorary doctorate from Mississippi State University in 2002, only the eighth person ever to receive the honor from the university.

Jack Cristil's 2011 university portrait.

Jack Cristil was the narrator of the university's 2009 investiture of MSU president Mark Keenum. Keenum and wife, Rhonda, are shown behind Cristil reacting to his quip that it was time to "wrap this investiture in Maroon and White."

MSU Head Coach Dan Mullen with Jack Cristil after the 2009 Egg Bowl. Shown with Mullen and Cristil, from left-to-right, are: Bryan Champlin, Bennie Ashford, Andy Sims, Ben Bailey, Alvin Ivy, Ralph Olivieri, Alex Byars, Jonathan Parrish, Will Simmons, Chris Sanders, Mike Godwin, Marc Rolph, and Jarrett Baker.

Clarion-Ledger editorial cartoonist Marshall Ramsey's cartoon marking Jack Cristil's retirement as the "Voice of the Bulldogs."

Jack Cristil took part in honoring longtime MSU sports information director Bob Hartley's induction into the Mississippi Sports Hall of Fame. Joining them is Hartley's successor Bo Carter.

Jack Cristil interviews Head basketball coach Rick Stansbury after his final broadcast in Knoxville, Tenn.

MSU President Mark E. Keenum thanks Jack Cristil for his 58 years of service to MSU as "Voice of the Bulldogs."

Shown at the dedication of the Jack Cristil Highway in Starkville on June 20, 2011 at the MSU Colvard Student Union were, left-to-right: MSU broadcaster Jim Ellis, Central District Transportation Commissioner Dick Hall, Northern District Transportation Commissioner Mike Tagert, Jack Cristil, and MSU President Mark E. Keenum.

Jack Cristil, center, at the MSU Colvard Student Union with daughters Kay Cristil Clouarte, left, of Baton Rouge, La., and Rebecca Cristil Nelson, right, of Augusta, Ga., on June 20, 2011. Joining them are grandson Jake Clouarte, a freshman at Northwestern State University in Natchitoches, La., far left, granddaughter Lindsey Newhall, a sixth-grader in Augusta, Ga., left front, and son-in-law Andy Nelson of Augusta, Ga., far right.

The Jack Cristil family shown at his Sept. 10, 2014 funeral in Tupelo included, from left: Daughter Kay Cristil Clouatre, grandson Jake Clouatre, granddaughter Lindsey Newhall, daughter Rebecca Cristil Nelson, and son-in-law Andrew Nelson. (Photo courtesy djournal.com by Lauren Wood)

Temple B'Nai Israel lay leader Marc Perler spoke of Jack Cristil's involvement in his synagogue and with the Jewish community in Tupelo. Perler conducted the religious portion of Cristil's funeral. (Photo courtesy djournal.com by Lauren Wood)

MSU President Mark E. Keenum spoke at Jack Cristil's funeral, noting the broadcaster's deep love of the university he served for 58 years. (Photo courtesy djournal.com by Lauren Wood)

The eulogy at Jack Cristil's funeral was delivered by former MSU athletic director Larry Templeton, who was one of Jack's closest friends. (Photo courtesy djournal.com by Lauren Wood)

Bully, MSU's canine mascot, attended Jack Cristil's funeral, curling up to the right of the casket and not so much as wagging his tail. The sight of Bully's entrance at the funeral brought many to tears. (Photo courtesy djournal.com by Lauren Wood)

Participating in the memorial service for Jack Cristil at the Humphrey Coliseum on Sept. 11 were: President Mark E. Keenum, MSU Athletic Director Scott Stricklin, MSU Head Baseball Coach John Cohen, MSU broadcaster Jim Ellis, former MSU head basketball coach and player Kermit Davis Sr., MSU Football Director of Player Personnel and former head football coach and player Rockey Felker, MSU Chief Communications Officer Sid Salter, former MSU basketball player and Starkville High School Head Basketball Coach Greg Carter, and Larry Templeton.

At the Sept. 11, 2014 MSU memorial service for Jack Cristil, the Humphrey Coliseum broadcast booth was empty and marked by a memorial wreath honoring the broadcaster.

Jack Cristil's daughters Kay and Rebecca, greeted the memorial service crowd in Starkville, along with grandson Jake Clouatre, granddaughter Lindsey Newhall, and son-in-law Andrew Nelson. The family received a standing ovation, led by Larry Templeton.

MSU Professor Michael Brown performed a solo rendition of the Frank Sinatra standard "My Way" in Jack Cristil's honor to conclude the MSU memorial service. Looking on were Larry Templeton, Jim Ellis, Kermit Davis Sr., and Rockey Felker.

Four vintage planes flew over the stadium prior to the Texas A&M game in the "missing man" formation in Jack Cristil's honor. Jack served his country in the U.S. Army Air Corps during World War II.

The MSU Famous Maroon Band led the Oct. 4, 2014 salute to Jack Cristil prior to the football game against Texas A&M by spelling out J-A-C-K for a crowd of 61,113 who were on their feet cheering the broadcaster.

A roaring, cowbell-ringing crowd at MSU's Davis Wade Stadium greeted Jack Cristil's family during the tribute to the veteran broadcaster. Shown are: Athletic Director Scott Stricklin, daughter Rebecca Cristil Nelson, granddaughter Lindsey Newhall, son-in-law Andrew Nelson, grandson Jake Clouatre, daughter Kay Cristil Clouatre, MSU President Mark Keenum, and Sid Salter, Jack's biographer.

will make the right ones."

Kay spoke of her father's attempt to bridge the void in the lives of his daughters after Mavis' death: "Since Mama's death, Daddy has had to step up to the plate and become mother and father. When Jake was born, Daddy was at my side as quick as he could drive to Baton Rouge. He stayed a few days at the house and helped me with Jake as much as he could. He fed him and rocked him so I could have some time to sleep and regain my strength. And, of course, when Rebecca and I both went through our divorces, he wasn't sure what he could do to help, but as always let us know if we needed anything, he would help in any way he could. Growing up, I would say that Daddy's job pretty much set the standard for our relationship. I respected Daddy for the simple reason that he was my daddy, and I respected him for his position in the public eye. It just came with the territory."

Asked to discuss his daughters, Jack's face takes on the same broad smile as when he speaks of the years before lupus with his late wife.

"Kay was always serious minded and capable of making decisions," said Jack. "She was a good student. We were always proud of her accomplishments. She's like Mavis in that when she tackles a problem, she brings it under control. But Kay does have some of my bad traits. She flies off the handle pretty easily; she's self-confident, and she readily makes friends.

"Rebecca is almost the image of Mavis and has so many of her traits. Like her mother, Rebecca tells you what she wants you to hear, and, like her mother, she keeps to herself. She was an excellent student. I really think both of our girls matured well and have been successful in their chosen professions. I can tell you this: they are both pretty solid parents," Jack said.

What about Jack Cristil's grandchildren, Kay's son, Jake Clouatre, and Rebecca's daughter, Lindsey Newhall?

Jack says of Jake: "I don't know Jake as well as I'd like. He's
got a level head, does well in school and is a fairly accomplished
athlete. He's been on a solid academic course in high school, and
he's signed a baseball scholarship to attend Northwestern State
University. I think they want him to walk on in football, too, but
who knows?"

Asked about granddaughter Lindsey, Jack beams: "She's kind of
following in Rebecca's footsteps in the Girl Scouts, going to camp,
all the things that Mavis would have been so proud about. She's
into computers."

At 85, Jack confronts some hard realities about his life and work
as it relates to his family.

"I was never able to spend the time with my daughters and my
grandchildren that I wanted," said Cristil. "I haven't spent a lot
of time with my grandchildren, and that bothers me. But it went
with the life and career I chose. I felt like I was paying the bills, and
Mavis was taking care of raising the children, and that was the way
of things. There are sacrifices. I try not to dwell on that."

Rebecca Cristil Nelson said that "distance is the biggest factor
in Daddy's relationship with Lindsey. Living 425 miles apart means
only three or four visits a year are doable. But Daddy gets weekly
reports about Lindsey when he calls on Sunday mornings, and he
always remembers to send cards for birthdays, Valentine's Day, and
Hanukkah.

"Lindsey was born three days prior to the Ole Miss game in
1999. And, of course, basketball had started by then, so finding a
few vacant days to come visit was not easy. He did get here when
Lindsey was maybe three weeks old. He was a godsend. I was suf-

fering from post-partum depression, and anxiety attacks came and went. Daddy was the constant in the house at that point. I watched as he held Lindsey with an easy, loving demeanor, and he kept me calm when I felt like I could not handle taking care of a newborn. His paternal instincts were far better than my maternal ones, but he assured me that I would learn as I went along, and the only thing I could do was take one day at a time.

"One thing Daddy does is that each summer when Lindsey goes to Mississippi to attend Girl Scout Camp Tik-A-Witha, he rides along with us to drop her off. As you can imagine, it's hotter than the hinges of Hades, and there is quite a bit of walking. Both of these factors make it difficult for even younger, healthier folks, much less an 80-something man. But he insists on going. He and Mama both had always taken Kay and me to camp, so I suppose he was just carrying on the tradition."

Kay shares her sister's assessment of the obstacles that impact her father's relationship with her son but is slow to heap all the blame on her father's demanding career.

"Daddy has been a part of Jake's life since the day he was born. The hardest part about establishing any relationship is distance. Daddy is not going to embrace the 21st century and its technology. When Mama died, Daddy made it a point to call us every Sunday. Of course there were times when Daddy knew he would be on the road, so he tried to remind us that he might not be able to call the following Sunday, or if he did, his call might be later that day. He has always followed this routine, and while Jake was living with me, I was able to let Jake talk to Daddy. Jake moved in with his dad six years ago, and at that point, Daddy just continued to call me, which meant he didn't speak to Jake. Then, the cell phone age came into existence. Daddy finally broke down and bought one, but he doesn't understand that it's ok to use it to call on any day of the week as well as call Jake on his cell phone. That type of relationship never got off the ground. Now, I know that road runs both ways. Jake could call his PawPaw, too.

"I blame myself for not trying to make their connection closer via cell phones, but I have had to face my own personal battles rearing Jake when I am not the parent in charge. But Daddy has never missed sending a birthday card or Hanukkah card to Jake as well as sending birthday money and Hanukkah money. Jake is the first name he mentions to me on the phone and the last name he mentions when he hangs up. He is very proud of Jake and all his accomplishments. Daddy has spent many summers watching Jake play baseball, but watching Jake play football hasn't been easy due to his MSU football schedule. However, with MSU playing LSU here this past fall, Daddy was able to rearrange his travel plans and ride with the trainers to Baton Rouge early that Friday afternoon prior to the football game on Saturday. I picked up Daddy at the hotel and got him to Jake's game. Jake was starting senior quarterback at his high school, Parkview Baptist, and knowing that Daddy was there to watch him play was a night Jake hasn't forgotten, and I know it's one Daddy truly enjoyed. Recently, Jake graduated from high school, and Daddy again made arrangements to get a ride to Baton Rouge as well as reschedule his dialysis treatment here so that he could be a part of Jake's graduation ceremony. I knew he had stressed about making the trip, and I was glad that he had been here with me on two of the biggest days of my life – Jake's birth and Jake's graduation from high school."

For so much of Jack Cristil's life, family defined him. There was the detached relationship with an immigrant father struggling with a dread disease and the adoration of a steadfast mother struggling to raise six children as a seamstress in the Depression. There were five brothers and sisters with whom Jack shared a difficult childhood. There was love and loss with his beloved wife, Mavis, and the quiet joy of his progeny – two smart, headstrong daughters so very much like their parents. With age, Jack's two grandchildren bring him pride and the realization that he has a legacy far more important than 58 years of consecutive service as a radio sports broadcaster for an NCAA Division I athletic program.

What sustained him? The vast majority of Mississippians didn't know and didn't care that the MSU broadcaster was Jewish. But despite his resentment of his father's dogmatic Orthodox Judaism, Jack Cristil has for the whole of his life been a man of deep faith and a leader in his synagogue in Tupelo. Politicians talk of "faith and family." For Cristil, the two institutions have long been at the core of his life. And while Jack is known for a sharp tongue and a pungently profane vocabulary when angered and admits to a propensity to "fly off the handle" easily, he is also known as a man for whom the Jewish word "Shalom" – which means to be safe or whole and at peace, hence to be complete as a state of mind or in a state of affairs – is appropriate. "Shalom" can be used idiomatically as a greeting or as a farewell.

After 85 years of living, Jack's sense of inner peace seems to be grounded in his faith, and the outward expression of his passions – love, regret, joy, sorrow, anger, or empathy – seem in no way contradictory of his faith.

CHAPTER SEVEN

SHALOM, MY FRIEND

"I marvel at the resilience of the Jewish people. Their best characteristic is their desire to remember. No other people have such an obsession with memory."

—ELIE WIESEL
NOBEL LAUREATE, HOLOCAUST SURVIVOR

TO UNDERSTAND WHAT IT'S LIKE TO BE JEWISH IN MISSISSIPPI, NUMBERS can provide a measure of context. In 2005, Mississippi was home to approximately 700,000 Southern Baptists, 186,000 United Methodists, 115,000 Catholics, and 1,400 Jews – and the Jewish community in the state continues a slow decline, according to scholars.

Stuart Rockoff, director of the history department at the Goldring/Woldenberg Institute of Southern Jewish Life, wrote in a November 2006 article for the website *Mississippi History Now*: "The Jewish population of Mississippi has been in decline for decades. It reached its peak in 1927, with 6,420 Jews. Since then, it has declined steadily. In 2001, only 1,500 Jews lived in Mississippi, with Jackson having the largest community."

Rockoff also noted: "Today, there are 13 Jewish congregations in the state, although only two, Beth Israel in Jackson and B'nai Israel in Hattiesburg, have a full-time rabbi. Despite their small size, most of the congregations continue to hold regular worship services with lay leaders, student rabbis from the Jewish seminary in Cincinnati, Ohio, or retired visiting rabbis."

MSU broadcaster Jack Cristil is the lay leader of his synagogue, Temple B'Nai Israel, in Tupelo. Cristil's heritage as the son of Eastern European Jewish immigrants has been documented. From his father's strict Orthodox upbringing and the conflict Benjamin Cristil's dogmatic interpretation of the daily practice of Judaism had on his children to his mother's eventual acceptance of the less stringent practices of Reform Judaism, religion has always played a part in Jack Cristil's life.

As a child, Cristil was raised in the Orthodox practice and attended Baron Hirsch Synagogue in Memphis. He was enrolled in Hebrew School there, but Jack's adherence to the Orthodox practice was buried, as he said, with his late father in 1939.

In a sweeping Aug. 26, 1995, interview on his Jewish faith with John Armistead of *The Northeast Mississippi Daily Journal*, Cristil spoke of the challenges of being a Jew in Mississippi. The interview examined Cristil's role as a lay leader or rabbi in Temple B'Nai Israel ("Children of Israel") synagogue.

Cristil told Armistead that despite the fact that his faith "lapsed a little" after his father's death, he has practiced his faith constantly since graduating high school and entering the military in the early 1940s. "I think everybody to a degree wants to maintain a sense of normalcy and you like to do those things which are meaningful to you and religion is one of them. It gives you a sense of security and strength," Cristil said.

After adopting the Reform practice, Jack also stopped trying to maintain the kosher dietary code, which he called "a very difficult thing to do in a rural area like Mississippi."

Even more difficult has been the fact that Cristil's chosen profession has put him in the position of having to work on the Jewish Sabbath, or Shabbat, which is Saturday. From a technical standpoint, Shabbat begins a few minutes before sunset on Friday evening and ends a few minutes after the appearance of three stars in the sky on Saturday night. For most of his career, the fall brought on Thursday night football broadcasts for Itawamba Community College, Friday night football broadcasts for Tupelo High School and Saturday MSU football broadcasts – meaning that Jack missed the observance of Shabbat entirely.

In a Sept. 7, 2007, article in *Y'all Magazine,* Jon Rawl wrote: "Cristil makes up for announcing Mississippi State football games for over a half-century on Shabbat by serving as a lay leader at his Tupelo synagogue. 'I get the best of both worlds,' Cristil said."

Cristil told Armistead in 1995: "I think God understands that I live in a predominantly Christian world and that I had to make a living for my wife and girls. I'm sure it's also difficult for Gentiles in retail who have to work on Sunday." Asked about his reaction to the phrase "Christian nation," Cristil replied: "Obviously, the Christian religion predominates, and the phrase really doesn't affect me much. If a person is truly a Christian, he's living by the Judeo-Christian ethic, and there won't be any problem."

In a broad series of questions about being Jewish, Jack revealed his ideas about prejudice and discrimination: "The word 'Jew' has been used detrimentally for so long that many people associate it with second-class citizenship. But Jews themselves have no problem with the terms (Jews or Jewish). A Jew is one who follows the Jewish teachings and way of life. In practice, the most important things are the moral and ethical teachings: kindness, compassion, understanding, tolerance. Basically, it is conduct which is pleasing in the eyes of God."

Jack told Armistead in 1995 and reiterated in 2011 to the author that he'd never experienced direct anti-Semitism.

"In our neighborhood in Memphis, there were many ethnic groups. Everyone had parents from the old country, whatever that old country was. In a big city, you can get lost. But in a small community, you're going to be involved whether you like it or not. You're going to be Jewish whether you like it or not. It's very important when you're in a vast minority that we remember that we are the Jews. We've all got to be the Jewish community," Jack said.

Tupelo's Temple B'Nai Israel was organized in 1939 and serves 10 communities in northeast Mississippi and northwest Alabama. The Reform congregation has never had a full-time rabbi. Lay leaders like Maury Stein in the 1960s and later Cristil accepted the task of leading Shabbat services on Friday nights and on special holidays. Between 30-35 families remain active in Temple B'Nai Israel. Cristil told the Memphis-based *Jewish Scene* magazine in December 2007: "It's all about being part of the Jewish community. The more I lead, the more comfortable I am. It's an ongoing personal experience for me. Any words of appreciation I've received from people are nice. You like to feel appreciated, whether it's for a ball game or a Friday night service."

But during his career at MSU, Cristil was only available April through August for Shabbat, and he led the services but did not serve as cantor. "I don't give the sermon," Cristil said. "I don't feel I'm qualified to tell people how to run their lives."

Just as Jack was featured in the 2002 book *Shalom Y'all: Images of Jewish Life in the American South* by photographer Bill Aron and writer Vicki Reikes Fox, he was also featured in the 2003 documentary film *Shalom Y'all* by New Orleans filmmaker Brian Bain. According to the National Center for Jewish Film, the documentary showcased Bain's "4,200-mile road trip through the American South. Traveling through Delta flatlands, small towns in Mississippi, suburban subdivisions, Texas ranches, and sprawling Sunbelt metropolises, what he uncovers is the unique and diverse history of Southern Jews. . . *Shalom Y'all* is peopled with interesting characters, including Zelda Milstein from Natchez, a hoop-skirted tour guide at a plantation; Leo Center, a Golden Gloves boxing champion from Savannah who learned how to box by literally fighting his way to get to synagogue; Tupelo's Jack Cristil, Mississippi State's football game announcer for a half-century; an African American-Jewish police chief; a kosher butcher; and musician provocateurs Kinky Friedman and the Texas Jewboys. Bain discovers a vibrant regional culture and hundreds of years of rich history in a film that is happily flavored with both its Jewish and Southern roots."

In an Oct. 3, 1983 story by the venerable Phyllis Harper of *The Northeast Mississippi Daily Journal,* there is an account of an honor Cristil won from his local temple for "promoting religious understanding."

"Though Cristil is known to sports fans as a radio voice, to members of the Jewish community in northeast Mississippi, he's the Hebrew scholar, lay leader, and teacher who has devoted more than a quarter of a century of service in the local temple," Harper wrote. "Cristil, as lay leader, leads the services that begin at sundown each Friday when he's in town. Other temple members take over when he's traveling. The Sabbath services follow a format of scripture reading and prayer, responsive reading with the congregation and singing traditional hymns."

As part of that honor, Ruben Copen, then president of Temple B'Nai Israel, presented Cristil with a plaque inscribed: "With deep appreciation for your distinguished and devoted service" to his temple. In talking with Harper for the story, Cristil said of his service as lay leader: "The world is undergoing change so rapidly and being thrown together as never before. Most people have a religion of some kind. We need knowledge of one another and of these different religions. It's vital that we know about one another if we're to live together in harmony, which is what we all desire. Basic understanding of people with different thoughts and ideas is of vital importance."

Another part of Jack's religious life has been his willingness to speak and visit in churches with youth and adult groups, telling Harper that he found the "Christian community in Tupelo to be always very open-minded."

One former Temple B'nai Israel member who first knew Jack as lay leader of the synagogue and later as MSU's football and basketball broadcaster was Booneville native Michael Rubenstein, currently the executive director of the Mississippi Sports Hall of Fame in Jackson. Prior to taking the post at the state's sports shrine, Rubenstein was arguably Mississippi's most recognized TV sports anchor and remains legendary among sports fans for his candor, courage, and audacity while anchoring Jackson NBC affiliate WLBT-TV's sports coverage for 15 years from 1977-92. Rubenstein told Nash Nunnery of *Mississippi Sports Magazine* in 2009: "I have fond memories of being a kid in Booneville. My dad, a Delta Jew, married my mom, a Delta Baptist, and we loved the area. It was a wonderful time in my life."

Part of that "wonderful time" in Rubenstein's life included attending the synagogue in Tupelo along with Jack Cristil. "My first knowledge of Jack Cristil was not as a celebrity, but as a very nice gentleman and a close family friend," said Rubenstein, who shared childhood experiences with Cristil along with his brother Ted Rubenstein, who became an Emmy-winning television producer for CNN in Atlanta.

"Jack's been to more Rubenstein funerals, funerals for my aunts, uncles, and cousins, than I'm sure he'd care to count," said Rubenstein. "I'd look up in the Baron Hirsch Cemetery in Memphis and the first person I'd see is Jack Cristil." Rubenstein also has memories of Jack's occasional flashes of temper in the press box, but he keeps the specifics to himself – as do most of Jack's younger contemporaries in an almost reverent fashion.

"Let's just say this," said Rube. "Jack Cristil was colorful and candid. But he never slipped in all those years. No words got on the air that shouldn't have and that requires a tremendous amount of discipline for a man with Jack's passions about everything."

While his grandparents in Belarus and Lithuania obviously dealt with religious persecution directly, Cristil at 85 maintains he's never dealt with anti-Semitism in a direct fashion. But indirectly, Cristil experienced it. "There may have been people out there who didn't like me because I'm Jewish, but if they had those feelings, they kept them to themselves," said Jack. "But right here in Tupelo, there was a time when Jews weren't invited to join the country club. Now I don't know if I was excluded from anything because of my Jewish faith, but if I was, it must not have mattered much."

One aspect of Judaism that Jack and his family did escape in Tupelo was attacks on their family or their synagogue during the state's civil rights struggles in the 1960s. Jewish synagogues in Meridian and Jackson were bombed in that era. Cristil said: "I don't know if it affected me as an individual, but I was always a little more liberal about accepting an integrated society than a lot of people in that era. As a Jew, we knew the discrimination that the white race had imposed on the black race. It made us more sympathetic and made us want to help them."

The broadcaster's empathy has a historical basis. Cristil told Armistead in 1995 that he has a long view of Jewish persecution: "Jewish people know of the past persecutions. They may not know how many Jews were slaughtered in the crusades, but they know about it. I think there's almost a subconscious feeling among non-Jews that Jewish people are not to be trusted, that they are somehow responsible for a lot of the illnesses of the world. Jewish people have often been the scapegoats. And that, in essence, is what causes anti-Semitism."

Perhaps the most significant expression of Cristil's self-awareness as a Jewish man in Mississippi comes from a trip that he and Mavis made to the site of the Nazi concentration camp at Dachau, Germany. Along with friends Joe and Wanda Veasey of Tupelo, the Cristils visited Dachau – where as many as 32,000 mostly Eastern European Jews were believed to have been murdered in the camp's infamous gas chamber. Mollie Kabakoff Cristil believed that she had relatives who had been imprisoned in the Nazi concentration camps, but Cristil said she was never sure.

In 2011, Cristil said he found it "impossible to imagine the horrors that took place" at Dachau and "the propaganda and fear that it obviously took to convince the Germans that treating fellow human beings in that manner was appropriate."

In the winter of his life, Cristil speaks of his faith like a familiar garment: "I have had to rely on my faith when there was nothing else. When troubles came, when burdens were heavy, and when it was difficult to understand the way of things, the reasons for suffering, there was that underlying faith. It's been a comfort to me. I believe if we hold to our faith, whatever that faith might be, it will sustain us in the darkest hours. That's been my experience, anyway."

CHAPTER EIGHT

THE COACHING CAROUSEL

"Winning is not a sometime thing; it's an all-time thing. You don't win once in a while, you don't do things right once in a while, you do them right all the time. Winning is habit. Unfortunately, so is losing."

—VINCENT LOMBARDI
FOOTBALL COACH

MISSISSIPPI STATE UNIVERSITY STUDENTS – KNOWN ALTERNATELY OVER the school's history as "Cadets," "Farmers," "Maroons," and finally "Bulldogs" – engaged in intercollegiate athletics before the arrival of Jack Cristil in 1953. But their exploits weren't described as adroitly, and it's safe to say that the vast majority of the university's athletic successes came during Cristil's long and distinguished tenure. Over 99 seasons through 2010-11, MSU has played 2,358 basketball games, winning 1,289 and losing 1,069 – a winning percentage of .546. Cristil called 1,538 MSU basketball games. Over 111 seasons through 2010-11, MSU has played 1,076 football games, winning 499, losing 538, and tying 39. Cristil called 636 MSU football games. Bulldog fans didn't give Jack Cristil their allegiance; he earned it game-by-game, year-by-year, and decade-by-decade.

The Cadets of Mississippi Agricultural and Mechanical College lost the university's first-ever football game on Nov. 16, 1895, to Southwestern Baptist (now Union University) 21-0 in Jackson, Tenn. A&M was winless and scoreless for both the 1895 and 1896 seasons. Football was suspended in 1897 due to a yellow fever outbreak and again in 1898 because of the Spanish-American War. The game disappeared from the A&M campus until 1901. That season would bring the school's first football victory, a 17-0 win over Ole Miss in Starkville. In 1903, Coach Dan Martin led A&M's storied "Boss Team" to an undefeated record of 3-0-2 for a team that didn't allow a touchdown. In that season, A&M tied Ole Miss 6-6 and tied Tulane 0-0 and defeated Meridian Athletic Club, Alabama, and LSU.

During the 1907-08 seasons, Pennsylvania native Fred Furman would post the first winning record of any A&M coach, going 9-7 over those seasons before leaving Starkville to enter the copper mining business in Montana. Furman was followed by W.D. Chadwick, an Ohio native who became A&M's first proper athletic director and the school's first professor of physical education. Chadwick posted a 29-12-2 record between 1909 and 1913. Yet it was not his success on the gridiron that earned Chadwick his greatest praise; it was his skill as an athletic administrator – a post he held for 21 years from 1909 to 1930. *The Commercial Appeal* wrote in 1914: "Since taking charge of the department of physical training and athletics, Coach Chadwick has greatly enlarged the work of the department, has put athletics on a sound footing and raised the standards of the athletic teams until they compare favorably with those of any Southern university." In his 1975 comprehensive history of Mississippi State football, *The Maroon Bulldogs*, Bill Sorrels wrote: "William Dean Chadwick accomplished an awful lot with a precious little."

Chadwick was the mentor of the university's second great athletic director, C.R. "Dudy" Noble, who in turn gave the green light to begin Cristil's storied career in Starkville. Noble held the athletic director's post at Mississippi State College from 1938 to 1959. Between them, Chadwick and Noble controlled MSU's athletic fortunes for 42 of the first 54 years that MSU played football.

Prior to Cristil's tenure at State, the football team enjoyed some landmark victories. Major Ralph Sasse's Maroons pulled one of the upsets of the decade when they defeated Army 13-7 at the U.S. Military Academy at West Point, N.Y., on Nov. 2, 1935, behind the running of Ike Pickle, the passing of Pee Wee Armstrong, and the 67-yard impossible catch-and-run by receiver Fred Walters. In 1937, Duquesne defeated Mississippi State 13-12 in the Orange Bowl in Miami, Fla. State had a 12-7 lead in the fourth quarter.

The 1940 Maroon squad won the 1941 Orange Bowl 14-7 over Georgetown behind the running of Billy Jefferson and an interception return by Big John "Spic" Tripson. The 1940 team's record was 10-0-1 with only a tie against Auburn marring their record.

Coach Allyn McKeen's 1941 Mississippi State team won the SEC championship with a 7-1-1 record and then defeated San Francisco in an exhibition game against the Dons 26-13 behind the running of Charles Yancey, Billy "Spook" Murphy, and Blondy Black.

McKeen led MSU to what for many years was considered the "golden age" of MSU football prowess. Between 1939 and 1948, McKeen's Maroons were 65-19-3 over nine seasons – ranking McKeen by percentage (.764) as the winningest head football coach in MSU's history.

After World War II, the 1947 squad posted a 7-3 mark with an exciting 10-0 win over Auburn behind Shorty McWilliams and Harper Davis. McWilliams, an All-American for the Maroons, was the prototype single-wing tailback who could run, pass, and kick. After several lackluster seasons, the 1952 season brought renewed hopes among the Maroon faithful as junior quarterback Jackie Parker showed his mettle against Auburn in a 49-34 victory, in which Parker ran for three touchdowns, passed for three more, and led the scoring drive for the seventh, according to The Associated Press account from Nov. 9, 1952. Parker went on to become a two-time SEC Most Valuable Player Award winner in 1952 and 1953 and was elected to the College Football Hall of Fame. He would later star in the Canadian Football League and become a CFL head coach and general manager.

Cristil's first season was Parker's last season. When Cristil inherited the Mississippi State radio announcing job from Dick Crago in 1953, Mississippi State had been playing football for 52 years. For the next 58 years, Cristil would call the action. That statistic, perhaps as much as any other, defines the scope of Cristil's accomplishments at MSU.

The same argument can be made for MSU basketball. MSU began playing basketball in 1908 and had been playing for 48 years – the university played neither football nor basketball in 1943 because of World War II – when Cristil took over announcing duties for the university's basketball program in 1957-58. For the next 54 years, Cristil was behind the microphone. Like the MSU football program, there have been more victories in the university's basketball program in the Cristil era than before it began. But there are, again, notable exceptions.

Basketball began at A&M in 1908 under Coach T.H. Werner

who promptly won his first five games – then just as promptly lost his last five. W.D. Chadwick was also the university's second basketball coach in 1909-10, compiling a poor 2-4 record. But Chadwick let one of his assistant football coaches, E.C. "Billy" Hayes, take over the basketball program in 1910-11, and Hayes reeled off six straight winning seasons in basketball on the way to a sterling 124-54 record over 12 seasons and four Southern Intercollegiate Athletic Association titles in 1912, 1913, 1914 and 1916 (A&M, like most of the current SEC schools, was a member of the Southern Conference from 1921-32). Hayes turned in a perfect 9-0 season in 1911-12.

The early decades of MSU athletics saw the school's scant number of hired coaches working in multiple sports – football, basketball, baseball, and track. In many instances, the head basketball coach was an assistant football coach. While many MSU fans remember that the late Paul Gregory was MSU's head baseball coach from 1954-74 – winning four SEC championships and a berth in the 1971 College World Series – fewer remember that Gregory was MSU's head basketball coach from 1947-55 with a record of 58-100 over eight seasons. Fewer MSU fans still will recall that Gregory was, for a brief time, a Major League Baseball pitcher for the Chicago White Sox who retired Babe Ruth in five at-bats in a game on May 26, 1933.

Cristil began his MSU football broadcasting career in 1953 with Murray Warmath in his last year as the Maroon head football coach. He began his MSU basketball broadcasting tenure in 1957 in legendary MSU head basketball coach James Harrison "Babe" McCarthy's third season. In the 58-year interim, 10 football coaches would come and go – as would seven head basketball coaches and nine athletic directors after Noble. In the early years, Cristil said broadcasters didn't have the interaction with coaches that came with the development of pre- and postgame shows and the coach's shows on both radio and TV. The lack of such personal interaction, along with Cristil's being new to the Mississippi State job, left him with few direct contacts with Warmath before he resigned after the 1953 season to take the Minnesota job.

"I just really didn't get to know Coach Warmath," said Cristil. "He had a significant amount of success. While I famously don't remember broadcasting my first game in 1953 when Mississippi State defeated Memphis State 34-6 in Memphis, I was really impressed with Coach Warmath's 26-0 win the very next week over Tennessee. That stuck with me. Other than that, I was still being indoctrinated and trained by Coach Noble and by Bob Hartley and just never had a personal relationship with Coach Warmath." Warmath posted a 10-6-3 record over two seasons in Starkville. In 1960, Warmath was National Coach of the Year at Minnesota, winning a national championship and taking the Golden Gophers to back-to-back Rose Bowls in 1961 and 1962.

Succeeding Warmath at Mississippi State in 1954 was Darrell Royal. Royal, a former All-American quarterback for the University of Oklahoma Sooners under Bud Wilkinson, had coached offensive backs for Warmath at State during the 1952 season before departing to coach the Canadian Football League's Edmonton Eskimos. Joining Royal's staff was fellow Oklahoma All-American lineman Wade Walker. Under the leadership of Royal and Walker, the Maroons turned in back-to-back winning seasons – going 6-4 in both campaigns.

Royal relied on a bevy of star players including Bobby Collins, Bill Dooley, Hal Easterwood, Scott Suber, Ron Bennett, Arthur "Art" Davis, Joe Silveri, and Levaine Hollingshead. The 1954 season

was marked by a 12-7 upset of previously unbeaten Alabama in
Tuscaloosa spearheaded by a 56-yard Collins punt return for a
score and a pitchout from backup quarterback Bill Stanton to Silveri for the winning score. In the rematch a year later, with State's
All-American Art Davis sidelined with a shoulder injury suffered
a week earlier against Kentucky, the Maroon squad was urged by
their fellow students to "Win for Arthur," and win they did, defeating the Crimson Tide 26-7 for back-to-back wins.

Art Davis was a player who made a keen impression on Cristil,
not just for his playing prowess but for his character. Cristil told
the MSU *Alumnus* magazine in 1969: "Arthur Davis to me personi-
fies Mississippi State students and athletes. I knew him when he
was a youngster in high school in Clarksdale. Watched him grow
up and remember the first play of his senior year as a high school
performer. He caught a pass in the flat and broke a leg. This would
have broken the spirit of many young men, but not Arthur Davis.
He came to Mississippi State as a tremendous performer, earned
All-American honors as he should have, played in his senior year
badly crippled and injured but certainly gave it – as the coaches always say – that 110 percent effort on and off the field. He has been
a true gentleman throughout his life, and I don't know of any one
single individual that I've been closer to, although we don't see a
great deal of each other and haven't for a number of years. But I've
always thought of Arthur Davis as being what I would like to think
of as typically Mississippi State in every way."

One losing effort from the Darrell Royal era resonated with
Cristil. In his 2008 oral history interview with MSU's Dr. Roy Ruby,
Cristil recalled: "I remember a game we played in the mid-1950s at
Auburn. We lost that game by one point, 27-26. We had a young
man by the name of Arthur Davis playing for us. Auburn was led

by Fob James, Frank D'Agostino, and Joe Childress. In those days, the athletes went both ways in football, offense, defense, and those guys really put on a show that afternoon. It was a marvelous, marvelous game. As we were coming back, we stayed the night in Montgomery, Ala., and I recall at the closing of the broadcast saying something to the effect you know how well the team had played, and so forth and so on and that they'd appreciate hearing from you, and we used Western Union telegrams in those days for communication . . .and suggested perhaps you might want to wire the team to the hotel, I think it was the Jefferson Davis, but I'm not sure. Anyway, we got over 400 telegrams congratulating the team, and the manager of the hotel wanted to know what happens when we win. But Coach Noble was not at all satisfied with it, in fact, that was the only time I can recall he really called me on the carpet. He said: 'We don't praise our team when we get beat. We expect to get a great effort out of them every time they play, and they certainly give that, but in the future, we just don't condone that type of thing.' So, that was the end of that."

Royal departed Starkville after two seasons in 1955 to become the head coach at the University of Washington in 1956. In 1957, Royal moved on to the University of Texas, where he won three national championships as the winningest coach in UT history on the way to the College Football Hall of Fame. Royal is also the last MSU head football coach to leave Starkville with a winning record and to land another Division 1 head coaching job after leaving State.

Cristil recounted another favorite story from the Royal era to *Dawgs' Bite's* David Murray in 2002. In 1955, Royal's Maroons led Kentucky 13-7 in Lexington. "Late in the game, Kentucky drove maybe 70 yards, scored and converted and led 14-13 with about a minute maybe left. I remember remarking that Mississippi State needed to get a good runback, and we ran it all the way out to the 17 yard line. I thought we were dead as a hammer. On the very next play, Bill Stanton threw a pass to William Earl Morgan on a dead run behind the Kentucky defender, it was an 83-yard touchdown pass and we won 20-14. We went back to the Phoenix Hotel and we were all in Coach Royal's room and were all elated. Then the phone rang and somebody said: 'Coach Royal, it's for you.' We all got quiet, he said 'hello, hey so-and-so, no, no, no, WE won the game!' Somebody had turned it (the radio) off when Kentucky was ahead 14-13 and had called the coach to console him after such a tough loss."

But there would be precious few such celebrations for MSU's football program between the end of the Darrell Royal era in 1955 and the 1974 season. Royal's assistant and former Oklahoma teammate Wade Walker succeeded him in 1956. Over the next six seasons, he won 22 games, lost 32, and tied two. Walker had four losing seasons, one winning season, and a 5-5 finish in his final year in 1961. That was also the final year that Mississippi State's athletic teams would be known as "Maroons," as the university officially adopted the "Bulldogs" mascot after an unofficial affiliation with the tenacious dog since the days of Major Ralph Sasse in 1936. After that season, Walker stepped down as head football coach and stayed on as the school's athletic director until 1966. Cristil's take on Walker's tenure is succinct: "Coach Walker tried to pattern Mississippi State's football program after Oklahoma's, but he just didn't have the resources, the facilities, or the players."

New Bulldog Head Coach Paul Davis, who had been Walker's assistant, succeeded him and promptly went 3-6. In 1963, Davis and his Mississippi State squad turned in a stellar 6-2-2 regular sea-

son that included ties with Florida and Ole Miss. The Rebels went
7-1-2 in 1963 and claimed an SEC title, but one of those ties was
a 10-10 standoff with their arch-rival Maroons. The 1963 success
carried State to the first bowl game since the 1941 Orange Bowl
22 years earlier, as the Bulldogs journeyed to Philadelphia, Pa., to
meet the Wolfpack of North Carolina State University in the 1963
Liberty Bowl. Behind the exploits of such Bulldog legends as Ode
Burrell, Hoyle Granger, Justin Canale, Pat Watson, Bill McGuire,
Tommy Inman, Tommy Neville, Sonny Fisher, and John Sparks,
Mississippi State defeated N.C. State 16-12.

For Cristil, the game lingers in his memory because of the frigid, bitter cold in which the game was played. Broadcasting from
an unheated press box, Cristil was only slightly better off than
the players and coaches on the field at Philadelphia Stadium who
were enduring temperatures of 22 degrees at kickoff dropping to
15 degrees by the end of the contest. Bowl organizers in 1963 lost
over $40,000 when only 8,000 fans braved the brutal temperatures
to attend the game. Coach Davis and the team had heaters on the
sidelines and a Plexiglas canopy to shield them from winds that
took the wind chill well below zero, but cups of coffee were literally freezing solid in the press box. It was in those environs that
Cristil uttered his famous "colder than a pawnbroker's heart" line
during the broadcast.

He would tell *Dawgs' Bite's* Murray in 2002: "It was colder than
a pawnbroker's heart to tell the truth. We put on everything we
could to keep warm. Joe Phillips, our producer, looked like a Russian with that big coat. We got to the stadium and set up, and they
were going to televise the game. There was a cable stretched over
where we were supposed to sit. I told Joe to grab one end and I'll
grab the other end and we'll move it. Some guy yelled 'Don't you

touch that cable, you're non-union people.' I said 'Joe, give me the hacksaw. I'm about to cut this cable.' That guy came over and moved the cable. Ballpoint pens wouldn't write, the coffee froze in the cups. We won the game over North Carolina State and there couldn't have been over 5,000 people in the stadium when it was over. But it was a big event for us."

One of the huddled mass of a half-dozen or so human pop-sicles in the broadcast booth with Cristil for the 1963 Liberty Bowl game was distinguished alumnus U.S. Sen. John C. Stennis, who rarely missed a Mississippi State athletic event of any kind that was played close to the Capitol in Washington. There was also the 1964 Davis era 20-17 victory over Ole Miss in Oxford – the first time since 1946 that State had defeated Ole Miss and the first time ever that Vaught had gone down to defeat to the Bulldogs since his career began in Oxford in 1947.

Despite the memorable if frigid bowl game win in 1963, Davis was unable to replicate the 1963 magic. That fact was borne out in the 1965 MSU season when the Bulldogs opened the season 4-0, in-cluding a win over a Steve Spurrier-quarterbacked Florida squad in Gainesville, only to lose the next six in a row. The first loss came at the hands of Memphis State in a 33-13 beating in Memphis. Cristil remarked late in the game when an airplane flew near the stadium: "I hope it's one of ours. Everything else has gone wrong tonight."

By 1966, then MSU president Dr. William Giles was forced to take a broom to the school's football program. Both Walker and Davis were let go as athletic director and head football coach, respectively. Several coaches turned town the MSU job after the dismissal of Davis, but Giles eventually hired Charlie Shira as the university's new athletic director and head football coach. Shira had been an assistant to former MSU Coach Darrell Royal at Texas for a decade and prior to that had been an assistant to Royal and Walker at MSU. Cristil recalls the Shira era as a difficult time in his own career. "Coach Shira knew what he wanted to do but had a very difficult time as a coach. He seemed to just not know how to go about achieving his goals and what he set out to do. It was just sad."

No single game epitomized the lackluster brand of football that Shira's leadership produced more than the 1969 MSU game with the University of Houston. Coach Bill Yeoman's Cougars mauled the Bulldogs 74-0. Yeoman, who invented the Veer offense that Rockey Felker would quarterback masterfully at MSU less than five years later, used his invention to annihilate the 1969 Bulldogs. Cristil told John Pruett of *The Huntsville Times* on Aug. 10, 1998: "It was a game you never forget. You don't forget that sort of embarrassment. It's burned into you forever. But what can you do? As accurately as you can, you tell the people what you saw. That's what you do if you're a professional broadcaster."

Shira, the school's sixth coach since 1949, went 16-45-2 over six seasons from 1967 to 1972, and he owns the lowest winning percentage of any MSU head football coach who held the post more than one season. Shira's lone winning season was in 1970, when the Bulldogs posted a 6-5 mark, and Shira earned SEC Coach of the Year honors. But his final season in 1972 was 4-7. Shira did oversee one key development during his tenure that laid the groundwork for future Bulldog victories, however. Shira recruited Frank Dowsing, MSU's first African-American football player.

Dowsing had been a standout athlete at Tupelo High School. As his teammate and current Tupelo Mayor Jack Reed, Jr., said of Dowsing in 2010 on the occasion of his induction into the Mississippi Sports Hall of Fame: "Frank Dowsing was a great

athlete, one of the greatest in Mississippi sports history. He was
an even greater person. He contributed more than any single
human being, black or white, to the peaceful, successful integration of the Tupelo public schools." Elected as the university's first
African-American "Mr. MSU" in 1973, Dowsing was an academic
All-American and made the All-SEC and All-American teams as
a player in 1972. Most MSU fans remember Dowsing best for a
spectacular one-handed interception in the end zone of Vaught
Hemingway Stadium to preserve MSU's 1970 upset win (19-14)
over nationally ranked Ole Miss.

Cristil, who covered Dowsing's exploits in high school and college, told *The Northeast Mississippi Daily Journal* in 1994: "The black
athlete was just coming onto the scene. They were under a micro-
scope. Frank lived up to the expectations. He did excellent work in
the classroom as well as the football field."

Shira's replacement was Water Valley native and Ole Miss
graduate Bob Tyler, who had just completed the 1972 season as
Shira's offensive coordinator after serving in 1971 as a first-year
assistant to Paul W. "Bear" Bryant at Alabama after breaking into
the college coaching ranks at his alma mater under Johnny Vaught
in 1968. Tyler was 4-5-2 in his first season in 1973 but shocked the
football world in 1974 with a sterling 8-3 record and a trip to the
Sun Bowl in El Paso, Texas, for a 26-24 victory over North Carolina. On the field, MSU went 6-4-1 in 1975, 9-2 in 1976, 5-6 in 1977,
and 6-5 in 1978. In 1974, Tyler took Rockey Felker, Jimmy Webb,
Walter Packer, Terry Vitrano, Harvey Hull, Ray Costict, Steve
Freeman, Dennis Johnson, Melvin Barkham, Mike Lawrence, Jim
Eidson, and Calvin Hymel and built the nucleus of a Top 20 Division I football team.

Tyler did it with relentless preparation and with motivation. He took a challenge from a player to write down why State would fare better under his leadership than it had under Shira's. One of the memorable Tyler catch phrases was: "Let's win something today." But an NCAA probe for alleged improper benefits to athletes saw the university eventually have to surrender most of the on-field wins from 1975-77. Tyler's official MSU record fell 21-44-2. The NCAA infractions cost State 18 games over three seasons.

Cristil didn't dwell on Tyler's troubles with the NCAA. "Coach Tyler was a very easy guy to get along with. He was always co-operative, gave you a little insight into what he was doing and from my standpoint as a broadcaster, he gave me good material to work with. Can't ask for better than that. He enjoyed a significant amount of success, and that made it enjoyable for me as well. Coach Tyler was an exceptional motivator."

Tyler's tenure did give Cristil one of his most memorable calls. Jack Cristil's broadcast of the final moments of the Oct. 19, 1974, game between MSU and Memphis State University (now University of Memphis) at Memphis Memorial Stadium was one for the ages – as was the final drive of the night. Following a Memphis punt, State was pinned on their own two yard line with 3:06 left in the fourth quarter trailing 28-21. The Bulldogs had already committed seven turnovers on the night. Despite the odds and despite the clock, Felker marched the Bulldogs 98 yards in 13 plays to score with just under a minute left to close the gap to Memphis 28, MSU 27. With 49 seconds left, Felker kept the ball on the Veer and sliced into the end zone. State won the game 29-28 on one of the most improbable, unbelievable drives in the annuls of MSU football. The drive forever cemented Felker's place in Bulldog football lore and was one of the superlatives that led to his easy selection as the 1974 SEC Most Valuable Player.

"It's a strange thing, but you're involved in a lot of games, and some stick out in your memory as if they were played yesterday and some you cannot recall at all," Cristil told David Murray. "That 1974 Memphis State game sticks in the memory. Memphis kicked the ball out of bounds on the two and we went 98 yards in 13 plays, one timeout to work with, it took three minutes or something like that. We elected to go for the two point conversion and scored on an almost identical play. Rockey Felker took it in. Memphis had an outstanding linebacker, he was intent on hitting Rockey on that play and obviously had mayhem on his mind because he tried to hit him up high, around the shoulders. Had he hit him around the waist we'd never have won that ball game. My friend John Rial had to miss it, he had a banker's convention in Hawaii. He was going to call me at the hotel at midnight, Hawaii time. It was five in the morning in Memphis."

Tyler's 1974 team featured future NFL players Jimmy Webb, Ray Costict, Mike Patrick, Walter Packer, Dennis Johnson, Richard Blackmore, Stan Black, and Steve Freeman. Webb was an anchor of the San Francisco 49er defense for six seasons. Freeman played 12 seasons for the Buffalo Bills and the Minnesota Vikings.

Succeeding Tyler at MSU in 1978 was former Texas A&M head coach Emory Bellard, the inventor of the Wishbone offense and a hard-nosed motivator. Bellard was a small man in stature but powerfully built and thoughtful. He spoke in Texas metaphors and called almost everyone "podnah." The pipe-smoking Bellard was the beneficiary of some of Tyler's recruiting successes and was blessed with some of the finest talent ever to wear the Maroon and White. Bellard went 37-42 in seven seasons at Mississippi State, including back-to-back Top 20 finishes in 1980 and 1981. In 1980, Bellard went 9-2 and took the Bulldogs back to the Sun Bowl in El

Paso, where the Nebraska Cornhuskers prevailed 31-17 after the MSU squad found themselves down 17-0 at the half.

But it was the 1980 game against Alabama that indelibly marked the careers of both Emory Bellard and Jack Cristil. For the Bulldog fans who did not remember the glories of the stunning 13-7 upset of mighty Army at West Point in 1935, MSU's 6-3 win over top-ranked Alabama on Nov. 1, 1980, at Mississippi Veterans Memorial Stadium in Jackson ranks as the greatest win in Mississippi State University football history. The game helped MSU to a 9-2 regular season, but cost rival Alabama dearly. Alabama Head Coach Paul "Bear" Bryant's loss to State ended Alabama's all-time school record 28-game winning streak and all-time SEC record 27-game conference winning streak. It also denied the Crimson Tide a share of the SEC championship, the first time since 1976 that they failed to win the conference title. It was Alabama's first loss to Mississippi State since 1957. Bryant had never lost to MSU since returning to lead his alma mater in 1958.

Some 50,891 souls watched the game according to official attendance records, but it is rare even in 2011 to encounter an MSU fan over 50 who does not claim to have attended the game. For MSU fans of a certain age, the bumper sticker claim "I Was There When We Beat The Bear" was as frequent and often as fraudulent as the claim by State students of an earlier generation to have roomed in "Polecat Alley" in Old Main Dormitory or to have been the roommate of Sen. John C. Stennis.

Before the game, Bellard told his Bulldog defense that he didn't fear Alabama's vaunted Wishbone attack: "I designed it, and I can stop it." Stop it Bellard's team did, holding a Crimson Tide offense that had averaged 349 rushing yards and 36.7 points per game to 116 yards on the ground and a field goal. The defense, led by Billy

Jackson, Tyrone Keys, Johnie Cooks, John Miller, and Rob Fesmire, played inspired football and the offense – led by a brash freshman quarterback from Valdosta, Ga., named John Bond – kept the ball away from the Tide for some 35 of the game's 60 minutes. Bond's reckless style along with his innate ability to make the big play made him a fan favorite. By his senior year at State, Bond would be the SEC's leading career rushing quarterback with 2,280 yards. The record stood for over 25 years.

After the game, Bellard told ABC sports broadcaster Bill Flemming of the post-game scene: "There was a complete explosion of a lot of pent-up emotion that's been floating around. It's been 22 years since Mississippi State had beaten Alabama. During that time, you get a lot of pent-up emotion. We had a heck of an effort out of our players and I'm extremely proud for them and thrilled to death for them and thrilled for everybody who loves Mississippi State University. We felt like we'd have to have a great defensive game because Alabama plays such great defense and points were going to be hard to come by. Our defense played a tremendous game."

Asked by Flemming what Bryant had said at the midfield exchange after the game, Bellard said: "He (Bryant) said just what you'd expect a class person to say, he said 'you whipped us.' He came to our dressing room and told the team we didn't get all we deserved, either. But that's the way it is, class always comes forth."

After a scoreless first quarter, Alabama's Woody Humphrey was forced to punt from deep in their own territory to Bulldog receiver Mardye McDole along the MSU 40. McDole lost the handle, and the Tide recovered at the 35. Four plays later, the Tide's Peter Kim connected on a 49-yard field goal, and Alabama took a 3-0 lead into intermission. In the third period, the Tide fumbled the exchange in their territory, and the Bulldogs' Billy Jackson recovered. The turnover led to a 37-yard Dana Moore field goal to knot the score at 3-3 with 11:59 left in the third period.

Early in the fourth quarter, Moore hit another 22-yard field goal to give State the lead 6-3. But the Tide wasn't done. Facing third and 20 from his own 42, Alabama quarterback Don Jacobs, who missed eight of his first nine passes, hit running back Major Ogilvie with a 25-yard pass into Bulldog territory at the State 33.

Cristil called the action, and it was a radio call for the ages: *"Third and 20 at the 42 and Alabama's ball in their own territory. Tide comes on the line of scrimmage. Two wide receivers, Mallard and Bendross, Mallard right and Bendross left, I-formation, Jacobs looks at a four-three defense, Jacobs long snap count, Jacobs uses motion, puts Ogilvie on the wing to the left, rolls back left to throw, is looking, is looking, fires to the left side, pass complete to Ogilvie at the 40, knocked off his feet at the 36 yard line. John Miller brought him down. First down Alabama at the 33 yard line in Mississippi State territory. For the Tide, their ninth first down. They'll not huddle with a minute and three seconds to go. Alabama's Jacobs, out of the I-formation again, Jacobs, long look, crowd is alive, Jacobs wants to throw, is looking, fires left side, pass complete at the 18, knocked off his feet immediately by Lawrence Evans, is the receiver, Bendross. Mississippi State has a man shaken up on the play, Glen Collins, but he's okay. Alabama first-and-ten at the 18, with 47 seconds to go. And Jacobs, again sets the I-formation with two wide receivers. Bulldogs leading 6-3. 40 seconds to play. Jacobs says he can't hear. Officials not calling anything yet. Jacobs, up underneath, long snap count, Jacobs wants to throw, under pressure, fires in the middle, pass caught at the five, knocked down at the four, Alabama's receiver knocked down at the four yard line. That was Krout, the tight end. First and four and goal to go for Alabama. They've stopped the clock with 25 seconds,*

Alabama gets on the goal line with 22 seconds, Wishbone offense, no time outs for Alabama, Jacobs says he cannot hear, Jacobs goes up underneath, Jacobs long snap count, goes to the fullback, fumbles the ball, BULLDOGS RECOVER! BULLDOGS RECOVER! BULLDOGS RECOVER! With six seconds left, the Bulldogs recover."

On the Nov. 2, 1980, broadcast of his Golden Flake / Coca-Cola-sponsored "Bear Bryant Show," Bryant first congratulated Bellard and the MSU team and then talked at length of the Tide's short-comings. "I think the whole thing was they wanted to win the game worse than we did. The coaches wanted to win it worse than we did, the alumni, the assistant coaches, everybody." But later in the broadcast, Bryant said that despite Alabama's poor effort, the team could have won the game "had it not been for the crowd noise, but that's something that's by the boards." Bryant's comments led many Alabama fans to refer to the loss as "the cowbell game" and to claim that Jacob's fumble had been the result of crowd noise rather than the Collins tackle and Jackson's second fumble recovery of the day. The 50,891 fans of both schools who attended the game knew better – as did Cristil.

Cristil told *Dawgs' Bite* in 2002: "The 1980 Alabama game stands out in the memory of all Mississippi State people. We won 6-3, three field goals kicked in the game with no touchdowns, we stopped the No. 1-ranked team in the country on our goal line when time elapsed. All the ingredients you want with outstanding play on both sides, a hard-hitting, hard-fought football game. And I was told the loudest cheer occurred in Lincoln, Nebraska. Alabama and Nebraska, depending on whose poll you read, were No. 1. Nebraska was playing Toledo Sub Normal or somebody in their stadium and were winning handily. People are sitting around waiting for the final score, it flashes up 'Mississippi State 6, Alabama

3.' A huge roar goes up. I was told it surpassed what was in the stadium in Jackson."

But not even the historic win over Alabama in 1980 and the successes that would follow in 1981 when the Bulldogs went 7-4 and defeated Kansas 10-0 in the Hall of Fame Bowl in Birmingham bought the Texas native any job security in Starkville. Four consecutive losing seasons from 1982 through 1985 – the final season winless in the SEC – brought about a parting of the ways. Bellard was 37-42 in seven seasons at Mississippi State.

Cristil would say of Bellard: "Emory Bellard was an outstanding coach, a tactician who invented and then perfected the Wishbone offense. Through our associations, I came to know Coach Bellard as a man with a great sense of humor who loved his family and really, really loved to win. He gave Mississippi State fans a moment they would never forget." Bellard died after a brief battle with Lou Gehrig's Disease in 2011 shortly before Cristil began to participate in interviews for this book. "There was a lot of sadness among Mississippi State people when they learned of Coach Bellard's illness and death. The fans remembered what he accomplished and they remembered the kind of man he was," Cristil said.

In looking for a successor to Bellard, MSU athletic director Charlie Carr settled on favorite son Rockey Felker, the Brownsville, Tenn., native whose meteoric rise through the college coaching ranks saw him begin his career at MSU after graduation by joining Tyler's staff as the junior varsity coach and later the varsity quarterbacks, receivers, and running backs coach. After Tyler's tenure ended, Felker joined the staff of Coach Rex Dockery at Texas Tech University in Lubbock, Texas. Felker followed Dockery to Memphis State in 1981-82. In 1983, after Bryant's retirement at Alabama, Felker joined the staff of new Crimson Tide Head

Coach Ray Perkins. Felker's future looked bright.

When his alma mater called after the 1985 season in which Bellard had been winless in the SEC, Felker answered. The Alabama squad he helped coach went 9-2-1 in 1985 and would go 10-3 in 1986. By then, at 33, Felker was the youngest Division I head football coach in the nation. Felker quickly won six of his first seven games, including wins over Syracuse, Florida; and a shocking 27-23 come-from-behind win over Coach Johnny Majors' eighth-ranked Tennessee Volunteers in Knoxville on the strength of quarterback Don Smith's 62-yard run to put the Bulldogs ahead 27-23 with 4:40 remaining.

Felker told the press after the game: "I was asked yesterday when we first got here, 'Do you really think you have a chance to win?' To somebody as competitive as me, that is really a slap in the face." Felker's approach to coaching was summed up in a 1985 *Clarion-Ledger* story heralding his hiring in which the young coach said: "I don't really feel pressure. I look at this as a great opportunity. I look at it as a lot of fun. I'm looking forward to putting together a great staff and working with the young guys, making them better players and better people. And if you don't look at it like that, I think you're looking at it the wrong way."

But after Felker's 1986 team went 6-1 through the first seven games, they proceeded to lose the final four games to Auburn, Alabama, LSU, and Ole Miss by a combined score of 144-12. The Bulldogs finished 6-5, but despite the November slide, Felker had managed to be the first Bulldog skipper to post a winning season in his first year since Darrell Royal in 1954.

In 1987, State went 4-7 and was winless in the SEC save the Egg Bowl, in which the Bulldogs defeated Ole Miss 30-20. In 1988, Felker endured the indignity of the infamous "Tech and 10" season, opening with a 21-14 win over Louisiana Tech and then losing 10 straight games to end with a 33-6 thumping from Ole Miss. The 1989 season saw the Bulldogs improve to a 5-6 record, including a satisfying 26-23 win over Brett Favre and the University of Southern Mississippi – but only one SEC win. The 1990 season was another 5-6 effort with another win over USM and Favre and an SEC win over LSU, but the season ended in a 21-9 loss to Ole Miss.

Succeeding Carr as MSU athletic director in 1987 was Larry Templeton, Cristil's former press box spotter as a kid and another acolyte of Bob Hartley in MSU's sports information shop. Templeton was a 1969 graduate of Mississippi State who worked his way up from sports information and served MSU as a golf coach, athletics business manager; and director for administration before becoming the university's athletic director in 1987 – a position he held for 21 years until 2008. Templeton grew up 50 yards from the Davis-Wade Stadium – his father was the university electrical foreman for 41 years. He had known Felker as a player, as an assistant coach and later head coach, but mostly as a close personal friend.

The Commercial Appeal's Ron Higgins observed in 2007: "The toughest day of Templeton's life – and maybe for Felker, too, for that matter – was the day they met at the end of the 1990 season and concluded Felker's coaching career was done. 'Rockey and I were best of friends, and that made it worse,' Templeton said. 'He was part of the decision. Neither one of us liked it, but we knew it was what had to happen.'"

Felker told Higgins in that 2007 story: "I think it took me a while to realize how thankful I was to have had the opportunity to be head coach at my alma mater. I was naive to think maybe I could stay here the rest of my life as head coach. It was tough when it happened, but I look back, and it was a blessing in disguise. It was time for me to move on." But by that time, Felker had returned to MSU as director of football operations under his successor, Jackie Sherrill, and later as a running backs coach under Sherrill's successor, Sylvester Croom. He presently serves as director of player personnel and high school relations for current head coach Dan Mullen.

Count Jack Cristil as speaking for many in the Bulldog family glad to see Felker in his fifth decade of association of MSU: "I had such a personal attachment to Rockey through his father, Babe, and Rockey's wife, Susan. He was a great player, sure, but I count him even more a personal and family friend. That was always far more on my mind than our relationship as broadcaster and coach. It was a lot of pressure on a young man, but boy, in that first season I enjoyed seeing a Tennessean lead Mississippi State to a win in Neyland Stadium over the Vols. I think everyone did. I'm glad Rockey's still on the MSU staff. He belongs there."

The next coach in the MSU coaching carousel during the Jack Cristil era was perhaps the most controversial – detractors referred to him as 'the Prince of Darkness" and terms less complimentary, as well – head football coach in the history of the institution. Jackie Sherrill was chosen to replace Felker for the 1991 season and proceeded to delight the MSU faithful with immediate successes, including a 7-4 record, a winning record in the SEC at 4-3, a Liberty Bowl berth, and a 24-9 win over Ole Miss before a home crowd.

Sherrill built national powerhouses at Pittsburgh and Texas A&M before coming to Starkville, but critics pointed to NCAA infractions at A&M and the fact that Sherrill resigned under fire there in 1988. Sherrill led the Bulldogs from 1991 until 2003, compiling a 75-75-2 record – the most wins of any coach in school history. He led MSU to six bowl games at a school that had only been to seven football bowl games in school history. His 1998 team won the SEC West and led eventual national champion Tennessee into the fourth quarter before losing 24-14 and earned a Cotton Bowl berth. Sherrill coached MSU to a 10-2 mark in 1999, the best overall record in the SEC. That mark included a school-record 8-0 start, MSU's first Top 10 ranking since the early 1980s, and six SEC victories. When State beat Clemson in the 1999 Peach Bowl, its 10 wins tied the 1940 Bulldog team for the most victories in school history.

Perhaps more than any other attribute for many MSU fans, Sherrill had a career knack for both defeating and needling the arch-rival schools of the universities where he coached. Sherrill infuriated Ole Miss fans by refusing to refer to the school by any other name than "Mississippi" and other perceived slights that made him a hated figure in Oxford, as he had previously been at State College, Penn. Pat Forde of *ESPN.com* wrote of Sherrill in 2004: "After all, Sherrill was forced out at A&M in 1988, shortly before sanctions came down. He was in charge when State went on probation in 1995 ... but on the field, the man was pure hell for his rivals. He was at his best on Thanksgiving weekend, when the biggest game rolled around. Sherrill became the first Pittsburgh coach to beat Penn State in Happy Valley in back-to-back seasons. He became the first Texas A&M coach to beat Texas five years in a row. And he took over a Mississippi State program that had lost the Egg Bowl to Ole Miss seven times in the previous eight years, then won seven of the next 11."

Sherrill retired after the 2003 season under the cloud of a second NCAA probe of MSU during his tenure. The Associated Press reported in 2004: "Mississippi State's football program was placed on probation by the NCAA for four years, stripped of eight scholarships over the next two seasons and banned from postseason play this season because of recruiting violations. The NCAA announced Wednesday that its infractions committee found two former assistants and several boosters broke recruiting rules between 1998 and 2002. But allegations of unethical conduct against former coach Jackie Sherrill were dismissed."

For Cristil, Sherrill's success on the field and his NCAA troubles were all part of the territory. But Jack remembers Sherrill as "perhaps the easiest coach I ever worked with. Coach Sherrill understood what we were doing; he wanted us to do well in terms of the broadcast and the playback show and wanted us to be successful. He understood that the broadcasts were good for the athletic program and good for the university, and he really put forth a lot of effort to be prepared, to put a lot of energy into his interaction with me and with the fans. I also had an excellent personal relationship with Coach Sherrill. He brought a lot of excitement to MSU."

With the university facing a disastrous four-year probation, Templeton faced the chore of bringing in a new coach to succeed Sherrill and to lead the crippled program during the period of NCAA punishment that reduced the number of scholarship players available to MSU. Templeton eventually settled on former Alabama All-American center Sylvester Croom, then the running backs coach for the NFL's Green Bay Packers. With that decision, Croom became the first African American head football coach in the SEC – a distinction that Croom addressed in his first press conference as the Bulldog skipper: "I am the first African-American coach in the SEC, but there ain't but one color that matters here, and that color is maroon."

After compiling a 3-8 record in both of his first two seasons and a 3-9 mark in 2006, Croom had a breakout season in 2007 as the Bulldogs went 8-5 and 4-4 in the SEC. The team's first winning season since 2000 earned State a Liberty Bowl berth, which resulted in a 10-3 win over Central Florida. In the final regular season game again Ole Miss, the Rebels held a comfortable 14-0 lead going into the fourth quarter only to see Croom's Bulldogs put up 17 unanswered points to win 17-14. Ole Miss Head Coach Ed Orgeron was fired the next day.

A year later, Houston Nutt was the head coach at Ole Miss and the Egg Bowl ended in a 45-0 start-to-finish humiliation at the hands of the homestanding Rebels and a 4-8 2008 record for MSU. Croom resigned in the wake of the loss, telling the media in a press release: "Five years ago, Mississippi State gave me the unprecedented opportunity to be a head football coach in the Southeastern Conference and to build a program based upon a strong foundation. We have tried to build a program the right way that can compete for conference championships. I believe the foundation has been set for those goals to be reached under the leadership of someone else, and it was my decision to resign."

Cristil was philosophic in assessing the Croom era at MSU: "I'm not sure Coach Croom ever separated himself from the pro game. He genuinely wanted to build a successful program but never really seemed to get that across to this staff and the players. Breaking the color barrier almost certainly increased the pressure on him from without and within. I think in many ways there was more expected of him than he was in a position to give."

The Croom era at MSU also saw a change in the leadership of the athletic program at the university as Greg Byrne succeeded Larry Templeton as athletic director in 2008 after Templeton stepped down. Byrne joined the university in 2006 as Templeton's associate athletic director for external affairs and brought with him a mastery of emerging social media, new ideas about the quality of the "game day experience," and a successful sports marketing strategy. Byrne brought in heralded University of Florida offensive coordinator Dan Mullen to succeed Croom. Mullen went 5-7 in 2009 and ended the season with a 41-27 thumping of Cotton Bowl-bound Ole Miss in Starkville. That result left high expectations for what would become Jack Cristil's final season calling MSU football in 2010.

Cristil's relationship with Templeton was an extremely close and personal one: "Larry Templeton is MSU. He grew up on the campus. He loves and understands MSU, and he's 100 percent maroon and white. Whatever Larry did as athletic director, he did with the very best interests of Mississippi State at heart. Often, the best interests of the university were not always the best interests of Larry Templeton. But he made the decisions and took the heat. I greatly admire him."

If MSU's football coaching carousel had spun fast and furious during Cristil's tenure, it was MSU's basketball program that brought Jack some of his fondest memories and deepest personal relationships. Paul Gregory led the Maroons in 1953 when Cristil took the job as State's broadcaster, but MSU did not begin broadcasting basketball until 1957-58 when Babe McCarthy was in his third season and Maroon basketball had begun to make some real noise in the SEC.

"Coach McCarthy was really ahead of his time," said Cristil in 2011. "He was a great innovator and a great motivator. McCarthy could get players to play above their talent level in the system they ran. McCarthy's teams challenged the best and generally came out on top. Of all the basketball coaches at MSU during my time there, I suppose I had the closest relationship with Coach McCarthy up until the time that Rick Stansbury took over. When looking at getting productivity out of players over and above their talent level, there's a reasonable comparison between McCarthy and Stansbury. Both have that ability to get a little extra out of the players."

McCarthy won 169 games and lost 85 at MSU, winning or sharing four SEC titles and earning SEC Coach of the Year honors three consecutive years from 1961 to 1963. He produced All-Americans Jim Ashmore, Bailey Howell, Red Stroud, Leland Mitchell, and All-SEC performers Jerry Graves, Charles Hull, Joe Dan Gold, and Doug Hutton. But McCarthy is best remembered, along with MSU President Dean W. Colvard, for leading MSU's team to break the barrier of segregation by accepting the automatic bid to meet Loyola University of Chicago in the 1963 NCAA basketball tournament in East Lansing, Mich.

In Bailey Howell, McCarthy produced one of the greatest athletes in MSU history. Howell was a two-time All-American and three-time first team All-SEC performer for the Bulldogs and keyed the university's 1958-59 team that went 24-1 overall and 13-1 in the SEC to finish third in the national rankings behind Kansas State and Kentucky. After a stellar 12-year NBA career, Howell would be voted into the NBA Hall of Fame, play on two national championship teams while a member of the Boston Celtics, and make the NBA All-Star team six times. Many of Howell's MSU records still stand more than a half-century after his career at State ended. Yet not even Howell's legendary status atop the pantheon of Mississippi State sports lore would surpass the exploits of another group of MSU cagers under the leadership of McCarthy a few years later.

For many, the courage that Colvard and McCarthy showed in defying the Mississippi Legislature and fiery segregationist Gov. Ross Barnett to enable the all-white MSU men's basketball team to compete against a Loyola team with four African-American starters represented the university's finest hours. For many, Mississippi State's 1962-63 basketball team, coach, and the university administration came together to create a defining moment not only for MSU athletics but for American civil rights and universal sportsmanship as well. Cristil told *Dawgs' Bite's* David Murray in 2002: "In 1963, Mississippi State for the third-straight year won the Southeastern Conference basketball championship. We had won the championship in 1959 and respectfully declined the NCAA invitation because of the integration policy that existed in Mississippi and other places. The same thing happened in 1961 and 1962, and Coach McCarthy and Dr. Colvard were determined Mississippi State was going to play in the tournament."

Cristil said he was naïve about the lengths to which Colvard and McCarthy would have to go to enable the MSU team to participate in 1963. "I had no inkling what was going on. But I did know they had told us to be at the airport in Columbus, and we boarded a C-54 cargo plane converted into an airliner. We took off without any difficulty and flew to East Lansing. There was a local paper emblazoned with the headline – big enough you'd have thought war had been declared – 'Mississippi State is on the way.'"

The incendiary racial climate in Mississippi during the 1962-63 college basketball season cannot be overstated. Less than six months earlier, the enrollment of James Meredith at Ole Miss on Sept. 30, 1962, led to three days of riots that left two dead and more than 180 injured. The 1963 assassination of Medgar Evers and the 1964 murders of Andrew Goodman, James Chaney, and

Michael Schwerner in Neshoba County had yet to occur. Tensions were high, and the dangers for those who bucked the status quo of segregation were real. To suggest that both Colvard and McCarthy risked their lives and their livelihoods to give the Maroons a chance to compete for a national basketball championship is not hyperbolic. Why did they do it?

Perhaps Loyola team captain Jerry Harkness, one of the four black starters for the Ramblers, best summed up the true motivation for the Maroons: "The (MSU) players are all right. I think that Mississippi State wants to play us. If they don't, they'll never know how good they are." Colvard's biographer Marion A. Ellis in the 2004 book *Dean W. Colvard: Quiet Leader*, wrote: "Colvard had several reasons for wanting the team to compete. First of all, it would give a positive boost to the MSU and Mississippi image. Second, he felt the four seniors on the team deserved a chance after having played together for three years and having won the SEC championship all three years." Leland Mitchell, the 6'4" forward and leading rebounder, told the media in 1963: "I don't see anything morally wrong playing against Negroes, Indians, Russians or any other race or nationality. Most of the boys have played against them in high school or in hometown sandlot games. In my opinion, it's just like playing against anyone else. You consider him just another player."

Loyola head coach George Ireland said: "I feel Mississippi State has a right to be here, no matter what the segregationists say. They may be the best basketball team in the nation and if they are, they have a right to prove it." Harkness, the Loyola All-American, and State's All-SEC team captain Joe Dan Gold met at center court in Michigan State's Jenison Field House for the opening tip. Gold extended his hand and Harkness shook it. "About a thousand flashbulbs went off," Gold would say after the game. The game saw

State jump to an early lead only to trail the Ramblers 26-19 at the half. The Maroons went on an 8-4 run to pull to within 30-27 in the second half, but would get no closer. State was down four with two minutes to go and missed the shot. Cristil said it was "a good shot that just didn't go down. We had to start shooting, and Loyola beat us by 10, 61-51. It was a disappointing loss, but it had been a marvelous opportunity for the young men."

Loyola would go on to win the 1963 NCAA national championship. Ron Miller, Loyola's 6'2"guard and one of the four black starters, told writer John Thomas on the 40th anniversary of the game: "I remember the (Mississippi State) guys being nice. I remember the guys wishing us luck (after the game), and wanting us to win (the national championship). And during the game it was polite. They played a very hard, very aggressive, very strong defensive game, very clean, and they didn't back off."

Cristil said the MSU's 1963 basketball team's trip to East Lansing "gave me insight into the different philosophies in Mississippi about how to best handle change. I thought MSU was much more open-minded toward making changes and much more willing to make changes in a positive way. I still think that's true even today." The MSU broadcaster also left the 1963 basketball season with a profound respect for Colvard: "I was tremendously impressed with Dr. Colvard and how he handled the broader issues of integration at Mississippi State, not just the 1963 NCAA tournament. He was a man with tremendous personal integrity, charisma, and great foresight. He had an innate ability to sway other people's ideas to his way of thinking."

But the magic of McCarthy's run in the late 1950s and early 1960s didn't last, and after two losing seasons Babe's run in Starkville was done when he accepted a job as head coach at

George Washington University in 1966. A year later, McCarthy became a head coach in the American Basketball Association in New Orleans, Memphis, Dallas, and ended his career coaching the Kentucky Colonels in Louisville, Ky. McCarthy died of cancer in 1975.

Succeeding McCarthy was his MSU pupil, Joe Dan Gold. Gold, 23, led the Bulldogs from 1965-1970, compiling a 51-74 record over five seasons. Gold's first season saw success with an overall 14-11 mark and a 10-6 SEC record, but the Bulldogs posted losing records the next four seasons. Gold died in 2011 after a successful career in public school administration in his native Kentucky. "Joe Dan was very inexperienced and just not ready to run a college basketball program," said Cristil. "He was thrust into an impossible situation. But he was a great young man, and his character was impeccable."

Another McCarthy disciple and MSU graduate succeeded Gold, as the personable Kermit Davis took over the Bulldog basketball program. McCarthy's first high school signee out of Walnut, Miss., Davis was a guard for McCarthy's MSU teams in the late 1950s and would lead the Bulldogs to a composite 91-91 mark over his seven seasons as head coach from 1970-71 to 1976-77. Cristil said of Davis: "I knew him friend to friend. Coach Davis did a good job with what he had in terms of talent and resources and ran the program about as well as he could."

Despite only two losing seasons and a .500 record, Davis was relieved of duty and replaced by Ron Greene, who built a sterling record first at Loyola of New Orleans and later at the University of New Orleans. With a team built around future NBA first rounder Rickey Brown, Wiley Peck, and Ray White, Greene led MSU to its best season since McCarthy's 1963 team. Greene's Bulldogs posted an overall 18-9 record with a 13-5 SEC mark. Greene won SEC Coach of the Year honors, but the Bulldogs were snubbed by the NCAA despite a second-place finish in the SEC to eventual national champion Kentucky. Despite a team laden with talent, Greene abruptly left Starkville after only one season to accept the head coaching post at his alma mater, Murray State. "I enjoyed that year," said Cristil. "Coach Greene was an interesting guy and a good teacher. He played an exciting brand of basketball."

Greene's departure opened the door for the Jim Hatfield era at MSU. Hatfield's first season saw the Bulldogs 1978-79 squad go 19-9 overall and 11-7 in the SEC with a season-ending loss to Coach Davey Whitney's Alcorn Braves in the first round of the National Invitational Tournament. That appearance was MSU's first post-season play since the 1963 NCAA bid. But Hatfield's fortunes soured the next two seasons, and after going 8-19 overall and 3-15 in the SEC in 1980-81, Hatfield's services were no longer required at the Humphrey Coliseum. Asked about Hatfield, Cristil said: "He had been on the Kentucky basketball staff. Coach Hatfield seemed to have the Kentucky playbook but not the Kentucky talent or staff or resources. It showed on the court."

Bob Boyd took the MSU men's basketball reins from Hatfield after 13 seasons at the University of Southern California. Cristil's assessment of Boyd, whose work at USC was impressive on paper, was frank: "Coach Boyd was an interesting character who just didn't quite fit in at Mississippi State. I got the impression he was sort of just going through the motions. It was frustrating for the fans and, honestly, frustrating for me as a broadcaster." Boyd posted a career 55-87 mark at MSU before returning to California. His lone winning season was in 1982-83, when he led the Bulldogs to a 17-12 season mark and a 9-9 record in the SEC behind future

NBA first-rounder Jeff Malone, who broke Bailey Howell's MSU career scoring mark and finished his career with 2,142 points.

State chose Richard Williams, one of Boyd's assistants and an alumnus of MSU, as its next head basketball coach. Williams would lead State to its second set of "glory years" by compiling a 191-163 overall mark over 12 seasons to become MSU's all-time winningest basketball coach and surpass even the legendary Mc-Carthy's records with five post-season appearances, including two trips to the NIT in 1990 and 1994 and three trips to the NCAA tournament in 1991, 1995, and 1996 when the Bulldogs made it to the Final Four for the first time in school history – losing to Syracuse 77-69 in Madison Square Garden in New York City. During the Williams era in 1996, Jack made two of his most heralded calls in basketball that echo today in the hearts of the MSU faithful. First was the call from the SEC Basketball Tournament in New Orleans: "This game is over! You can wrap it in maroon and white. The Mississippi State Bulldogs are the champions of the Southeastern Conference, beating the Kentucky Wildcats 84-73." The second historic Cristil call came in Rupp Arena in Lexington, Ky., at the 1996 NCAA Southeast Regional Final: "This game is over. Mississippi State is on its way to the Final Four with a 10-point win over the Cincinnati Bearcats. There are Bulldogs all in the center of Rupp Arena, hugging one another, and some are on the floor. A little bit of all of it." In that call, MSU fans could literally hear Jack's pleasure, feel his pride, and share his slight uncertainty as Bulldogs everywhere asked themselves: "Is this really happening?" It was as if the Children of Israel had just crossed over and were surveying the Promised Land.

"In that Final Four run in 1996, Williams did his greatest coaching job by teaching those kids how to win games rather than how to not lose them," said Cristil. "Each player gave all they could. They beat Cincinnati and Connecticut at Rupp Arena, and I guarantee you they were the best two teams in the country that year. They beat them both in a week's time. Those two games were the best back-to-back games Mississippi State ever played."

Williams was twice chosen SEC Coach of the Year. He won one SEC title outright and won two SEC West titles. Cristil said: "Coach Williams was a great student and a great teacher of the game of basketball. He was classy, educated, and a gentlemen in every respect in my book. He's a winner, that's about all you can say. He's a winner." Yet two seasons after the historic Final Four run, Williams resigned his post at MSU under controversial circumstances about which he never commented. Chosen as his successor was Williams' chief assistant, Kentucky native Rick Stansbury.

On the topic of Stansbury, Cristil is animated and authoritative: "Rick Stansbury is a remarkable story. He'd done more with less than any coach in the league has ever done. He's a great recruiter. Rick's teams are always competitive and successful. He's had continuity in the coaching staff. Mississippi State has been really lucky to have Rick head up the university's basketball program."

Since 1998 when he took over from his mentor Williams, Stansbury led the Bulldogs to 10 post-season tournament appearances in 13 seasons including six trips to the NCAA tournament and four trips to the NIT. He became the first MSU coach in history to lead the squad to five consecutive post-season appearances from 2000 to 2004. Stansbury has led MSU to five SEC West titles in posting 11 winning seasons, one losing season, and one break-even season. He also coached the Bulldogs to two SEC tournament titles and the 2004 SEC regular season championship – when he garnered

SEC Coach of the Year honors. At the end of the 2011 season, Stansbury was the all-time winningest coach in MSU basketball history with an overall record of 272-151 with a 114-92 record in the SEC.

Beyond his impressions of the signature games and the coaches who led Bulldog football and basketball players over six decades, Jack Cristil had an opportunity to work with MSU's athletic directors and university presidents from a unique vantage point.

Dr. Ben Hilbun was president of Mississippi State when Noble hired Cristil in 1953, and they only saw each other in passing. Colvard, who Cristil admired, took over in 1960. Dr. William Giles, who succeeded Colvard and served from 1966 to 1976, was also a man Jack said he didn't get to know well. "I enjoyed the few interactions I had with him, and he was very gracious to me when Mavis died," said Cristil. "But our time together was limited."

Dr. James McComas was MSU's president from 1976 to 1985 when Cristil's daughter Kay was a student. "Dr. McComas was very down to earth, and I spent a good bit of time with him," said Jack. "He had great executive ability and tried to represent the best interests of MSU. I knew him not only as a broadcaster, but as the parent of an MSU student. I had confidence in him."

Dr. Donald Zacharias, the lanky, cerebral Indiana native who came to MSU from Western Kentucky, succeeded McComas and served as MSU's president from 1985-97. Zacharias led the university to new heights in enrollments, and national research status and raised over $143 million in private endowment. He was a tireless and fearless advocate for higher education in Mississippi during his tenure and remains, in retirement in Starkville at age 75, one of MSU's most beloved chief executives. Cristil views Zacharias as one of the institution's most able leaders: "Dr. Zacharias is an

outstanding individual. He was a great administrator and had a superb knowledge of how a university should function and serve the
state. I think his greatest attribute was that he had great credibility.
When he talked about the needs of the university, people believed
he was sincere and that the need was real and they somehow wanted to help him when they could."

Zacharias was succeeded by MSU alumnus Dr. Malcolm Portera
from 1998 to 2001, but Cristil said their paths didn't cross. Portera's
successor was Dr. Charles Lee, a North Carolina native who had
a long professional affiliation with MSU prior to assuming the
presidency from 2002 to 2006. "Dr. Lee was a very nice man and I
enjoyed my association with him. I think he knew he was filling a
niche for a short time, but he was a class act."

Following Lee was Gen. Robert H. "Doc" Foglesong, a former
four-star general in command of the U.S. Air Force in Europe.
Cristil's impression of Foglesong's tenure at MSU is the adminis-
trative equivalent of Jack's infamous "Sonic Drive of the Game"
call: "Gen. Foglesong was the only general I had an opportunity
to talk to and still come away feeling that I was at least his equal if
not his superior." Foglesong abruptly stepped down amid con-
troversies great and small on the campus in 2008. After a long
presidential search and the service of interim presidents Dr. Vance
Watson and Dr. Roy Ruby, Dr. Mark E. Keenum was named the
19th president of MSU in January 2009.

Keenum, an MSU alumnus, came to MSU after serving as
Under Secretary of the U.S. Department of Agriculture and as the
former chief of staff to U.S. Sen. Thad Cochran, R-Miss. Cristil's
assessment of Keenum was also blunt: "When Dr. Keenum's po-
tential is fully realized, I think he may well turn out to be the most
remembered and honored president Mississippi State ever had. He

understands Mississippi and Mississippi State and the problems that challenge both the state and the university. He has a unique ability to bring State's alumni together and get them pulling in the same direction together. He is a tremendous asset to MSU and to the state as well."

As the fall of 2010 rolled around, Cristil was anxious to broadcast the second season of Bulldog Head Coach Dan Mullen's career in Starkville: "I've never been around a guy with more energy. He's going to be very successful. He surrounds himself with good people, and he's taught the players that hard work, doing the right thing, pays dividends."

Stansbury's 2010-2011 basketball team was expected to be competitive. In addition to a young, exciting football coach heading into his second season in Mullen and a proven winner at the Humphrey Coliseum in Stansbury, MSU entered the 2010 football season with a new athletic director. Scott Stricklin, a 1992 State graduate who was employed in media relations and marketing positions at Auburn, Tulane, Baylor, and Kentucky before returning to MSU to head fundraising for the Bulldog Club and serve on Greg Byrne's executive staff in 2008, proposed to build on Byrne's changes in the "game day experience" in Starkville and to grow the university's athletic programs in ways the university had never before experienced. Cristil liked Stricklin's chances.

"Scott's got marvelous credentials and has a great opportunity to make his mark on this university," said Cristil. "Based on what I've seen, my bet is he does it."

As football season neared, Jack's energy was waning, and his kidney function was decreasing. But he was game at age 84 to try another season as MSU's football and basketball broadcaster – and what a season it turned out to be.

CHAPTER NINE

THE FINAL SEASON

"We do not remember days. We remember moments."

—CESAR PAVESE
ITALIAN POET AND NOVELIST

ENTERING WHAT WOULD BE HIS FINAL SEASON AS THE VOICE OF
Mississippi State University's football and basketball programs
in 2010, Jack Cristil had already reached a level of professional
accomplishment that rated him one of America's top play-by-
play radio broadcasters of all time. The walls of Cristil's den in
his Tupelo home were already covered with more plaques and
awards than the one room could accommodate. Some of Jack's
awards are literally stacked or filed in his home – not from lack of
appreciation but from a simple lack of space.

In 2010, as had been his habit for decades, Cristil's tools of the
trade were a pen, a stenographer's notepad to chart the play-by-
play, a two-deep roster with colored push pins to keep track of the
athletes who were actually on the field, and a yardage wheel to
compute distances on kicks and long gainers. The tools served him

well.

During his first 12 years as MSU's sports radio announcer, Cristil was named Mississippi's Sportscaster of the Year four times by the National Sportscasters and Sportswriters Association (NSSA) in Salisbury, N.C. He would win that award a total of 22 times over the course of his career. By 1965, only sports information director Bob Hartley and business manager "Doc" Pattey had more seniority in the MSU Athletic Department than did Cristil. The awards had not come without decades of hard work and sacrifice.

Pick Noble – who in 1965 along with Bill Hamlin was a spotter for Cristil – wrote about Cristil's work ethic in the Oct. 15, 1965, edition of the MSU student newspaper *The Reflector*: "Every year, Jack has at least one trip which causes him to cover several games and travel many miles in a weekend. This season, Jack has a freshman football game to broadcast on Friday afternoon with Auburn on campus. Immediately following the freshman game, the crew will load up the car and head for Greenville where Jack will broadcast the Tupelo High School game. Returning to Tupelo after the high school broadcast in Greenville, the crew will rise early Saturday morning and drive to Birmingham to report the play-by-play of the Mississippi State-Auburn varsity clash." Noble's account didn't address the fourth game of Jack's broadcast routine in that era – Itawamba Community College on Thursday nights.

The Sept. 11, 1982, edition of *Dawgs' Bite* recounted that Cristil also was called into duty for MSU baseball broadcasts: "(Cristil) even had the pleasure of broadcasting Mississippi State University's 1971 baseball playoffs in which the Bulldogs captured the NCAA District III regionals and advanced to the NCAA College World Series in Omaha." In the same article, Cristil spoke about his deep friendship with the late Joe Phillips of Starkville. A Starkville native and U.S. Air Force officer during World War II, Phillips was for 30 years the producer and director of Mississippi State sports radio broadcasts for the Mississippi State University Network. In 1948, Phillips built and held the Federal Communications Commission operating license for WSSO-AM and would later build and operate WMPA-AM in Aberdeen and WSMU-FM in Starkville, along with a cable television system and other businesses.

In Cristil's kitchen in Tupelo, the walls are decorated with family photos that include a shot of Jack and Joe and their wives in a celebratory pose at a social gathering – all smiles and embraces. Jack called the relationship between the Cristil family and the Phillips family "special."

Jack said that like Hartley and Larry Templeton, Joe Phillips treated him as a true friend and colleague, not as an employee. "We traveled together, took our meals together, roomed together on occasion, and had a lot of fun along the way," said Cristil. "If we had driven all night and were afraid to fall asleep for fear of missing the kickoff, Joe would hang with you, and he'd go without sleep, too. Our wives were very compatible as well, so the four of us enjoyed a lot of good times together over the years along with the Hartleys in that era."

One former MSU Athletic Department staffer who has insight into Cristil's relationship with Phillips was Bo Carter, the longtime assistant to Hartley who eventually succeeded him as MSU's sports information director. In remarks at the 2002 banquet held in tribute to Cristil's 50th anniversary at MSU, Carter told the crowd: "It was so hot and steamy in the old steel press box at Florida Field that Jack and the beloved late Joe Phillips locked the door to the tiny MSU radio booth on the top level. A puzzled public relations person sneaked a peek around the side area of the booth and there were Joe and Jack – in their skivvies. They quickly put back on their pants (they had kept on their dress shoes and socks) at the end of each quarter and had spotters fetch water and soft drinks."

But Carter knew, as did Hartley and Templeton, the dedication which Cristil and Phillips shared in maintaining a high level of quality and reliability on the old Mississippi State University Network: "Jack and Joe Phillips were the true 'twin towers' of MSU broadcasting ... the road warriors during the 1950s and 1960s when Mississippi State athletics' and radio networks' finances were tight." Templeton told *The Commercial Appeal's* Ron Higgins in a 1994 interview about Cristil's "indestructible" work ethic that often led him to calling games on Thursday, Friday, and Saturday night regardless the outrageous distances between venues: "I roomed with Jack on the road and one time at Tennessee he was extremely sick all day the day before the game. You would never have known that listening to his broadcast."

By 2010, Jack's memories were filled with family, loved ones, and friends who were no longer around to enjoy his incredible ride as MSU's broadcaster. Gone were the friends and colleagues with whom he made memories – Hartley, Phillips, and a host of other MSU friends had died or retired. Gone was his beloved Mavis, and daughters Kay and Rebecca were busy with families of their own in Louisiana and Georgia. After Phillips and his Mississippi State University Network came Steve Davenport and TeleSouth Communications, with whom Jack had a long and positive relationship. In 2008, MSU and multimedia collegiate sports rights holder Learfield Sports inked a 10-year pact that would come to include the radio broadcast rights for MSU sports in addition to ancillary radio and television exposures, game and facility signage, and various sponsorship and promotional opportunities.

Cristil recalled one story that made him laugh with gusto. His siblings had taken his mother, Mollie Cristil, to the only one of the Mississippi State football games he broadcast that she ever attended. Asked how she liked the football game, Mrs. Cristil replied that she liked the halftime show very much. Jack said: "Somebody asked her 'What about the ball game, Momma?' She answered: 'What do I care who catches the ball?'"

Jack's health was deteriorating. Close friends and colleagues knew it. His physicians knew it. Most of all, Jack knew it, but the drive within him to complete one more year was strong. His memories drifted occasionally back to the kindnesses of his professional colleagues and the Bulldog Nation over his long career.

In 1973, then MSU Alumni Association president Tommy Everett led an effort to organize "Jack Cristil Appreciation Day" on the 20th anniversary of Cristil's tenure at MSU. Everett's letter to his fellow alumni promoted an event to honor Cristil on the day of the 1973 MSU spring football game: "Our plans are to present Jack with an attractive plaque and also a cash gift. No one, that I can recall, has been so faithful and done so much to create good will for Mississippi State as this man has done. The ability he has of announcing an athletic contest so vividly and selling Mississippi State at the same time has been invaluable to our great university."

Again in 1983, when Cristil hit his 30-year milestone at MSU, the university made an effort to honor Jack. Then-MSU president James McComas presented Cristil with a handsome plaque with the broadcaster's image etched upon it at the 50-yard line during halftime homecoming festivities of MSU's 31-7 loss to the University of Miami.

Cristil's peers among SEC broadcasters in 1988 voted Jack as the league's best broadcaster – edging out his friend Cawood Ledford of Kentucky, who entered the league the same year as did Jack. Four years later, Cristil would become the first non-athlete to be inducted into the Mississippi Sports Hall of Fame in 1992. The 1992 class of inductees included: former Alcorn State University basketball coach Dave Whitney; former Ole Miss quarterback Jimmy Lear, tennis champion Lester Sack, Olympic gold medalist and Greenwood native Glenn "Slats" Hardin, and former USM basketball coach Lee Floyd. The induction, held at the Jackson Coliseum Ramada Inn and emceed by former Gov. William Winter, led *The Clarion-Ledger's* Orley Hood to quote Jack on April 30, 1992: "People say, 'I've listened to you all my life.' Next football season will be my 40th at Mississippi State. So a lot of them, they're right."

Hood's column coincided with another Cristil milestone. A month after his historic induction into the Mississippi Sports Hall of Fame, Cristil won the first Ronald Reagan Lifetime Achievement Award from the NSSA. The award was created to honor a "grassroots" sports reporter for career excellence and dedication. Other NSSA national winners that year included NBC sportscaster Bob Costas and *Sports Illustrated* columnist Rick Reilly.

Cristil retired from his last full-time job in advertising as sales manager of WTVA-TV in Tupelo on Jan. 1, 1995, at the age of 69. Jack had stepped down from play-by-play football and basketball duties at Itawamba Community College after 30 years (1955-85) and the same duties at Tupelo High School (1955-85) a decade earlier. From 1995 until his final MSU call in Knoxville in 2011, Cristil's time and attention was totally directed at his connection to Mississippi State. He told Vincent Pride of the *Clarksdale Press-Register* on Feb. 24, 1996: "Larry Templeton, the athletic director of MSU, and I are very good friends and we had a talk to discuss my status. I told him that I'd like to continue to represent Mississippi State University the way you would like for me to do. If I can't handle that option, please let me know and I will retire from broadcasting. Larry agreed."

A Feb. 14, 1995, MSU basketball game indicates just how much fun Cristil was still having as the Bulldog broadcaster. State had beaten the Kentucky Wildcats in Lexington, Ky. The following was the MSU broadcast call after the game as Cristil intoned: *"The game is over. The Bulldogs have won it 76-71– a historic night here at Rupp Arena. Mississippi State has never won in the Rupp Arena, and you've never heard such silence. The silence is absolutely deafening. The silence is deafening . . . I don't know who's happier – obviously Richard Williams, these basketball players, everybody involved with Mississippi State athletics, all the fine folks that follow the Maroon and White, they're rejoicing in this thing. And the Kentucky band is playing something that sounds like a funeral dirge."*

Color analyst Jim Ellis replied: *"Well, it's Old Kentucky Home."* Cristil replied: *"Oh, it sounds like a funeral dirge. I was right to begin with. We owe a bunch of commercials, I don't know how many, so right now let's pause for two minutes for network commercials and our local commercials."*

In the late 1990s, Cristil still mowed his own lawn and worked in Charlie Robison's wood-working shop making birdhouses in the off-season to be sold for charity or given as gifts. Another major honor, perhaps the signature honor of his professional life, came in 1997 when the College Football Hall of Fame named Cristil the second winner of the Chris Schenkel Award. Schenkel, the late longtime ABC announcer for whom the award was named, was the first recipient. Schenkel died in 2005. Georgia announcer Larry Munson, the only other SEC announcer to win the honor, received it in 2003 before his retirement.

Cristil lost one of his dearest friends when Bob Hartley – who had served MSU athletics for 39 years prior to his retirement in 1985 – died at the age of 77 on Aug. 27, 1997. A year later, Cristil would tell Larry Liddell of the *Clarkdale Press Register*: "Bob meant more to Mississippi State University than anyone who ever lived. For 50 years, he gave of himself to Mississippi State. When the university needed friends in the 1960s and 1970s, Bob Hartley got them friends because he had friends all over the country. Bob Hartley is one individual to which Mississippi State owes everything. I will be forever indebted to him."

In 1998, Cristil had the opportunity to call the games that saw No. 23 MSU win the SEC West title in football and play No. 1 Tennessee for the SEC Championship title at the Georgia Dome in Atlanta. State took a 14-10 lead into the final quarter, but UT's Tee Martin threw two touchdown passes in the span of 32 seconds in the fourth quarter to win 24-14. Tennessee would win the national championship with a 23-16 win over the Florida State Seminoles in the Fiesta Bowl. During the run-up to the SEC Championship game, Cristil told *The Northeast Mississippi Daily Journal's* Christopher R.C. Bosen on Dec. 5, 1998: "I enjoy watching Mississippi State people happy – that's my enjoyment – seeing those people having the opportunity to rejoice in the success of the team and the program." The 1999 season saw Cristil call his 500th game for Mississippi State – a 14-9 road loss to Arkansas.

In 2001, Cristil, then 75, faced his greatest health challenge when he was diagnosed with prostate cancer. The cancer diagnosis led to the tests that revealed both the aneurysm and his kidney disease – a diagnosis that in truth saved Jack's life.

The cancer diagnosis brought with it every medical test imaginable, Cristil said. The tests revealed a potentially deadly abdominal aneurysm and revealed that Jack's left kidney had atrophied or been injured and was no longer functional. Cristil would undergo surgery to repair the aneurysm and the renal artery to the right kidney. The dangerous surgery required a significant hospital stay during the summer that left Cristil's status for the 2001 football season in doubt. But Cristil rallied and returned to duty behind the microphone.

In a mid-season Oct. 25, 2001, interview with *The Northeast Mississippi Daily Journal's* Parrish Alford, Cristil told the reporter that a 30-minute daily regimen of walking around his Marquette Street neighborhood in Tupelo had helped his recovery: "Basically, I'm doing very well. I really have no major problems, and I've got most of my strength back. Everything being said and done, I've got no room to complain."

A year later, Cristil would be honored once again by MSU for his service, as the broadcaster observed his 50th anniversary as the "Voice of the Bulldogs." On Nov. 1, 2002, Cristil was honored by a sold-out banquet in which his broadcast partner Jim Ellis, sideline reporter John Correro, former MSU president Charles Lee, Bo Carter, South Carolina play-by-play announcer Charlie McAlexander, Auburn broadcaster Jim Fyffe, then-MSU Foundation president Leo Seal, Larry Templeton, and daughters Kay Cristil Clouatre and Rebecca Cristil Nelson took part in the program. The next day, at halftime of MSU's 45-22 loss to Kentucky, Cristil was honored on the 50 yard line with the presentation of a large photo montage celebrating his career and the keys to a new Buick LeSabre.

Charlie Mitchell, the longtime executive editor of *The Vicksburg Post*, worked with Cristil briefly as an MSU student employed at Joe Phillips' WSSO-AM in Starkville in the early 1970s. Mitchell's

Nov. 17, 2002, statewide syndicated political column celebrated
Cristil's 50th anniversary at MSU: "Cristil, now 79, tells us what is
happening in the game with depth and specificity. It's only through
the slightest change in his tone that you can tune in and tell
whether the Bulldogs are ahead or stinking up the place. Cristil is
all MSU, but his commentary contains no editorializing."

Less than a month after being honored for his golden anniversary with MSU, Cristil became only the eighth person to receive
an honorary doctoral degree in the university's history. On Dec.
13, 2002, Cristil received his honorary doctorate in creative and
performing arts from Charles Lee, who said: "Jack Cristil has been
telling an important part of the Mississippi State University story
for the past half century. In the process, he has become an important part of a major segment of the university's 124-year history.
That unmistakable voice on the radio is as familiar and as comforting to multitudes of Bulldog fans as that of a dear friend. It gives
one pause to reflect on all the history that Jack has witnessed, but
that escalates into amazement when we stop to consider that he
has been much more than a passive observer."

The 2002 fall commencement at MSU was made even more
memorable by the fact that Cristil's honorary doctorate would be
presented after a commencement speech delivered by one of the
most beloved figures in the university's history – Roy Ruby, who
served the university from 1964 until 2004 in varying administra-
tive and academic capacities including education dean and vice
president. Ruby came out of retirement in 2009 to serve as interim
president of the university. Ruby, like Cristil, enjoys a larger-than-
life reputation with MSU partisans and is an engaging and delight-
ful public speaker. With Cristil in the audience awaiting his degree,
Ruby told the 2002 MSU fall graduates: "You are today in the top

99th percentile of the world's educated," Ruby said. "While you have an obligation to your professional success and to your family, as an educated person you also should assume a strong obligation to be of help to mankind and to those who are less fortunate than you ... you must give back."

In 2003, Cristil was one of three honorees into the MSU Sports Hall of Fame – the second non-athlete ever inducted into MSU's sports shrine behind his friend Bob Hartley. Cristil's class included former Bulldog baseball legends Will Clark and Jeff Brantley. Clark helped lead State to its best showing ever – tied for third – in the College World Series while starring for MSU from 1983-85. He was the second player chosen in the 1985 Major League Baseball draft. Over 15 seasons of professional baseball as a first baseman, Clark was an MLB All-Star six times and won a Gold Glove in 1991. Clark hit .391 over his career at MSU, still the university's all-time record career batting average. Brantley was an All-American pitcher at State and pitched a record 18 wins in 1985. His 45 career SEC wins set a league record that has been tied but not broken. Brantley, an MLB All-Star in 1990, enjoyed a 13-year pro baseball career with the Giants, the Cincinnati Reds, the St. Louis Cardinals, and the Philadelphia Phillies.

Cristil took a star turn in 2003 when he was asked to play fictional high school football radio play-by-play announcer "Buck Coffey" in the Random House audio edition of John Grisham's small, intimate novella *Bleachers*. Grisham's story examined the complexities of a talented but flawed high school quarterback named Neely Crenshaw who returns to his hometown of Messina 15 years after his glory years as his coach, Eddie Rake, is dying. Grisham's tale of life and the cult worship of high school football's fleeting heroes in a small town had a special appeal to every boy or man who had ever played high school football for a hard-bitten, demanding coach. Grisham recalled how he came to involve Cristil in the project: "For years, Bantam Audio (a division of Random House) wanted me to read one of my books, but I was not tempted until *Bleachers*, primarily because it had the fewest words of any novel I had written. I reluctantly agreed to do so. I have found few things to be as tedious as getting locked in a sound room for eight hours a day and reading, without the slightest mistake, an entire novel. Never again.

"In the midst of the process, I came to the scene that included a radio announcer calling a high school football game, and as I practiced I found myself imitating Jack Cristil. I used such standards as 'he cannot go' and 'knocked down at the line of scrimmage.' At some point, I decided to contact Jack and see if he had any interest in doing it himself. He did not hesitate. I hope he enjoyed the process. Because of a deadline, we did not have the time to rework the dialogue and allow Jack to call the game his way. That is something I will always regret," Grisham said.

The cavalcade of awards, honors, and career superlatives continued for Cristil in 2004, as the Knoxville Quarterback Club tapped him as the winner of the Lindsey Nelson Award, given annually to one of the nation's premier sports broadcasters. Other broadcasters who have won the award include: ABC's Keith Jackson, CBS's Verne Lundquist, Tennessee's John Ward, and Kentucky's Cawood Ledford.

Awards weren't the only part of Cristil's broadcasting career at Mississippi State. There was routine – mind-numbing routine. Jack's schedule made travel, particularly the drives during the early years of his career on two-lane roads, brutal both from road conditions and distance. The early years also required heavier, bulkier tube-based radio equipment. There were cables and telephone wires to be dealt with and primitive press boxes – baking hot in the early season games and freezing as fall gave way to winter. Cristil told ESPN.com's David Albright in 2007: "The technical end has changed considerably. When we began, we used to lug in huge pieces of equipment which was all vacuum tubes. After they invented the transistor, we got it down to the size of a little cigar box. And now with the expanded technology it's gone right back to the other extreme. And I'm completely lost in this technological era."

There were also countless hard landings, turbulent flights, delays, and the other realities of frequent air travel. Lewis Halbert of the MSU Television Center recalled one experience with Jack in 1999: "When the football team traveled by air for an out-of-state game, for 17 years, his seat was always in the back, usually a row or two across from where I was seated. Every time the jet would land on the runway, Jack would say 'Another great day for flying,' even if we were arriving at night. The only time he didn't make that comment was when we were returning to Golden Triangle Regional Airport in Columbus from a game against Arkansas. The fog was so dense and close to the ground that we couldn't see the runway, and we knew the pilot couldn't, either. We could feel the jet descending at an odd angle when all of a sudden the jet touched down like it was landing on an aircraft carrier. Everyone was so freaked out from this experience, and I looked over at Jack, who for the first time did not say 'great day for flying.' He said: 'Damn, he must have been a Navy pilot.'"

Then there was the infamous "tornado" game in the Georgia Dome in Atlanta during the 2008 SEC Basketball Tournament. On Friday, March 14, 2008, the National Weather Service issued a tornado warning for the downtown area at 9:26 p.m., after radar indicated a storm six miles west of Atlanta capable of producing a tornado. The storm blew a hole in the roof of the Georgia Dome, delaying MSU's 69-67 overtime win over Alabama for more than an hour and forcing the SEC to move the remainder of the tournament to the campus of Georgia Tech. NWS meteorologists said the tornado produced winds between 110-135 m.p.h., making it an EF2 tornado. For his part, Cristil calmly filled air time talking with Templeton and analyst Bart Gregory.

Yet there were also game memories and moments that linger, as he shared with *The Commercial Appeal's* Ron Higgins in 1994. Cristil fondly remembered a 1962 McCarthy-era 49-44 basketball win over Kentucky: "It was a real slowdown game, but it was the first time we'd ever won in Lexington." An 11-10 football win over Auburn in 1961 in Birmingham stuck with him: "Johnny Baker scored a two-point conversion to win the game. State broke a 22-game SEC winless streak."

Recordings of Cristil's famous calls can take MSU fans back to their own memories and moments, some of elation and some of utter despair. Cristil's call of the 1983 Egg Bowl in Jackson is an example: *"Out of the hold of Brent Parker, Artie Cosby will attempt a 27-yard field goal. The ball is down, the kick is up. He's high enough! It's being held up by the wind. It is no good! The wind blew it completely out of the ball park. Ole Miss wins 24-23."*

Not all of Cristil's memories as the "Voice of the Bulldogs" involve sporting events. On Oct. 16, 2009, Cristil had a command performance at the Lee Hall Auditorium as MSU officially installed Mark Keenum as the 19th president of the university. At the request of Keenum and his wife, Rhonda, Cristil served as the "voice" of the event and stole the show at the event's conclusion when he said: "Let's wrap this investiture in maroon and white!"

Born in Starkville while his father was a student at MSU, Mark Keenum grew up listening to Cristil. Keenum, who played football at Corinth High School and later at Northeast Mississippi Community College in Booneville, said that one of the moments he remembers from his youth was when Corinth played Tupelo: "That was always a big game for Corinth, but as a Bulldog it was even more special to me because I knew that Jack Cristil would be calling the game on the radio and might, if I played well, call my name. You can't imagine what an honor that was for me. I had a tape of the game that I played over and over."

Cristil's final football season was a memorable one. The team finished the season 9-4 overall and 4-4 in the SEC with league wins over Georgia, Florida, Kentucky, and Ole Miss. Against eventual national champion Auburn, the Bulldogs recovered an onside kick after narrowing Auburn's lead to 17-14, but the offense stalled. Cornerback Corey Broomfield dropped an interception on what would likely have been a touchdown. On State's final drive, receiver Leon Berry dropped a pass that would have put the Bulldogs in field-goal range.

Regardless, the 2010 Bulldogs turned in a stellar season as clearly the most improved team in the SEC and won the right to face Michigan in the Gator Bowl. With Bulldog fans invading Jacksonville, Fla., in record numbers, State annihilated the Wolverines 52–14 in Cristil's final football game and finished with a No. 15 final ranking in the final AP poll. The successful season left MSU head coach Dan Mullen as one of the hottest coaching properties in the country and helped spur an increase in private sector pledges and gifts to MSU athletics. During the 2009-10 fiscal year, MSU sports brought in an athletic department record $17.6 million in private giving. In fiscal year 2011, Mississippi State University received private gifts and pledges totaling more than $80.3 million – making 2011 the most successful giving year and a 23 percent increase over the previous year's $65.1 million.

A significant portion of that came in the form of a school-record $37 million-plus to athletics through the Bulldog Club and the Bulldog Foundation.

Was Jack expecting a nine-win season in 2010? "I learned a long time ago not to analyze the schedule and project wins and losses," Cristil said. "What I appreciated from the season was the Florida victory. The manner in which we played, the superb game plan, was just magnificent. Coach Mullen shortened the game by running the ball and by doing so disrupted what Florida wanted to do. The defense bent but didn't break. It was marvelous."

It's not surprising that Cristil picked the Florida win as his favorite from the 2010 season. The MSU win in Gainesville was the first since 1965, snapping a 16-game losing streak at "The Swamp" and came over a Gator team that had won two of the last four national titles.

Despite increasing fatigue and weakness as his kidney function decreased, Cristil continued to meet his obligations. He continued to delight longtime fans by his signature accounts of the Bulldogs being "three yards from the land of milk and honey" or "knocking on the door" when the football team was driving toward the end zone and touchdown.

During MSU's 2010 homecoming celebration, Jack was chauffeured in the antique car "Cowbell Cruiser" as the grand marshal of the Homecoming Parade. Just before the start of the college season, Tupelo High School sponsored "Jack Cristil Day" and presented the broadcaster a THS letterman's jacket in recognition of his 30 years as the "Voice of the Golden Wave."

Despite the carnival-like celebration in Jacksonville by MSU fans after the Gator Bowl, Cristil's memory of it is tainted by the fatigue that plagued him. "After the basketball road trip and the necessary travel immediately following that to get to Jacksonville, I was in a situation in which I had no pep, no vitality, and everything was just gray matter. It meant the world to me to see the success of the team and coaching staff, and certainly the absolute joy of our fans, but I was just physically and mentally exhausted," Cristil said.

After the Gator Bowl, Cristil and his doctors knew it would be a race against time over whether he could finish the Bulldogs' 2010-11 basketball season before he was forced to begin kidney dialysis. Coach Rick Stansbury's squad eventually battled to a 17-13 overall mark and a 9-7 finish in the SEC West but missed post-season action for the first time in five years and only the second time in 11 seasons. "There were distractions during the course of the season, no question, but Coach Stansbury got those kids to play competitively in spite of the distractions," said Cristil. "For my money, it was one of the best coaching jobs of his very successful career."

Cristil's unique voice never failed him, but over the six weeks following the Gator Bowl in Jacksonville, his 85-year-old body finally did. His kidney function dropped to dangerous, life-threatening levels. Fatigue gripped the old Army Air Corps mechanic. The clock, as it were, had finally run out on his broadcasting career.

Jack Cristil made his final call of MSU's 70-69 win over Tennessee in Knoxville on Feb. 26, 2011. He left the profession as he had entered it – on his own terms.

His thoughts on the night he retired from service to MSU? Remember what Cristil said that night after his last call in Knoxville?

"No deep thoughts, no regrets, I was just so pleased that we won the ballgame," said Jack. "I was ready to get on the bus and head for home and get on with whatever awaited me."

CHAPTER TEN

"WRAP THIS ONE IN MAROON AND WHITE!"

"There comes a special moment in everyone's life, a moment for which that person was born. That special opportunity, when he seizes it, will fulfill his mission – a mission for which he is uniquely qualified. In that moment, he finds greatness. It is his finest hour."

—SIR WINSTON CHURCHILL
BRITISH STATESMAN

IN HIS OWN CHARACTERISTICALLY BLUNT WORDS, WHAT AWAITED JACK Cristil in Tupelo was: "Fifteen hours a week of dialysis, and 153 hours a week thinking about dialysis. It is pure and unadulterated agony. Other than that, it's fine."

Cristil explained the process. "It's cold in the dialysis unit while you're being treated, and all the patients are wrapped up in blankets because they cool your blood while it's running through the machine. Two large needles are inserted in your arm, the arm needs to stay immobile during the process and if it doesn't, the machine shuts off and you have to start over. In spite of everything the staff does to make you comfortable and as nice as they are, it's

uncomfortable having to sit in a chair for 4-5 hours total and sub-
mit to the treatment. It's a mental process, learning to live essentially on a machine and be tethered to it." His words come sharp
and staccato, as if he's calling the action in a ball game. Then Jack's
voice softens and the smile comes back to his face: "But, you look
around the room at the dialysis unit and you realize, you're not in
as bad a shape as a lot of the people there."

Cristil's right. He's fit and trim, eats a healthful and careful diet,
follows doctor's orders (with the decided exception of his choice to
smoke) and does his part to make the dialysis regimen worthwhile.
"I'm not ready to die," said Cristil with a wry smile. "I've got a
choice. If this becomes such a chore that I don't want to do it any
longer, well, you can come and visit me and Mavis in Verona (at
the cemetery). Bring flowers. But not yet."

In life, as in broadcasting, routine remains important for Cristil.
"Dialysis saps your strength," Jack said. "The next day, you feel better and stronger and you try to go about your errands to the bank,
the Post Office, the drug store, and so on." Cristil reads the newspaper daily and glances at a few magazines. When he reads books, he's
a fan of John Grisham's legal thrillers. He watches sporting events
on TV and splits his news viewing between Fox News and CNN.

As has been the case for a number of years since the death of
Mavis Cristil in the late 1980s, there is a special friend and companion in Jack's life – Waurene Heflin, a vivacious widow who is
an accomplished realtor, a Baptist Sunday School teacher, and the
familiar figure who has accompanied Jack to countless sporting
events and social engagements on the MSU campus.

"I've known Waurene for a long time," said Jack. "She's been
good for me, and I hope I've been good for her. We have a wonderful time together. I admire her dedication to her daughter, Rhi-

annon, and really enjoy the time we've had together." They met while Jack was on a sales call at Tupelo Auto Sales after Waurene's husband died – a man Jack had known when Mr. Heflin came to WELO-AM to sing in a quartet on the radio. In addition to the MSU travels, Jack and Waurene like to explore restaurants and fish houses in and around Tupelo, particularly the Estes Fish House in Plantersville.

In Tupelo, despite the obvious pride many in the city feel for Cristil, he is by his own description "just one of the guys." Jack's a member of a coffee club comprised of men of his generation who gather frequently to "solve the world's problems" over a cup of coffee at Danver's on West Main Street. Although he's lost some dear friends on Marquette Street and in other environs in Tupelo, he loves his neighborhood: "You couldn't ask for better neighbors. I had a good relationship with the town's business community for many years, and I've always been treated with respect. We made a wonderful life in Tupelo."

Cristil is a Republican. "I've been a Republican since Eisenhower in 1952," Cristil said. "But I have voted for some conservative-minded Democrats." Jack maintains an adamant view on taxes, one befitting the son of immigrants who sacrificed so much for their citizenship: "Taxes? No matter how much it is, it's cheap rent to live in this country. There's no such thing as a free lunch."

In short, the retired MSU broadcaster is the same man, the same neighbor, the same father and grandfather, the same friend, and the same Jewish lay leader that he was before Cristil made his final call in Knoxville. Dialysis has irreparably changed his routine and limited his ability to travel and to stray from his routine, but his mind remains crystal clear, his observations sharp, his wit keen, and his speech quick and salty.

Cristil's retirement set in motion a flurry of honors and tributes. Shortly before the announcement, Jack was honored by the Mississippi State Alumni Association during a gala banquet attended by his daughters and by Waurene Heflin and her daughter, Rhiannon, along with a host of his friends and fans. On March 16, "Jack Cristil Day" was proclaimed by the Mississippi Legislature, and the broadcaster was flown to Jackson along with Waurene, MSU president Mark Keenum, and MSU athletic director Scott Stricklin.

While addressing the House following a standing ovation, Jack said: "This is awesome. I'm so completely overwhelmed to be receiving here today an honor deeply cherished. I share this recognition with an untold number of ladies and gentlemen on the campus of Mississippi State University. We touch a lot of lives that we know about, and we touch a lot of lives that we don't know about, as well. From the depths of my heart, I thank you."

Jack received formal legislative resolutions from both houses of the Mississippi Legislature and addressed both the House and the Senate. In Washington, U.S. Sen. Thad Cochran, R-Miss., commended Cristil from the Senate floor, saying in part: "For the better part of six decades, Mississippi State fans welcomed Jack's professionalism and his unambiguous play-by-play descriptions, free from hyperbole or favoritism, onto their radios. His distinctive voice and irreplaceable wit will be missed." Cochran's remarks, and a Rick Cleveland front page story on Cristil's retirement from *The Clarion-Ledger*, were read into the *Congressional Record*. Similar sentiments were expressed on the floor of the House and read into the *Congressional Record* by U.S. Rep. Gregg Harper, R-Pearl, and U.S. Rep. Alan Nunnelee, R-Tupelo.

But beyond the dignitaries, reaction from lesser known and often anonymous MSU fans commenting on newspaper websites, blogs, message boards, Facebook, and Twitter were eloquent and heartfelt, as in these comments on *Dawgs' Bite's* website:

"I am 64 years old and have been listening to you, Jack, all 58 years. I bought one of the first transistor radios in Houston, Mississippi, and would take it to the cornfield and listen while pulling corn. Jack, you are MSU," wrote one commenter posting as 1maddog.

Another commenter, posting as "Gerald Scarborough," wrote: "I have never known a MSU voice other than Jack's. As a kid, my dad and I always looked forward to finding Jack's voice on the radio. When I was in school at State, I went to The Club in Columbus one night and there was Jack, celebrating his daughter's birthday. A great time was had that evening partying with Jack Cristil. When I moved to Tennessee in 1985, I would drive to the highest hill in town or I would start driving in the direction of Mississippi until I could pick up that voice, pull over and listen to the game. My wife thought I was crazy. The things I enjoyed most about Jack were the unmistakable voice and his ability to be unbiased in his reporting of the game. Mississippi State broadcasts will never be the same."

A *Dawgs' Bite* reader posting as "b woffer" shared this story: "In the days before other modern communications methods, I often found myself a great distance from a station broadcasting MSU football. However, sometimes I managed to get just a weak signal on a Saturday night. When I was a graduate student in Boulder, Colorado in 1967, I was able to listen to a game on a Memphis station by going up on Flagstaff Mountain. The same happened when I was at Fort Sill in 1969. Later, when living in Decatur, Ala., we were able to catch the games on the clear channel station out of Houston, Miss. It was always weak and often faded out, but you could always know when you were on the right station when you heard Jack's distinctive voice.

"The farthest away that I ever listened to Jack was in Vietnam in 1970. My mother made a tape of the Ole Miss game and sent it to me. Joe Reed and the boys laid it on the Rebels that day and I enjoyed hearing that familiar voice of Jack calling the game even if it was not live. I still have the tape. I have been unable to find a reel-to-reel player to listen to it again. I'll keep it as a memory of all the Bulldog games that Jack brought to life for me."

David Kellum, the respected Ole Miss radio broadcaster who has the only numerically realistic chance to break Cristil's record of SEC sports broadcasting longevity, said he believes Cristil's record will endure. "I really don't think Jack's record will ever be broken, and I'm not going to try," said Kellum. "Honestly, if I ever got close, I think I'd stop one game short out of respect for him. Jack was one of the first five people to call to congratulate me and encourage me when I got the Ole Miss job, and I've learned so much from him. He has a unique voice, an amazing voice. Honestly, Jack Cristil and Jack Eaton were two of the people who got me interested in pursuing a career in broadcasting. It has been an honor and a privilege to come to know Jack as a friend as well as a colleague."

Perhaps one of the most elegant expressions of what Jack Cristil's career meant to Mississippians came in the prose of the 2010 formal obituary of Mississippi State alumnus David Earl Brewer of Jackson. The obituary for Brewer, 84, a civil engineer who retired as chief bridge engineer for the Mississippi Department of Transportation and once taught engineering at MSU, included this passage: "He preferred listening to Jack Cristil announce Mississippi State football on the radio to watching on TV. He always loved his Bulldogs."

When Cristil's retirement became a reality, MSU officials faced the daunting task of making decisions about "Life After Jack" in terms of the future of the Bulldogs sports radio broadcasts. To the great pleasure of Cristil and the relief of the majority of MSU stakeholders, the decision was made to promote Jack's color analyst and veteran MSU broadcaster Jim Ellis to the lead role as play-by-play broadcaster. As MSU campus radio station WMSV General Manager Steve Ellis – a longtime colleague but no relation – said of Jim Ellis: "It's the perfect choice. With Jack and Jim, you essentially had two play-by-play announcers working together, with Jim playing a very important supporting role. MSU fans know and respect Jim Ellis, and he's more than earned the right to have this opportunity. It will definitely be different for State fans without Jack, but I believe they will embrace Jim as he moves over to first chair."

Steve Ellis said the mutual respect between Cristil and Jim Ellis is obvious: "Jim's as much a son as Jack's ever had. He learned the craft of broadcasting at this level at Jack's elbow. I believe Jack will enjoy listening to a guy he helped to train." Jim Ellis, a 1969 MSU alumnus, already has 33 years of service to the university broadcasting MSU baseball and has spent three decades working with Cristil. Joining Ellis in the broadcast booth for MSU football in 2011 as color analyst will be former Bulldog quarterback Matt Wyatt. Wyatt hosted his own morning show, "First Call," in Tupelo; has hosted pre- and post-game shows for MSU in the last two years; and launched a statewide sports talk show after Cristil's retirement. John Correro, who has been associated with the MSU radio broadcasts since 1979, will continue his role as the football sideline reporter. Joining Ellis for Bulldog basketball broadcasts as the new color analyst for men's basketball will be Bart Gregory, the play-by-play voice of the Lady Bulldog basketball team. Gregory will also join Ellis in the baseball booth beginning in the 2012 season.

Ellis told Brad Locke of *The Northeast Mississippi Daily Journal*: "From a professional standpoint, I've always wanted to be the Mississippi State guy. I can't emulate Jack Cristil, he was one-of-a-kind, and he was an icon. But I think that we can hopefully as a team put a product out that Mississippi State people will be proud of, that will be informative, and maybe bring to the fore some things around the game that they will like to hear about."

What did Cristil think of the changes? "I couldn't have asked for a better successor than Jim Ellis," Jack said. "They don't come any better. Jim has been a part of Mississippi State since he was a student. He's highly professional, and Mississippi State will be very well represented. I came to know him like I came to know a lot of my closest Mississippi State friends – people like Larry Templeton, Bob Hartley, John L. Long, Bo Carter, Straton Karatassos, and finally Jim Ellis – as roommates on road trips. Jim watched my grandson Jake grow up over the years. We are very close friends, and I'm immensely proud of him. Bart is improving dramatically, and while I haven't been able to hear as much of Matt's work, I'm sure he'll approach this responsibility as he did when he was a Bulldog athlete. He'll give it all he's got."

After his retirement, Jack's daughters spoke of their hopes for their father. Daughter Rebecca Cristil Nelson said: "Daddy has said for many years that he is in the fourth quarter and time is running out. My hope is that he will go into double-overtime. I pray that his health allows him to remain active to whatever extent makes him happy, that he will enjoy his retirement, and that Lindsey and I will have many more visits with him. I expect that he will still listen to the games because he has complete confidence in Jim Ellis. I must admit that I might have had trouble getting adjusted to a new voice if anyone but Mr. Jim had been chosen to take over. I would love for him to attend games on campus whenever possible, but he will need to get lessons on how to be a spectator. I've seen him as a spectator at a game only one time at the 1974 Sun Bowl, and he wasn't very good at it, nor has he had much practice with a cowbell, so we have much work to do. I know beyond a shadow of a doubt that he will continue to follow his beloved Bulldogs and be 'True Maroon' forevermore."

Daughter Kay Cristil Clouatre offered a more poignant answer to questions about her father's future and his legacy: "Daddy's legacy is his voice. There will never be another 'voice' like his. His voice is distinct and 'Cristil clear.' Beyond 'the voice' is Daddy's love for his Mississippi State Bulldogs not only in athletics, but also in academics, and most definitely in family and friends. Daddy's love and passion for MSU extends far beyond the playing field and court. Time is my hope and expectation for the future. 'Time' is Daddy's response when asked: 'Do you need anything? Is there anything I can get for you?' His response is always 'time,' so that is my answer, too. I hope Daddy will continue to be a part of the MSU experience and hopefully get to attend a few games and enjoy being on the 'other side' for a change."

There is an obvious but painful question when telling the life story of an 85-year-old man battling kidney disease – the question of the inevitable end of life.

Does Jack Cristil have fears or expectations when he contemplates coming to the end of his life? "Mavis taught me to have my affairs in order, the bank book balanced, and to anticipate problems so as not to be a burden to anyone. Like everyone my age, I'm concerned that a day will come when I can't take care of myself. But for the most part, that's out of my hands. I firmly believe that the Almighty gave each of us a soul. It belongs to Him. How he dispenses with it is up to Him. I don't want to die, but I'm ready if He decides I'm done with the things He put me here on Earth to do."

Cristil looks back over his life with a measure of wonder. His greatest accomplishment? "I got Mavis to marry me." His greatest failure? "I was always too self-centered, too egotistical, and never felt I gave as much as I received." His greatest regret? The answer is at once revealing and illuminating for the boy who grew up resenting a stern, intractable, and mostly absent father: "I regret that I had no real opportunity to get to know my father better. If circumstances had been different, if I had come to know him better, I might have known myself better. I think about that a great deal at this stage of my life."

His favorite interview? Without reservation, Cristil says his most memorable interview was the late entertainer Bob Hope on Oct. 31, 1970. Alabama was hosting MSU at Denny Stadium in Tuscaloosa. Hope was on a tour of college campuses in the wake of the shootings at Kent State University months earlier promoting a more peaceful dialogue, and was to perform later that night on the Alabama campus, unbeknownst to Jack. What Jack did know was that Bear Bryant's charges were in the process of administering a 35-6 beating to Cristil's Bulldogs when one of Alabama's sports information employees whispered in Jack's ear: "Hope is available at halftime if you want him." Cristil replied: "Fella, I need some hope right now."

Finally, what would Jack Cristil say at age 85 if it were possible for him to encounter his boyhood self – the little boy in the north Memphis working class neighborhood during the Great Depression wearing his Chickasaw Buddies cap and bouncing a tennis ball against the steps as he pretended to broadcast a baseball game on a radio station he was creating solely from his imagination?

What would Jack Cristil the man – the man who became a legendary broadcaster on college football's biggest and brightest stage in the SEC – say to the boy whose father's greatest gift to him was a radio that inspired the child's dreams?

Contemplating the question, Jack Cristil smiled, took a drag on his cigarette and exhaled. He was quiet for a time, then said: "I'd tell him to be a banker! The hours are better! No, honestly, I'd tell that boy to do whatever his conscience dictated. I have no qualms about the path I chose. I've had a marvelous life. Who could ask for anything better? My life's been so much better than that little boy I once was ever dreamed it could be. That little boy didn't know there was so much more to life than being a broadcaster. There's family, friends, responsibilities, joys, sorrows, time for laughter, and time for serious thinking. The good, the bad, I wouldn't have missed a minute of it."

For generations of Southeastern Conference sports fans, there will never be another Jack Cristil. He is unique, original, and talented in a way that cannot be imitated. The little boy bouncing the ball on the stoop in Memphis while broadcasting imaginary games willed himself not only to realize his dreams, but to mold those dreams into a historic career in American broadcasting and into iconic status as a goodwill ambassador of Mississippi State University.

Asked about his legacy, Cristil said: "I would like to think my legacy would be that I was a good son to my mother and that I carried out her wishes that I do my best. I think I've done that. I was 100 percent true to my wife and tried to provide the material things that made my family's life easier. I tried to be a counselor to my girls. I wasn't 100 percent successful, but I tried. I tried to help solve problems and ease the pains of my neighbors and friends when I could. I think those are the real things that one should consider when you talk about 'legacies' for anyone."

As to his enduring legacy as a broadcaster – one of the last of the truly great announcers from the Golden Age of radio – Cristil said he knows the legacy he would prefer: "Simple. He told it like it was."

For Mississippi State fans, Cristil's legacy will be far more. Jack's legacy will be the unfailing honesty, integrity, and fairness of his broadcasts. Jack's legacy will also be an irascible sense of humor and a dogged determination to represent the university to the very best of his ability. Perhaps more than anything else, Cristil's legacy is that he was the trusted guide and companion of generations of MSU alumni and friends – and also fans of our bitterest rivals – who knew they could trust him to "cut out the bull" and tell us the score, who had the ball, the time remaining, and to praise excellence from athletes representing both the Bulldogs and their opponents. For those of us who love Mississippi State University, Jack's voice will forever echo across our collective memories of six decades of joys, sorrows, victories, and defeats – and those memories will leave us inextricably wrapped in maroon and white.

As he faces the future, the fervent, singular prayer of the Mississippi State family is that when his days are done, Jack Cristil finds that magical place that he spoke of so often to us over the airwaves all these years with such constant trust, belief, and hope – "the land of milk and honey."

Jack will get there soon enough. After all, he's only three yards away, and he's knocking on the door.

EPILOGUE

SIGNING OFF ON HIS OWN TERMS

"I've been around a long time. I played here, I coached here, I have been involved with the alumni association at Mississippi State University for over 36 years. I can say Jack Cristil is by far the greatest ambassador this university has ever had."

—JOHN CORRERO
MSU RADIO BROADCASTER,
MSU ALUMNI ASSN. EXECUTIVE, AND CLOSE FRIEND

JACK CRISTIL DIED ON SUNDAY, SEPT. 7, 2014, AT SANCTUARY HOSPICE House in Tupelo at the age of 88. The causes of death were complications from kidney disease including congestive heart failure and late stage lung cancer that was diagnosed only weeks before his death.

The final years of Jack Cristil's life were hard for him physically, emotionally, and spiritually. The grueling, unrelenting pain and mind-numbing routine that is kidney dialysis was a constant source of aggravation. Jack's arms ached from the dialysis needles. Fatigue gnawed at his strength, his patience, and his usual good nature.

Jack was never able to achieve a tolerance for being "tethered to a damn machine" and lamented the loss of his freedom and independence. "I can't travel to any extent and I have increasingly less time that I actually feel well as a result of the treatments," said Cristil. "I'm prolonging my life, yes, but the quality of the life I'm lengthening is pretty debatable."

After his retirement and the beginning of dialysis, Jack mentioned often to John Correro, Jim Ellis, Straton Karratossos, Larry Templeton, this writer, and others within his circle of family and close friends that he "didn't know how much longer I'm going to keep doing this (dialysis)."

But Jack's other routines continued in retirement. As long as his health allowed, Jack remained active as a lay leader of the reform congregation of Temple B'nai Israel – his synagogue in Tupelo.

He continued to join the afternoon coffee klatch at Danver's in Tupelo, but the number of participants grew smaller as more of his friends died or became physically unable to attend. Jack, Waurene, and Rhiannon continued to keep company in their familiar haunts like the Estes Fish House in Plantersville.

But Cristil's routine – along with that of much of the city of Tupelo – was broken on the afternoon of April 28, 2014, when an EF-3 tornado slammed the city. Jack's home sustained substantial damage from trees felled by the storm – including roof, exterior, and interior wall damage, and the loss of the tall trees behind the house that Jack and Mavis had planted more than a half-century ago.

Jack was uninjured, but the storm left the home that he and Mavis built forever changed. Neighbors on Marquette Street, friends, and MSU fans looked in on Jack and a number of them brought rakes, chain saws, and other equipment, and volunteered their time to help clean up the broadcaster's yard. Many of them were senior citizens themselves. They did it without being asked. For them, it was a show of respect for a loved one.

But the felled trees were massive and required heavy equipment to be removed. Like many of his neighbors and fellow Tupelo townspeople, Jack's home was without power for several days. He waited his turn for insurance adjusters and for the things he needed to get his home repaired and back to normal.

Friends brought non-perishable food, ice, flashlights, batteries, and survival supplies to Jack, but he wouldn't discuss leaving his home. Others contacted Jack's daughters and tried to get them to prevail on their father to leave the house until repairs could be implemented – but like Jack's friends, Kay and Rebecca were unsuccessful.

"I can't leave," Jack said. "This is my home, these are my possessions. Somebody has to be here when the adjuster comes. I have to go to dialysis, that's the bottom line."

The house was eventually repaired. But the tornado really marked the beginning of Jack's final decline. It's as if the tornado that slammed Jack's beloved Tupelo changed things in a way that Cristil simply couldn't abide. The house on Marquette Street and the neighborhood he cherished had represented stability, sanctuary, and served as the reliable repository of his memories. Now, along with his retirement from broadcasting and the changes that reality brought, even the back yard view was different.

Jack's retirement from broadcasting MSU sports never rocked him as much as many believed that it would. On Sept. 1, 2011, the first football game the Bulldogs played in the post-Cristil era was against the University of Memphis Tigers in Liberty Bowl Stadium. The game was telecast and Jack watched it on TV, but turned the sound off and listened to his old partner Jim Ellis make his first solo broadcast. Mark and Rhonda Keenum sent Jack a tailgate spread for the evening. Jack said he was surprised that MSU's president had given any thought to the retired broadcaster "with all the things he has on his plate." But the gesture obviously pleased him.

Yet when the game began, Jack got quiet and listened intently to the MSU radio broadcast. "I'm so proud of Jim," Jack told the small group gathered in his home that night for the game. "I hope the fans will be as good to Jim as they have been to me." If Jack felt any remorse about not being behind the microphone, he never said a word about it.

Jack continued to follow MSU sports tirelessly in retirement. In his daily routines, people still sought his opinions about Bulldog athletics, and he was constantly confronted with well-meaning fans who told him how much they missed his broadcasts. In reply, Jack would thank them, but say: "Jim Ellis is doing a really marvelous job and I'm listening to him."

The routine continued. Jack endured three dialysis treatments each week from the time of his retirement until just days before his death. There were visits from his daughters and their families, there were occasional visits from MSU friends, there were his phone conversations with his daughters, his surviving sisters Zelda Cristil Esgro and Mimi Cristil Lapides, and close friends. There were small adventures out to the fish house. He attended MSU sporting events through the 2013 football season, including having his name unveiled in the "Ring of Honor" in Davis Wade Stadium and having a banner with his name raised to the rafters of the Humphrey Coliseum alongside those of his friends Babe McCarthy and Bailey Howell.

MSU Athletic Director Scott Stricklin left no stone unturned in keeping Cristil's legacy tied firmly to the school's athletic program. When the Bulldogs win in Davis Wade Stadium, fans still celebrate with Jack's signature "Wrap It in Maroon and White" call being played over the sound system and flashing on the video and ribbon boards.

On Nov. 23, 2013, Jack attended the wedding of Kate Salter
and Nathan Gregory at the First United Methodist Church in
Starkville, sitting with Keenum during the ceremonies. He came to
the reception afterwards at the MSU Hunter Henry Center to give
the bride a hug and to meet the groom, but left shortly after the
reception began. To his father-of-the-bride biographer, Jack said: "I
wouldn't have missed this for the world, but I'm just so tired that
I'm going to have to leave it with you."

Jack's final public appearance in the Humphrey Coliseum came
on Dec. 1, 2013, when he took part in MSU's celebration of the
50th anniversary of the 1963 "Game of Change" as MSU hosted
the Loyola University of Chicago Ramblers to commemorate the
1963 NCAA basketball tournament game the two teams played
in East Lansing, Michigan. The loudest applause of the day came
when Cristil was invited onto the court to take a bow.

But not even Jack's love of Mississippi State could keep him
from the inevitable ravages of kidney disease and the health im-
pacts of decades of smoking. The vaunted Cristil longevity – a gift
from the gene pool of Mollie Kabakoff Cristil – likely gave him
more years than anyone facing his physical challenges could have
expected.

Two weeks to the day before Jack died, I called and asked if he
felt like a visit. Leilani and I left Starkville after church headed to
Tupelo. We stopped and picked up some ridiculously rich and dec-
adent chocolate cupcakes. Back to his childhood in Memphis, Jack
always enjoyed "something gooey and chocolate" as he'd shared
years ago with fellow broadcaster Joe Phillips.

When we arrived at the house on Marquette Street, Jack's appearance was distressing. His skin had yellowed, his breathing
was labored and his pain was obvious on his face. Jack's eyes were
bloodshot and swollen. We sat down together at the kitchen table

where we'd worked together to produce Jack's biography. In the process, we had become friends and our families had bonded. Leilani unwrapped the cupcakes and we exchanged pleasantries and caught up with news of our respective families.

As we ate, I dreaded the conversation that I knew was about to transpire. Jack's daughters, Kay Cristil Clouatre and Rebecca Cristil Nelson, had told me that time was short and why. We had talked regularly the last few weeks, and they had shared Jack's recent diagnosis of lung cancer.

Jack lit a cigarette and said in a calm, strong voice: "I've got lung cancer. They want me to try radiation treatments and I guess maybe I'll do that. But I'll tell you this – if I try it and don't think it's worth it, I'm simply going to stop taking dialysis and be done with it. They tell me that within a few days of stopping dialysis, there's renal failure and that's it.

"Sid, I'm tired. I'm just worn out. And as I've told you before, there are a lot of things worse than death. I'm not afraid of death. But I really don't want to be a burden to my family and my friends and that's about where we've come to. I don't want to be remembered like this. So let's just say our goodbyes and you head on back down to the campus."

Leilani embraced Jack for a long time and then walked toward the door. When the time came for me to tell him goodbye for what I knew would be the last time, I could hardly speak. Jack turned to go back to his old tan recliner and said over his shoulder: "Give Kate a hug for me."

I walked out onto the carport and eased the storm door closed. I didn't dare look back. Joining Leilani in the car, we drove south in silence for a long time.

Jack faced his final days with the support of his family and neighbors. Rebecca and Andy Nelson had moved back to Tupelo from Augusta, Georgia, in July 2014. Kay Clouatre had retired after a long teaching career in Denham Springs, Louisiana.

Kay remembered the last six months as a period of almost constant decline.

"He just didn't feel well. He lost weight, his appetite, his interest in conversation, his zest for life. He was a man who was in pain, yet he didn't want to burden anyone," Kay said. "He never asked me to come to Tupelo. He never asked Rebecca or Andy for any help. He was stubborn and proud.

"I don't know if he was scared because I didn't ask. I listened when he called. I answered questions when he asked," she said. "He had been saying for years 'the clock was ticking' and he was in the fourth quarter. But this time, he knew. I could hear it in his voice.

"I saw the look on his face when we talked at the kitchen table. I knew that no matter what God's plan was, Daddy was not going to linger. He had already made up his mind that when it was over, it was over," said Kay.

Kay's sister, Rebecca, agreed: "I saw Daddy becoming more realistic that the end was close. I really think the tornado took his emotional will away. The cumulative loss of his neighbors to death or to them moving into nursing homes took a toll. Daddy loved his Marquette Street neighbors."

Rebecca said that after his cancer diagnosis, Jack still had some fight left in him.

"When he was diagnosed with cancer, Daddy decided he wanted to try the radiation, but he died the day before radiation treatments were to begin," Rebecca said. "After several years of constant pain, I think he had some fear about stopping dialysis. He wanted to know what it was like and whether he would be in pain. Malinda Ingram, one of my childhood friends from the neighborhood, was a nurse practitioner and she came to see him to try to answer those questions. Daddy talked to Malinda and asked questions in the manner that someone would use if they were about to buy a new lawn mower."

On Sept. 2, Jack's remaining kidney essentially stopped functioning. That hard reality threw his congestive heart failure into overdrive and weakened an already very tired elderly man.

Malinda Ingram told Jack he'd "last about a week" if he ceased his dialysis treatments.

Jack's son-in-law, Andrew Nelson, was present for that discussion on Friday, Sept. 5.

"Jack was ready to talk about it," said Nelson. "He wanted to know the truth. Would it hurt? Malinda gave him the respect of honesty. She didn't sugar coat what she had to say. I could see a change in Jack. He went from the Jack who was tough and could take it to the Jack who was in a lot of pain and didn't really know what to do."

Later that evening, Jack fell in his bedroom. The fall was hard enough that it broke the sheetrock wall.

On Saturday, Sept. 6, Rebecca, Andy, and daughter Lindsey were preparing to go to Starkville for the MSU-University of Alabama-Birmingham football game at Davis Wade Stadium. Rebecca got a call from Jack, who said: "Well, I fell again last night."

Cristil told his family to go ahead to the game, but when they pressed he said they could "swing by if you want to." Rebecca asked if he wanted to go home with them, but her father declined. "I just don't want to go anywhere," Jack said.

Andy said he "could tell Jack was in pain. He never could get comfortable in the recliner. We decided not to go to Starkville. We watched the first half of the UAB game, then brought home take out for lunch. But Jack said he needed to go lie down. I could hear him in there, he was obviously in pain. He could not get comfortable in bed, either."

It was Andy who decided that regardless his father-in-law's protestations to the contrary, it was time for Jack to go to the hospital and he called the ambulance. When two female EMTs arrived, Andy laughed that his father-in-law "turned on the charm."

But Jack obviously knew that his time was short. When the EMTs got him on the gurney and were rolling him out to the waiting ambulance, Rebecca said he threw up his left arm, waved, and said loudly: "Goodbye, House!"

During the ambulance ride, Andrew Nelson said his father-in-law was reciting orders to make sure the lawn man and housekeeper were paid, and other business and personal obligations met. To the last moment, Jack intended for his affairs to be in order – a lifetime trait.

When they arrived at Northeast Mississippi Medical Center in Tupelo, doctors found a bruised and battered man in his late eighties suffering from lung cancer, congestive heart failure, a recent fall, and kidney disease. They offered little hope. But they stabilized Jack and eventually were able to help him manage his pain after a difficult night. Several times on Saturday night, Jack would drift in and out of sleep and asked the score of the SEC football games.

"I was amused that even in that pain and with the meds, Daddy knew the opponents and the location of all the SEC games being played," said Rebecca. "It was also a great comfort to me that he never lost his voice. As long as he had any consciousness, his voice still filled the room and was strong."

On Sunday, Sept. 7, the decision was made to move Cristil across town to Sanctuary Hospice House in Tupelo. Kay remembered: "Daddy was in the hospital a few hours, then we took him to hospice. As soon as we got him to hospice, the nurses got him settled while we completed the paper work. Rebecca and I left for about an hour and returned to find Daddy resting comfortably. I took his hand and told him we all would be just fine and he could cross over, see the light, go find Mama . . . do whatever you need to do."

Rebecca recalled: "When the EMTs were moving him from the hospital to hospice, one of the hospital nurses told Daddy they hoped he would feel better. Daddy said: 'Lady, where I'm going you don't feel better!' That was kind of Daddy's last moments to be the Jack that the public knew."

After only a few hours in the care of Sanctuary Hospice House, Jack Cristil died peacefully in his sleep on the night of Sunday, Sept. 7, 2014.

Andy Nelson called to let me know that Jack had passed away. On Twitter, I shared the news with the Bulldog Nation in a 10:49 p.m. tweet: "My friend Jack Cristil passed away peacefully in Tupelo tonight. Funeral arrangements are incomplete. . . ."

Fans across Mississippi reacted – and not just MSU fans, either. The entire state was moved. Jack Cristil dominated the front pages of the state's newspapers and was the lead story on TV stations across the state as well. ESPN noted Jack's passing during their *Sports Center* program and fellow broadcasters all over the country paid tribute to him.

But on that Sunday night, Cristil's most poignant mourner was his young granddaughter, Lindsey Newhall, who was experiencing the real grief of a loved one's passing as she cried for her PawPaw. Grandson Jake Clouatre, a college senior at Northwestern State University in Louisiana, felt the sting of the loss of his famous grandfather, too.

Kay said her father's death was in no way shocking or surprising: "When I got the call from Rebecca that Andy had called the

ambulance to take Daddy to the hospital, I just knew. I had prepared myself for this day for 26 years. I don't think anyone is ever
really ready to say goodbye, but I just wanted Daddy to be comfortable and not in pain. Rebecca, Andy, and I had discussed that
many times. Our goal was to adhere to all of Daddy's wishes and
make certain he was not in pain."

Mississippi State University released Cristil's formal obituary
shortly after he died: *STARKVILLE, Miss.-Jacob Sanford "Jack" Cristil,
the beloved former sports broadcaster of six decades of Mississippi State
University athletics, died Sunday [Sept. 7] at the age of 88 at Sanctuary
Hospice House in Tupelo of complications from kidney disease and cancer
after an extended illness. Cristil, who served MSU from 1953 to 2011, was
known throughout the South as "the Voice of the Bulldogs."*

*"As a lifelong Bulldog, my heart is heavy at learning of the passing
of legendary MSU broadcaster Jack Cristil," said MSU President Mark
E. Keenum. "Jack's deep love of this university was always evident in
his words and in his deeds. He was a tireless ambassador for Mississippi
State and he brought great honor and distinction to our university as one
of the most revered radio announcers in American history. I join every
member of the Bulldog family in extending our sincere respects and deepest sympathies to his daughters, Kay and Rebecca, and to his grandchildren, Jake and Lindsey. Surely, Jack's remarkable life and work is now
forever wrapped in Maroon and White."*

*With a 58-year association with MSU, Cristil was the second-longest
tenured college radio play-by-play announcer in the nation at the time of
his 2011 retirement due to health problems.*

*During his legendary career as the voice of the Bulldogs, Cristil called
636 football games since 1953, or roughly 60 percent of every football
game played in the history of the institution. He was in his 54th season
as the men's basketball play-by-play voice, having described the action of
almost 55 percent of all the men's basketball games played at the school.*

In all, Cristil delivered game descriptions to Mississippi State fans across the Magnolia State and around the world for more than 1,500 collegiate contests.

"Jack Cristil connected with generations of Bulldog fans and remains an icon for all who love the Maroon and White," MSU Director of Athletics Scott Stricklin said. "No school's broadcaster was as synonymous with their institution as Jack Cristil was with Mississippi State. Jack's passing leaves a large void, but I think all Mississippians appreciated his dedication and talent, and Jack will always be the Voice of the Bulldogs."

After his retirement, Cristil lent his time to the production of a biography called "Jack Cristil: Voice of the MSU Bulldogs." The book, written by MSU journalist in residence Sid Salter with a foreword by author and MSU alumnus John Grisham, sold 10,500 copies and raised over $170,000 for the Jacob S. "Jack" Cristil Scholarship in Journalism at MSU.

Earlier, Jack and Mavis Cristil had established a need-based scholarship in their name to benefit Lee County students at MSU with academic talent who needed help with tuition, books and fees.

"Jack Cristil was a courageous, tenacious man possessed of a great love for Mississippi State University," said MSU Chief Communications Officer and Cristil's biographer Sid Salter. "His tired body finally failed Jack, but his keen mind and that great staccato baritone voice never failed him. I count his friendship as a tremendous gift to me and to my family. We all loved him."

It was in August 1953 that Cristil sent audition tapes to then-Mississippi State Director of Athletics C.R. "Dudy" Noble, and just one month later the association between Cristil and the university began. His announcing career began with a 34-6 win over then-Memphis State in his Tennessee birthplace Sept. 19, 1953. Appropriately, his last football game was State's 52-14 win against Michigan at the Gator Bowl in Jacksonville, Fla., in Jan. 2011.

Cristil's first basketball season was 1957-58, the third of legendary

*head coach Babe McCarthy's tenure. Like football, his first men's bas-
ketball game was an 80-56 win at Union, in Jackson, Tenn., the city in
which he launched his broadcasting career 10 years earlier. His final basketball call came on Feb. 26, 2011, at the University of Tennessee in Knoxville – a game that was a 70-69 win for the Bulldogs.*

*A winner of numerous broadcasting laurels during his career, Cristil
was most recently presented the Lindsey Nelson Award, given annually
to the nation's premier sports broadcaster. He was honored with the pres-
tigious College Football Foundation Chris Schenkel Award in 1997 for
excellence in college sports broadcasting. Nelson and Schenkel were longtime national award-winning broadcasters. In 1992, Cristil received the
Ronald Reagan Lifetime Achievement Award from the National Association of Sportscasters and Sportswriters. That same year, he was also the
first non-coach/non-athlete to ever be inducted into the Mississippi Sports
Hall of Fame. Cristil was inducted into the Mississippi State Sports Hall
of Fame in 2003.*

*A winner of the Mississippi Sportscaster of the Year Award a record
21 times, Cristil was named the Southeastern Conference's Broadcaster of
the Year in 1988.*

*During his early years working at Mississippi State, Cristil served in
advertising sales at WELO Radio and later WTVA-TV in Tupelo, where
he has resided since 1955.*

*Cristil was a veteran of World War II, serving as an aircraft engine
mechanic in the U.S. Army Air Corps.*

*Prior to coming to Mississippi State, Cristil broke into the profession as
a minor league baseball broadcaster, working in Jackson, Tennessee; Anniston, Alabama; Clarksdale, Mississippi; and Memphis. He also broadcast countless high school and junior college games through the years.*

*From 1947-48, Cristil studied broadcast journalism at the University
of Minnesota before returning home to Memphis and eventually launch-
ing his professional career.*

Born in Memphis in 1925, Cristil is survived by daughters Kay Cristil
Clouatre of Baton Rouge, Louisiana, and Rebecca Cristil Nelson (An-
drew) of Tupelo and grandchildren Jake Clouatre of Baton Rouge and
Lindsey Newhall of Tupelo. He is also survived by two sisters, Zelda Cris-
til Esgro of St. Louis, Missouri, and Miriam "Mimi" Cristil Lapides of
West Palm Beach, Florida, and a number of nieces and nephews.

Cristil was preceded in death by his wife of 33 years, Mavis Kelly Cris-
til, in 1988. He was also preceded in death by his parents, Mollie Kabakoff Cristil and Benjamin Herman Cristil of Memphis; by a sister, Charlotte Cristil Hiller; and by brothers Harold Cristil and Stanley Cristil.

Jack's Sept. 10 funeral would be directed by State Rep. Steve
Holland, D-Plantersville, the proprietor with his family of Holland
Funeral Directors in Tupelo – a beautiful facility that had been
converted into a tasteful 20,000 sq. ft. funeral home from its previous existence as what Rep. Holland said had formerly been "the
largest honky tonk in the city limits of Tupelo."

Holland turned his funeral home into a virtual Mississippi State
University shrine, bringing items from home and borrowing other
items. He covered the cross in the stained glass window in the chapel with a cloth with a Star of David on it for Jack's services.

Mourners filed past an open casket in which the broadcaster
was displayed wearing his tan embroidered *yarmulke*, a gray blazer,
and maroon tie, and holding two very familiar talismans – a microphone in his left hand and a cigarette in his right.

Sister Zelda Cristil Esgro, 92, of St. Louis, Missouri was unable
to attend her brother's funeral because of her husband Sam's ill
health, but sister Miriam "Mimi" Cristil Lapides, 89, of West Palm
Beach, Florida was able to come.

The funeral began with the traditional procession into the
chapel, but the casket was followed by Larry Templeton leading
MSU's canine mascot Bully on a leash. Templeton delivered the

eulogy at the services, but Bully curled up near the casket when the services began and never moved and made not a sound. The dog's loyalty and reverent behavior was at once comforting and devastating. Even Bully knew that things were forever changed in Starkville.

Templeton was eloquent in his remarks: "There are heroes and there are legends. Heroes at Mississippi State University we remember by the hundreds, but our legend will always be our friend who told us to 'Wrap It in Maroon and White.'"

MSU President Mark E. Keenum spoke for the university as one who had not only grown up listening to Jack call MSU games, but who had played in north Mississippi high school games that Cristil called. Keenum said: "His passion for his Bulldogs was never far from the surface, and his intensity came through to those of us who clung to every colorful turn of phrase. That wonderful baritone voice – gruff, perhaps, but musical to all who knew it so well."

Temple B'Nai Israel lay leader Marc Perler spoke to local friends and the Jewish community when he said: "I, along with his close friends and his family, know also the private Jack. This Jack Cristil is somewhat quieter, often very witty, sometimes quite grumpy. Yet, a caring man intensely devoted both to his family and to his Jewish faith."

The funeral service was brief, only about a half-hour long – as Cristil had planned it. Interment followed the service at Lee Memorial Park in Verona, six miles south of Tupelo. There, Jack was reunited with his beloved Mavis. Holland had one more touch in store for Cristil's family and friends. The burial vault was painted maroon and white – meaning that the broadcaster's body would be eternally "Wrapped in Maroon and White."

Kay Clouatre said of her father's funeral: "Daddy had planned

his funeral since the day Mama died. He kept a running list of pall
bearers and throughout the years, he would draw a line through
the ones who passed away and write in a new name. This continued until a few days before he passed away. Daddy told Rebecca
the final names of the ones who would be his pallbearers. We followed his wishes.

"Daddy was not an extravagant person. He didn't care for pomp
and circumstance. He liked to keep things simple. When we sat
down to discuss the funeral with Steve Holland, we planned everything as Daddy wanted: simple. We incorporated the roots of his
Jewish faith along with his deep-rooted love for Mississippi State
in the service. Larry Templeton and Bully's processional down the
aisle touched my heart more than I can ever express. That was the
icing on the cake as far as funeral services go. You can't get more
Mississippi State than that. I know Daddy was smiling. The out-
pouring of friends, family, and fans who took time from work to
attend the visitation and/or the funeral were amazing. We can't
thank everyone enough for all their love and support during that
emotional time."

A day later, on Sept. 11 in MSU's Humphrey Coliseum, a memorial service was held in Jack's honor. Cristil's broadcast booth was
illuminated with a spotlight and decorated with a floral wreath and
black banner with the word "JACK" on it. Another spotlight focused on Jack's banner hanging in the rafters. The Cristil memorial
service marked the first time the new center court message boards
in the Humphrey Coliseum were used, creating an impressive yet
intimate backdrop for the service.

Participating in the celebration of Jack's life and work were:
Keenum, MSU Athletic Director Scott Stricklin, MSU Head Baseball Coach John Cohen, MSU broadcaster Jim Ellis, former MSU
head basketball coach and player Kermit Davis Sr., MSU Football

Director of Player Personnel and former head football coach and player Rockey Felker, MSU Chief Communications Officer Sid Salter, former MSU basketball player and Starkville High School Head Basketball Coach Greg Carter, Larry Templeton, and Jack's daughters, Kay Cristil Clouatre and Rebecca Cristil Nelson.

Carter said: "I'll forever be indebted to Mr. Cristil; he made those basketball games come alive for my grandfather, and now, he's gotten to meet him. Many other MSU fans have gotten to meet him now that he's gone from us, and he's wrapping it up one more time in maroon and white."

Davis observed that "I don't believe we've ever had another person at Mississippi State who was loved and appreciated like Jack Cristil. He was a guy that I respected as much as any person I've ever met at Mississippi State University, and he was good; he was a tremendous person."

Felker pointed out what many felt was the undisputed truth for longtime MSU fans: "Think about all the good games and the bad games that we're all familiar with, but Jack didn't have bad games."

Kay addressed the memorial service crowd, responding on behalf of her family: "It has been a whirlwind the past few days, but I cannot tell you how much Mississippi State has meant to us as a family. My home is not just in Tupelo: it will always be at Mississippi State University." After the memorial service - which was concluded by MSU Professor Michael Brown's haunting solo trumpet rendition of the Frank Sinatra standard "My Way" – Rebecca said: "We were in a daze, a guy came out of the stands. He told me about how he and his dad would be out on the tractor working and they would listen to Daddy's broadcast together. He was listening to my daddy with his daddy. What joy in those memories for him and for me! The fact that he bothered to come tell me the story, I just couldn't express what it meant. It was a big moment for me. I hope when others pass away that I can comfort someone that much."

Andy Nelson was moved by a tableau he witnessed at the funeral home visitation. "This guy came in wearing slacks and a plaid shirt. None of us knew him, family or friends. He is just pitifully upset, I mean gone to pieces. He tried to speak to us, but couldn't find the words. He walked over to the casket, looked at Jack, and just rushed out. He was a State fan. Just a fan. And he was distraught. It's really rare to see that kind of reaction and it speaks to the connection people felt with Jack."

There was one final formal salute to Jack Cristil and it came as MSU took the field to begin in earnest a football run for the ages, one never witnessed by the beloved broadcaster. Going into the MSU game against Texas A&M on Oct. 4 at Davis Wade Stadium, the Bulldogs were 4-0 and coming off an open date after upsetting the Louisiana State University Bayou Bengals in "Death Valley" on national television by a score of 34-29. Most of LSU's points came after the game had been decided and MSU dominated both sides of the line of scrimmage.

The university planned to honor Jack in the pregame ceremonies. The MSU Famous Maroon Band spelled out J-A-C-K prior to the usual "State" spellout. A special video presentation honoring Cristil's life and work was played to a sellout afternoon crowd that was on their feet. Kay, Rebecca, Andrew, Jake, and Lindsey were escorted onto the field by President Keenum, Scott Stricklin, and Sid Salter for a presentation of a framed portrait of Jack to each of his daughters. The Bulldogs wore helmet stickers in Jack's honor that had been worn in each game since his death.

As the on-field recognition of Cristil reached a crescendo, four vintage aircraft approached the stadium in formation before one peeled off in the "missing man" formation. The fans, already loud and at a fever pitch, caught another gear and the din of ringing cowbells and applause was deafening.

"What I remember vividly is that everyone stood up," said Rebecca. "I remember thinking that they really liked Daddy. It's like everything in the Davis Wade Stadium world stopped and it was all about Daddy."

"I wasn't surprised, it was emotional. The missing man, the fact that those pilots volunteered to do this and honor him. Breathtaking. But this wasn't my first time on the field. I was with Daddy when he was honored on his 20th year and again on his 50th year. It really made me miss him. It filled the void to have Lindsey, Jake, and Andy with me and Kay."

For Kay, the flyover in front of 61,113 Bulldog fans was mesmerizing. "What a wonderful tribute to Daddy! The missing man formation is something I have seen many times, but I did not know it had a name or what it meant until it was explained to me before the presentation on the field. I anticipated that moment from the time we stepped on the field. What a tribute to Daddy! He loved this country. I had tears in my eyes when the plane flew out of formation. I missed him so much, yet I felt his presence . . . such a surreal moment."

Months after Jack's death, the 2015 Mississippi Legislature unanimously passed Senate Concurrent Resolution 511 honoring Jack's life and work. The resolution's title: "A Concurrent Resolution Paying Tribute to Former 'Voice of the Mississippi State Bulldogs'" Jack Cristil and Extending the Condolences of the Mississippi Legislature to His Surviving Family."

Kay and Rebecca, along with Andrew and the grandchildren, were left with their memories for a time. They faced going through their father's memorabilia and the normal estate handling matters.

But after a time, they realized that Jack Cristil's shadow was long and strong and that Mississippi State people still held tightly to his famous phrase: "Wrap It in Maroon and White!"

The family formed wrapitinmaroonandwhite.com as a means of continuing Jack's philanthropic interests and protecting his name and image.

Andrew Nelson said: "Jack's philanthropies, the organizations he's given to, we would like to continue Jack and Mavis's giving. They gave to their community. They gave to their faith. I thought it was important to continue that in some form.

"Trademarking the 'Wrap It in Maroon and White' phrase and protecting Jack's name and likeness in a way that helps his family continue to help students is a good thing," said Nelson. "Kay, Rebecca and I are north Mississippi natives and we believe in giving back to the community as well. So we see this as something that Jack would embrace."

That assumption is likely spot on, given a discovery Jack's family made while cleaning out his old radio station WELO briefcase. Taped to the briefcase was this quote: "No man has a right to live in a community, take unto himself all of the good things of life - social advantages for his family, educational opportunities for his children - without GIVING SOMETHING of his own . . . time, talent, and energy . . . to benefit the common good."

Jack Cristil lived that philosophy. He was the ultimate self-starter, a man for whom "good enough" never really was. There will never be another Jack Cristil. He was unique, original in a way that cannot be imitated. As to his enduring legacy as a broadcaster, as one of the last truly great broadcasters, it's simple – Jack Cristil told it like it was.

For Bulldogs of a certain age, there will always be something missing on game days. But most State fans take great solace in the fact that our Jack finally found that magical place that he spoke of so often to us over the airwaves all these years with such constant trust, belief, and hope – "the land of milk and honey."

Doubt that? A week after MSU honored the late Jack Cristil prior to a 48-31 thumping of Texas A&M, the Bulldogs manhandled No. 2 Auburn 38-23 – which propelled MSU to the first No. 1 national ranking in school history. MSU maintained that No. 1 ranking for five straight weeks. The 2014 MSU Bulldogs finished the regular season 10-2 and earned a trip to the Orange Bowl in Miami for the first time since 1941.

All of that football magic in the wake of the loss of MSU's most beloved figure just weeks before. Coincidence? Maybe. Whatever one thinks, you have to admit that Jack Cristil had a heavenly seat for the greatest season in Bulldog football history – a seat he earned over 58 years of excellence in broadcasting and excellence in life.

Shalom, Jack. *"The Lord bless thee, and keep thee. The Lord make his face to shine upon thee, and be gracious unto thee. The Lord lift up his countenance upon thee, and give thee peace."* Numbers 6:24-26.

SELECTED BIBLIOGRAPHY

Abrams, Jeanne. "Jewish Consumptive's Relieve Society." Creatingcommunities.denverli-
brary.org. Creating Communities, n.d. Web. 15 June 2011.

Albright, David. "Cristil's wrapped it in maroon and white since 1953." ESPN.com. 12
October 2007. Web. 21 July 2011.

Alford, Parrish. "The voice: Still strong."_The Northeast Mississippi Daily Journal. 25 October 2001. Print. C1.

Antonik, John. "Unique Game." MSNsportsNET, 22 June 2005. Web. 18 July 2011.

Barner, William G. The Egg Bowl: Mississippi State vs. Ole Miss. Jackson: UP of Mississippi,
2007. Print.

Bosen, Christopher R.C. "Cristil ready for new memories." The Northeast Mississippi Daily
Journal, 5 December 1998. Print. A1.

Brandt, David. "Legendary Voice Of The Bulldogs Cristil To Conclude Career Saturday."
myFOXmemphis.com. myFOX Memphis, n.d. 24 Feb. 2011. Web. 7 March 2011.

Branston, John. "Just the call...that's all: Broadcasting 32 years of SEC football." The Commercial Appeal, 19 Aug. 1984: 12-14. Print.

Brumfield, Patsy. "Keenum era official at MSU." The Northeast Mississippi Daily Journal, 17
October, 2009.

Carter, Sam T. (Bo). Letter to Jack Cristil. 24 February 2011.

Carter, Sam T. (Bo). Letter to Sid Salter. 11 July 2011.

Clouatre, Kay Cristil. Personal interviews with Sid Salter, 22-25 June 2011.

Cleveland, Rick. "It's a wrap for Mr. Maroon and White." clarionledger.com The Clarion-
Ledger, n.d. 26 Feb. 2011. Web. 25 March 2011.

Cleveland, Rick. "Storm disrupts MSU-Alabama game." The Clarion-Ledger, 15 March
2008.

Cristil, Jack. Interview with Roy H. Ruby. 12 Aug. 2008.

Cristil, Jack. Personal interviews with Sid Salter. March-August 2011.

Corder, Charles. "Cristil's career on radio spans many landmarks." The Clarion-Ledger, 30
March 1996.

Dunn, Lori. "Peers vote Cristil as SEC's best broadcaster." The Columbus (Ga.) Ledger-
Enquirer, 24 August 1988.

Ellis, Steve. "Wrap this one in maroon and white." Mississippi State Alumnus, Spring 1992:
25-28. Print.

Ellis, Steve. Personal interview with Sid Salter. 19 August 2011.

Esgro, Zelda Cristil. Personal interview with Sid Salter 19 June 2011.

Everett, Tommy. Letter to MSU Alumni. 26 January 1973.

Ferris, Marcie Cohen. "A Biblical People in the Bible Belt: The Jewish Community of Memphis, Tennessee, 1840s-1960s." *American Jewish History*, Dec. 1999. Web. 16 June 2011.

Forde, Pat. "Sherrill played the rivalry game perfectly." ESPN.com, 8 October 2004. Web. 21 July 2011.

Harper, Phyllis. "Cristil cited for promoting religious understanding." *The Tupelo Daily Journal*, 3 October 1983. Print.

Hayden, Mark. "Jack Cristil - The Voice Behind the Mississippi Bulldogs." *Jewish Scene*, Dec. 2007: 22. Print.

Higgins, Ron. "Cristil reaches 50th year as voice of Mississippi St." *The Commercial Appeal*, 1 Nov. 2002. Print.

Higgins, Ron. "Close ties to MSU keep Felker bound." *The Commercial Appeal*, 23 Nov. 2007. Web. 20 July 2011.

Higgins, Ron. "Voice of the Bulldogs Cristil clear." *The Commercial Appeal*, 7 October 1994.

Hiller, Roy. Personal interview with Sid Salter. 18 July 2011.

Hood, Orley. "Big Stan was a man for all seasons." *The Clarion Ledger*, 2 July 2006. Web. 25 March 2011.

Hood, Orley. "Poetic justice – Jack Cristil wins 1st Reagan Award." *The Clarion-Ledger*, 30 April, 1992.

Higgins, Ron. "Ward, Cristil keep mike hot." *The Commercial Appeal*, 4 November 1994: D1-D3. Print.

Horn, Barry. "Seasoned Voices." *The Dallas Morning News*, 15 Dec. 2000: B1-B15. Print.

Hunt, Rebecca. "Dr. Charles David Spivak: A Jewish Immigrant and the American Tuberculosis Movement." Rev. of *Dr. Charles David Spivak: A Jewish Immigrant and the American Tuberculosis Movement* by Jeanne Abrams. coloradowest.auraria.edu Center for Colorado & the West at Auraria Library, n.d. 5 Oct. 2010. Web. 16 June 2011.

Jones, Paul. "Jack Cristil." *Mississippi Sports Magazine* Sept./Oct. 2008: 28-32. Print.

Kelly, Todd. "It's Cristil clear: Only 1 voice can call State games." *The Clarion-Ledger*, 2 September 2001. Web. 28 March 2011.

Kelly, Todd. "State honors 'Voice of Dogs.'" *The Clarion-Ledger*, 3 November 2002. Print. D5.

Kieffer, Chris. "Cristil addresses THS students." *The Northeast Mississippi Daily Journal*, 27 August 2010.

Knobler, Mike. "Radio royalty: MSU's Rock of Gibraltar is pure Cristil." *The Clarion Ledger*, 5 April 1992: 1C-3D. Print.

Lapides, Miriam "Mimi" Cristil. Personal interview with Sid Salter. 14 June 2011.

Liddell, Larry. " 'Voice of the Bulldogs' Jack Cristil entertains large crowd of local alums and fans." The Clarksdale Press-Register, 26 August 1998.

Locke, Brad. "Ellis to replace Cristil in football, basketball." *The Northeast Mississippi Daily Journal*, 30 March 2011. Print. B3.

Lopresti, Mike. "Their voices make fall Saturdays come alive." *USA Today*, 19 October 1994: 12C. Print.

Marcello, Brandon. "In his words: Cristil signs off from Humphrey Coliseum." clarion-ledger.com *The Clarion-Ledger*, n.d. 23 Feb. 2011. Web. 28 March 2011.

McDavid, Sammy. " 'Voice' Cristil, Dean Ruby have key parts in MSU Dec. graduation." 22 November, 2002. Mississippi State University, Office of University Relations. Print.

Mikaberidze, Alexander. *The Battle of Berezina: Napoleon's Great Escape*. Barnsley, UK: Pen & Sword Military, 2010. Print.

Mississippi State History: *MSU Men's Basketball Media Guide 2010-2011*. Mississippi State University. Print.

Mississippi State History: *MSU Men's Football Media Guide 2011*. Mississippi State University. Print.

Mitchell, Charlie. "Jack Cristil's 'outcues' can thrill the fans." *The Clarion-Ledger*, 17 November 2002. Print. G3.

Mize, Buzzy. Letter to MSU official. August 1990.

Mord, Russell. "Cristil doing exactly what he always wanted to." *Starkville Daily News*, 18 April 1997.

Morgan, Ruth. "Remember WSSO Radio and 'Turntable Spin': the favorite 50s-60s hangout." *Starkville Daily News*, 20 February 2011.

Morris, Marty. "MSU honors its 'voice.'" *Starkville Daily News*, 17 October 1983. B1.

Mule, Marty. "Cristil's 'no-frills' style has stood the test of time." *The Times-Picayune*, 20 October 2000.1D.

Multiple entries. *Ancestry.com*, 2011. Web. 26 May 2011.

Murray, David. "THE VOICE...in His Own Words." *Dawgs' Bite*. 9 November 2002. Print.

Nelson, Rebecca Cristil. Personal interviews with Sid Salter. 22-26 June 2011.

Nelson, Rebecca Cristil. Personal interview with Sid Salter. 11 July 2011.

Noble, Pick. "The voice of the Bulldogs: Jack Cristil." *The Reflector*. 15 October 1965. A13. Print.

Nunnery, Nash. "Rube." *Mississippi Sports Magazine* September 2009: 40-42. Print.

Pepper, Bobby. "Change in the airwaves." *The Northeast Mississippi Daily Journal*, 23 October 1996: 1E-10E. Print.

Phelps, Gene. "OPINION: Frank Dowsing - His was a life that touched many others." *The Northeast Mississippi Daily Journal*, 22 October 2009. Web. 18 July 2011.

Pride, Vincent. "It's Cristil clear he's Mr. Bulldog." *The Clarksdale Press-Register*. 24 February 1996.

Pruett, John. "Jack Cristil: Crystal clear for Mississippi State." *The Huntsville Times*, 10 August 1998: D1-D2. Print.

Pruett, John. "Radio still a joyful part of football." *The Huntsville Times*, 21 August 1996: D1-D2. Print.

Rappaport, Ian R. "MSU radio voice Cristil silenced by pneumonia." clarionledger.com *The Clarion Ledger*, n.d. 17 March 2005. Web. 25 March 2011.

Rawl, Jon. "The Voices of Southern Glory." *Y'all: The Magazine of Southern People*, Sept. 2007: 21-26. Print.

Reikes Fox, Vickie, and Bill Aron. *Shalom Y'all: Images of Jewish Life in the American South*. Chapel Hill, NC: Algonquin Books of Chapel Hill, 2002. Print.

Reno, Jimmy. "The Top 10 College Football Radio Announcers of All-Time." bleacherreport.com *Bleacher Report*, n.d. 14 Aug. 2009. Web. 21 March 2011.

Rockoff, Stuart. "Jews in Mississippi." mshistory.k12.ms.us Mississippi History Now, n.d. Nov. 2006. Web. 18 May 2011.

Rubenstein, Michael. Personal interview with Sid Salter. 4 March 2011.

Slater, Grant. "Belarus helping to restore cemeteries." jta.org *JTA: Jewish & Israel News,* n.d. 3 June 2008. Web. 7 June 2011.

Smith, Danny C. "Golden anniversary: Cristil honored by MSU for 50 years behind mike." *The Commercial Dispatch.* 29 October 2011. Print. B1.

Sorrels, William W. *The Maroon Bulldogs: Mississippi State Football.* Huntsville, AL: The Strode Publishers, 1975. Print.

State of Colorado. Dept. of Public Health and Environment. *Locations of Historical TB Sanatoriums in Colorado and Possible Relationships with the Current Distribution of Asthma Cases: Draft report, September 2004.* Comp. Ingrid Asmus, LeeAnn Wilkins, Mark Egbert. Print.

Stukenborg, Phil. "Cristil to celebrate 40th year as Bulldog voice." *The Commercial Appeal,* 4 September 1992: D3. Print.

Stockstill, E.H. "MSU radio man still Cristil clear after 40 years." *The Sun-Herald.* 27 December 1996. Print. B1.

Swinhart, Earl. "The North American AT-6 Texan." aviation-history.com The Aviation History Online Museum, n.d. Web. 7 July 2011.

Talbert, Mike. "Jack's voice isn't Cristil clear, but his story-telling is." *The Northeast Mississippi Daily Journal,* 6 April 1992: 1B-3B. Print.

Talbert, Mike. "Jack makes it Cristil clear: Class is first." *The Northeast Mississippi Daily Journal,* 26 April 1990. Print.

Thomas, John C. "Forty Years Ago Today." ramblermania.com, Ramblermania.com, n.d. 15 March 2003. Web. 1 August 2011.

Tingwald, Scott. "Keynote speaker, award recipient announced for Hall of Fame Enshrinement Banquet." 5 August 1997. College Football Hall of Farm. Print.

Vaughan, Andrew. "This Day in Music Spotlight: Elvis Sells for $35,000." gibson.com Gibson, n.d. 21 November 2010. Web. 14 June 2011.

Veazey, Kyle. "Storm disrupts MSU-Alabama game." *The Clarion-Ledger,* 15 March 2008.

Vincent, Fay. "Fay Vincent: Baritone of longtime announcer at former Dodgertown will be missed." *TCPalm,* 4 July 2011. Web. 5 July 2011.

Walsh, Christopher J. *Where Football is King: A History of the SEC.* Lanham, MD: Taylor Trade Publishing, 2006.

Yanushewskaya, Anastasiya. "News Article: National Tourism Agency to Offer Minsk Ghetto Excursion." belarus-misc.org, A Belarus Miscellany, n.d. 3 March 2008. Web. 7 June 2010.

"1955 Sun RCA Deal." elvispresleymuseum.com. Elvis Presley Museum, n.d. Web. 14 June 2011.

"Clark, Brantley and Cristil will be inducted into the MSU Hall of Fame." Mississippi State University Athletic Department. 2003. Print.

"Coahoma County World War I Draft Registration, page 8." usgwarchives.com. USGen-Web Archives, n.d. Web. 13 June 2011.

Congressional Record. "Tribute to Jack Cristil." 4 March 2011: S1262-S1263. Web.

"Cristil recovering from pneumonia." clarionledger.com *The Clarion Ledger,* n.d. 1 April 2005. Web. 28 March 2011.

"History of National Jewish Health." nationaljewish.org. National Jewish Health, n.d. Web. 8 June 2011.

"History of Temple B'nai Israel, Tupelo." msje.org Goldring/Woldenberg Institute of Southern Jewish Life, n.d. Web. 28 March 2011.

"Interview With Our Man Jack." Mississippi State University *Alumnus* Magazine, Fall 1969.

"Jack Cristil presented Lindsey Nelson Award." *Starkville Daily News*, 17 April 2004.

"Jack Cristil: 50 Years Wrapped in Maroon and White." Mississippi State, MS: Mississippi State University, 2003. Print.

"Jack Cristil: Wrap It In Maroon And White!" scout.com Gene's Page, n.d. 26 February 2011 Web. 7 March 2011.

"Kabakoff." kabakoff.com. Kabakoff, n.d. Web. 13 June 2011.

"Legendary Voice Of The Bulldogs Jack Cristil To Conclude Career Saturday." mstateathletics.com Mississippi State Athletics, n.d. 23 Feb. 2011. Web. 19 Apr. 2011.

"Line-Up For Yesterday by Ogden Nash." baseball-almanac.com. Baseball Almanac, n.d. Web. 16 June 2011.

"LSU beats Mississippi State 84-82." The Associated Press, 24 February 2011. Web. 25 March 2011.

"Mississippi Sportscasters of the Year." nssafame.com National Sportswriters and Sportscasters Hall of Fame, n.d. 11 April 2011. Web. 14 August 2011.

"Mississippi State beat Tennessee 70-69." clarionledger.com *The Clarion-Ledger*, n.d. 27 February 2011 Web. 25 March 2011.

"MSU play-by-play man hits 500." The Associated Press, 20 November 1999. Web. 28 March 2011.

"News article: Holocaust Memorial unveiled in Dokshitsy." belarus-misc.org, A Belarus Miscellany, n.d. 24 May 2008. Web. 7 June 2011.

"Official basketball box score." *utsports.com* UT Sports, n.d. 26 February 2011. Web. 10 May 2011.

"Plot Summary for *Shalom Y'all*." imdb.com IMDB, n.d. Web. 28 March 2011.

"Ruby gives MSU graduates perspective." *The Clarion-Ledger.* 14 December 2002. Print. B3.

"Tupelo, Mississippi." msje.org Goldring/Woldenburg Institute of Southern Jewish Life, n.d. 2006. Web. 28 June 2011.

"'Voice of the Bulldogs' heard in Ripley." *The Southern Sentinel.* Print. 10A. 31 March 1994.

"Voice of MSU Bulldogs Jack Cristil 1997 Chris Schenkel Award winner." *Starkville Daily News*, 6 August 1997.

"What is Lupus." lupus.org Lupus Foundation of America, n.d. Web. 6 July 2011.

"Whitney and Floyd are among six headed for Mississippi Sports Hall." *The Clarion-Ledger.* 18 November 1991.

"Zagare." jewishvirtuallibrary.org. Jewish Virtual Library, n.d. Web. 6 June 2011.

"Zagare, Lithuania." shtetlinks.jewishgen.org. JewishGen, n.d. Web. 6 June 2011.

INDEX

Abraham, Jimmy 16
Adams, Jeanne 56
Alcorn Braves 185
Alumnus 23, 26, 40, 48, 58, 89, 120, 159, 163, 186, 189, 214-215, 221, 225
American League All-Star Team 80
Anniston Rams 78
Archer, Pattye 16
Armistead, John 50, 144
Armstrong, Pee Wee 155
Aron, Bill 73, 147, 223
Ashford, Bennie 15, 133
Atlantic Coast Conference 32
Ballard, Mike 16
Barber, Red 25
Barkham, Melvin 165
Barnett, Ross 181
Baron Hirsch Synagogue 144
Belue, Buck 30
Bennett, Ron 158
Bidwill, Charlie 102
Black, Blondy 155
Blackmore, Richard 167
Black, Stan 167
Boggs, Otis 29
Bond, John 169
"Boss Team," 154
Bost, Dee 41
Boston Celtics 180
Boyd, Bob 185
Branston, John 78
Brooklyn Dodgers 25, 77
Brown, Rickey 184
Buck, Jack 5, 102
Buffalo Bills 167
Bulldogjunction.com 22

Burrell, Ode 162
Byrne, Greg 178, 190
Cade, John 15
Canadian Football League 93, 156, 158
Canale, Justin 162
Caray, Harry 5, 102
Carr, Charlie 172
Carter, Bo 26, 71, 90, 134, 193, 199, 216
Center, Leo 147
Chadwick, W.D. 154, 157
Chaney, James 181
Chattanooga Lookouts 80
Chicago White Sox 157
Chickasaw Buddies 65-66, 218
Childress, Joe 160
Christensen, Ray 29
Cincinnati Bearcats 186
Ciraldo, Al 32
Clarksdale Planters 81
Cleveland, Rick 16, 43, 60, 212
Clouatre, Jake 105, 138
Clouatre, Kay Cristil 15, 37, 103, 105, 109, 111-112, 129, 199, 217
CNN 149, 210
Cochran, Thad 189, 212
Coleman, Frances 16
Collins, Bobby 93, 158
Collins, Glen 170
Colvard, Dean W. 180, 182
Cooks, Johnie 169
Copen, Ruben 148
Correro, John 125, 199, 215
Costict, Ray 165, 167
Crago, Dick 84, 156
Crawford, Joan 98
Crimson Tide 34, 159, 168, 172

Cristil, Benjamin Herman 45, 49, 114
Cristil, Harold 61-62, 118
Cristil, Mavis 99, 101, 103, 105, 107-110, 116, 210
Cristil, Mollie Kabakoff 45, 48-49, 52, 58, 114, 150
Cristil, Stanley 62-63, 118
Croom, Sylvester 131, 175, 177
Curtis, Bob 29
Davenport, Steve 15, 194
Davis, Art 93, 159
Davis, Harper 156
Davis, Kermit 184
Davis, Paul 161
Dawgs' Bite 15-16, 41, 48, 58, 60, 71-72, 76, 83, 89, 97, 160, 162, 171, 181, 192, 213, 223
de Havilland, Olivia 62
Dockery, Rex 172
Dooley, Bill 93, 158
Dowsing, Frank 164, 223
Duke, Wee Willie 65
Easley, David 16
Easterwood, Hal 93, 158
Edmonton Eskimos 93, 158
Egg Bowl 133, 173, 176, 178, 204, 221
Eidson, Jim 165
Ellis, Jim 15, 21, 23, 34, 38, 108, 125, 130, 136, 197, 199, 215-216
Ellis, Marion A. 182
Ellis, Steve 15, 23, 32, 40, 48, 58-59, 67, 71, 76, 92, 103, 215
Ells, Paul 34
Esgro, Sam 64
Esgro, Zelda Cristil 15, 48, 56, 59, 63, 118
ESPN 18, 22-24, 36, 38, 176, 203, 221-222
Evans, Dinky 93
Evans, Lawrence 170
Falkenstien, Max 27
Fallon, Frank 31
Favre, Brett 174
Felker, Rockey 6, 15, 128, 164-165, 167, 172
Ferguson, John 31
Ferrell, Kirby 65
Fesmire, Rob 169
Fighting Irish 32

Final Four 173, 186-187
Fisher, Joe 34
Fisher, Sonny 162
Flemming, Bill 169
Forney, John 34
Fox, Vicki Reikes 73, 147
Freeman, Steve 165, 167
Friedman, Kinky 147
Fulton, Bob 29
Furman, Fred 154
Fyffe, Jim 34, 199
Gaelic Sports Results 35
Georgetown 89, 155
George Washington University 184
Georgia Tech 32, 204
Geuder, Maridith 15
Giles, William 110, 163, 188
Gold, Eli 34
Golden Gophers 29, 158
Gold, Joe Dan 180, 182, 184
Goldring/Woldenberg Institute of Southern Jewish Life 143, 225
Goodman, Andrew 181
Goodrich, Bill 32-33
Granger, Hoyle 162
Green Bay Packers 177
Greene, Ron 184
Greenwood Dodgers 82
Gregory, Bart 85, 204, 215
Gregory, Paul 157, 179
Grisham, John 3, 7, 16, 22, 201, 210, 227
Halberstam, David J. 24
Hall of Fame Bowl 172
Happy Valley 176
Harkness, Jerry 182
Harper, Phyllis 147
Hartley, Bob 42, 90, 97, 105, 121, 134, 158, 174, 192, 198, 201, 216
Harvey, Paul 25
Hatfield, Jim 185
Hearst, Garrison 92
Helena Seaporters 82
Higgins, Ron 14, 22, 174, 194, 204
Hilbun, Ben 188
Hillary, Sir Edmund 40
Hiller, Charlotte Cristil 51, 62, 118

Hofmann, Freddie 65
Hollingshead, Levaine 158
Hood, Orley 33, 51, 92, 196
Horn, Barry 32, 35
Hot Springs Bathers 82
Howell, Bailey 180, 186
Hull, Charles 180
Hull, Harvey 6, 165
Humphrey Coliseum 36, 42, 185, 190, 222
Humphrey, Woody 169
Hymel, Calvin 165
Inman, Tommy 162
Ireland, George 182
Itawamba Community College 97, 101, 125, 145, 192, 196
Jackson, Billy 170
Jackson, Keith 35, 202
Jacobs, Don 170
James, Fob 160
Jefferson, Billy 155
Jenison Field House 182
Jewish Virtual Library 50, 225
Johnson, Dennis 6, 165, 167
Jones, Paul 22, 27, 89
Kabakoff, Jacob 48, 51
Kabakoff, Mendel 48
Karatassos, Straton 15, 216
Keenum, Mark 11, 16, 133, 204-205, 212
Keenum, Rhonda 16
Kellum, David 34, 214
Kelly, Todd 19
Kentucky Colonels 184
Keys, Tyrone 169
Khrushchev, Nikita 39
KITTY League 40, 78
Kim, Peter 169
KMOX 5, 102
Knobler, Mike 33, 79-80, 89
Kopach, Joe 82
Krzyzewski, Mike 31
Landis, Kenesaw Mountain 25
Lapides, Bernard 65
Lawrence, Mike 165
Ledford, Cawood 31-32, 123, 195, 202
Lee, Charles 130, 189, 199-200
Lee, Martin 21, 36

Lewinsky, Monica 39
Lewis, Wendell 41
Long, John L. 100, 216
Los Angeles Dodgers 84
Louisiana State University 31
Loyola of New Orleans 184
Loyola University 180
Madison Square Garden 186
Major League Baseball 84, 157, 201
Majors, Johnny 173
Malone, Jeff 186
Marcello, Brandon 41
Martin, Dan 154
Martin, Tee 198
McAlexander, Charlie 33, 199
McCarthy, Clem 24, 26
McComas, James 188, 195
McDole, Mardye 169
McGuire, Bill 162
McKeen, Allyn 67, 155
McNamee, Graham 24
McRaney, Bob 83, 87
McWilliams, Shorty 156
Memphis Chicks 65, 78-81
Memphis Memorial Stadium 166
Meredith, James 181
Meridian Athletic Club 154
Mikaberidze, Alexander 46
Miller, John 169-170
Miller, Ron 183
Milstein, Zelda 147
Minnesota Vikings 167
Mississippi History Now 143, 223
Mississippi Sports Hall of Fame 33, 127, 134, 148, 164, 196
Mississippi Sports Magazine 22, 27, 89, 148, 222-223
Mississippi Veterans Memorial Stadium 124, 168
Mitchell, Charlie 199
Mitchell, Leland 180, 182
Mize, Buzzy 110
Moore, Dana 170
Morgan, William Earl 161
Motlin, Stirka "Tillie," 49
Mule, Marty 14

Mullen, Dan 133, 175, 179, 190, 205
Munson, Larry 29-30, 197
Murray, David 15, 48, 58, 60, 71-72, 76, 83, 89, 97, 99, 103, 109, 160, 167, 181
Natchez Indians 82
National Center for Jewish Film 147
National Invitational Tournament 185
NCAA 11, 14, 27, 31, 141, 166, 175-177, 180-181, 183, 185-187, 192
Nebraska Cornhuskers 168
Nelson, Rebecca Cristil 15, 38, 101, 105-106, 112, 129, 136, 138, 199, 216
Nemeth, Mike 15
Neshoba County 182
Neville, Tommy 162
Newhall, Lindsey 105, 136, 138
Newsom, Louis Norman (Bobo) 79
New York Giants 77
Neyland, Bob 42
Neyland Stadium 175
Nix, Jack 67
Noble, Dudy 27, 85, 87-89, 111
Noble, Pick 192
Norgay, Tenzing 40
North Carolina State University 162
Northwestern State University 105, 136, 138
Northwestern University 76
Nunnery, Nash 148
Nutt, Houston 178
O'Ceallachain, Sean Og 35
Ogilvie, Major 170
Oklahoma State University 29
Old Main Dormitory 168
Olson, Andrew 17
Orange Bowl 88, 155, 162
Orgeron, Ed 178
Osmond, Donny 105
Packer, Walter 165, 167
Parker, Brent 204
Parker, Col. Tom 64
Parker, Jackie 92, 156
Parkview Baptist 140
Patrick, Mike 167
Peach Bowl 176
Pearl, Bruce 28

Peck, Wiley 184
Penn State 176
Perkins, Ray 173
Phillips, Joe 121, 126, 162, 192-194, 199
Phillips, Sam 64
Pickle, Ike 155
Pine Bluff Cardinals 82
Polecat Alley 168
Portera, Malcolm 189
Presley, Elvis 64, 97, 224
Presley, Vernon 64
Pruett, John 35, 164
Rial, John 167
Robertson, Bob 29
Roberts, Tony 32
Robison, Charlie 197
Robison, Kay 108
Rockoff, Stuart 143
Roosevelt, Franklin 72
Royal, Darrell 93, 158-159, 161, 163, 173
Rubenstein, Michael 148
Rubenstein, Ted 149
Ruby, Roy H. 44, 221
Rupp, Adolph 103, 105
Rupp Arena 186-187, 197
Rush, John 16
Ruth, Babe 157
Sasse, Ralph 155, 161
Schenkel, Chris 27, 197, 225
Schmanke, Jack Dale 29
Schwerner, Michael 182
Scully, Vin 35
SEC Coach of the Year 164, 180, 185, 187-188
Shalom Y'all: Images of Jewish Life in the American South 73, 147, 223
Sherrill, Jackie 129, 175, 177
Shira, Charlie 126, 163
Siegal, Florence 68
Silveri, Joe 158
Slutsky, Yehuda 50
Smith, Bonnie 68
Smith, Don 41, 173
Sorrels, Bill 92, 155
Southeastern Conference 10, 27, 32, 103, 122, 178, 181, 186, 219

Southeastern League 78
Spanish-American War 154
Sparks, John 162
Spivak, Charles David 55-56, 222
Stansbury, Rick 28, 41, 135, 180, 187, 207
Stanton, Bill 159, 161
Starkville Daily News 16, 223, 225
Steele, Alfred 98
Stein, Maury 146
Stennis, John C. 120, 163, 168
Stern, Bill 24, 26
St. Louis Cardinals 102, 201
Stricklin, Scott 11, 15, 85, 190, 212
Suber, Scott 93, 158
Sun Records 64
Tabachnik, Sara Liba 49
Talbert, Mike 73, 83
Temple B'Nai Israel 57, 101, 144, 146, 148, 225
Templeton, Larry 15, 122, 130, 174, 178-179, 193, 196, 199, 216
Texas Jewboys 147
Texas Tech University 29, 172
The Associated Press 156, 176, 225
The Clarion-Ledger 16, 19, 33, 41, 43, 60, 79-80, 89, 196, 212, 221-225
The Commercial Appeal 16, 22, 65, 78, 80, 154, 174, 194, 204, 221-222, 224
The Dallas Morning News 32, 35, 222
The Huntsville Times 164, 223
The Jackson Five 105
The Maroon Bulldogs 92, 155, 224
The Northeast Mississippi Daily Journal 16, 50, 73, 83, 98, 144, 147, 165, 198-199, 216, 221-224
The Partridge Family 105
The Times-Picayune 14, 223
The Vero Beach Press Journal 84
Thomas, John 183
Time magazine 24
Tomlinson, Jim 16
Torgerson, Stan 32-33
Tupelo High School 125, 145, 164, 192, 196, 206
Tutor, Julie 103
Tyler, Bob 126, 165

Tzuchman, Sarah Kabakoff 48
Ufer, Bob 32
University of Alabama 34
University of Florida 30, 84-85, 179
University of Iowa 29
University of Kansas 27-28
University of Kentucky 31, 103, 123
University of Minnesota 29, 93
University of Oklahoma 29, 158
University of Tennessee 18, 20, 31
University of Texas 93, 160
University of Washington 93, 160
U.S. Military Academy 155
Vaughan, Andrew 64
Vaught Hemingway Stadium 165
Vaught, Johnny 165
Veasey, Wanda 150
Vitrano, Terry 6, 106, 165
Walker, Wade 158, 161
Walters, Fred 155
Ward, John 18, 31-32, 36, 202
Warmath, Murray 92, 157
Washington Senators 80
Watson, Pat 162
Watson, Vance 189
Weaver, Robin 83
Webb, Jimmy 165, 167
WELO 96-98, 120, 125
Werner, T.H. 156
West Point 155, 168
West Virginia University 31
Westwood One Sports 24
White, Ray 184
Whitney, Davey 185
Wilkinson, Bud 158
Williams, Richard 128, 186, 197
Winfield, Sim 69, 82
WLBT-TV 148
WROX 82-83, 93, 95-96, 119
Y'all magazine 145
Yancey, Charles 155
Yeoman, Bill 164
Zabel, Jim 29
Zacharias, Donald W. 110
Ziskind, Esther Kabakoff 48